this is the place

this is
the place

women writing about home

edited by Margot Kahn *and* Kelly McMasters

SEAL PRESS

Seal Press
Hachette Book Group
1290 Avenue of the Americas, New York, NY 10104
sealpress.com

Printed in the United States of America
First Edition: November 2017

Published by Seal Press, an imprint of Perseus Books, LLC, a subsidiary of Hachette Book Group, Inc.

The Hachette Speakers Bureau provides a wide range of authors for speaking events. To find out more, go to www.hachettespeakersbureau.com or call (866) 376-6591.

The publisher is not responsible for websites (or their content) that are not owned by the publisher.

Print book interior design by Jack Lenzo

Library of Congress Cataloging-in-Publication Data has been applied for.

ISBNs: 978-1-58005-668-7 (paperback), 978-1-58005-758-5 (ebook)

LSC-C

10 9 8 7 6 5 4 3

For my mother.
—MK

For my grandmothers,
Anita Brackett & Betty McMasters,
and
for my sons, my forever home,
Emerson & Angus.
—KM

Contents

Introduction

As women coming of age in the modern era, moving out of our parents' homes and into spaces of our own was exhilarating and terrifying. We looked to the past, to the homes our mothers and grandmothers had defined for us by example, and we looked forward into something new we were going to create. Our wishes and daydreams were defining not only the kinds of spaces our homes would be, but the kinds of women—wives, partners, mothers, and citizens—we could become.

As we got older, moving out of homes where we thought we'd be forever, or feeling stuck in places we didn't mean to be for so long, we realized that home is a loaded word, a complex idea: it's a place that is safe, sentimental, difficult, nourishing, war-torn, and political. There are so many ways to define it: we might have an ancestral home or homeland, and the place we're living at the moment, and also the place we feel our soul belongs. Home can be a place whose memory remains trapped in our bones, a notion that may be passed down in our very DNA. Home can be where we learn to first understand our place in the world, and a place we return to, again and again, for answers about how to be.

Home is a place constantly evolving alongside our concepts of work, family, gender roles, the economy, and the environment. It is a concept worthy of ongoing reflection and renegotiation.

In her essay "On Moving Home," Kirsten Sundberg Lunstrum says of the place she chooses to call home: "I am more myself here . . . than I could be anywhere else in the world." This may be the home feeling we seek, most distilled. And yet, as we collected the essays that ultimately make up this book, we realized the work we were reading overwhelmingly contained an electric current of complicated beauty and love, as well as unease, dissatisfaction, and displacement. These are the stories at the core of our sense of being and belonging, and they are not all happily-ever-after.

The majority of these essays are original, written specifically for this anthology, from a collection of women writers who are diverse on many levels: geography, ethnicity, culture, religion, age, sexuality. What we found, despite our differences, were incredible commonalities in the ways we consider home. Indeed, though we did not suggest or expect it, mothers appear in nearly every essay in this book—in these pages, women remember the mothers, grandmothers, and maternal figures who made or unmade homes for them, while other mother-writers reflect on the homes they are making for their families and for themselves.

Other themes circulate, as well. "Home is the language you are loved in," says Naomi Jackson in "Between My Teeth." The language in which we are first loved, the language in which we dream, the accents, aphorisms, songs, and silences we associate with home never leave us, even if the actual language does: for instance, in "A Family Business," Jane Wong remembers growing up in her parents' Chinese American restaurant, saying "hello in Cantonese because you haven't forgotten your language yet."

Danielle Geller's "Annotating the First Page of the First Navajo-English Dictionary" takes on formalized language as a way to marshal facts and memory, using the rigidity of an institutionalized format to tell the story of her home in a new way.

Moving—moving out, moving in, moving across the country, moving across continents, and simply being on the move—was another constant source of storytelling. Sarah Viren contemplates the comfort and confusion of returning to a place she's lived before in "Some Notes on Our Cyclical Nature;" and Tara Conklin's "The Explorer" interrogates that space between the urge for adventure and the tension of staying still. Lina María Ferreira Cabeza-Vanegas ("Allá En La Fuente") confronts a flawed view of her homeland Colombia while in Iowa; as a little girl sitting in a church pew in North Carolina, Hasanthika Sirisena ("Of Pallu and Pottu") imagines the ways her mother's new life compares to her old in Sri Lanka. Desiree Cooper describes the ghosts that follow a tight military family through their many moves in "Away from Dangerous Things," reminding us that ultimately, "Home is culture, tradition, and memory—not mortar."

Jennifer Finney Boylan celebrates the freedom of choosing to return home or not for the holidays in "Freeing Thanksgiving from My Family," while in "Subjunctive" Naima Coster explores the inevitability of certain patterns laid out by the family history that precedes us. In many instances, moving is not a choice, but a necessity: in her essay "The Stars Remain," about her childhood in El Salvador, Claudia Castro Luna remembers, "On a windy afternoon Mami comes home and tells us that our petition for US Resident Status has been approved. To leave means survival."

Landscape becomes story in many pieces, from Terry Tempest Williams's political land purchases in "Keeping My Fossil

Fuel in the Ground" to Miranda Weiss's choice to raise her family in far-flung Alaska in "Cold, Comfort." In Pam Houston's essay "The Sound of Horse Teeth on Hay in the Snow," a snowed-in ranch that seems like a dangerous setting to others offers only peace and insulation, while Leigh Newman's Brooklyn garden becomes the unexpected center for intersecting lives in "Vesica Piscis." Elissa Washuta, in "Undergraduate Admissions Essay Draft," charts the experience of leaving home for college, illustrating the transition by the absence of the home landscape she'd taken for granted: "I didn't know, then, that there were places without crickets, without mothers."

In many ways, a home can be defined by the objects we choose to live alongside us, but sometimes those objects wind up defining home for us. In "The Inheritance," Elisabeth Eaves describes the way an object can contain both person and place when losing a home is helixed with losing a loved one. Akiko Busch artfully links objects to the ways in which we build home and the ways objects remain even as home changes in "Home in Four Acts," while in "The Privilege Button," a simple garage-door opener triggers Maya Jewell Zeller's conflicted emotions of her personal history moving from homeless to homeowner.

Home can also be a dangerous place, as we learn in Amanda Petrusich's eerily comforting essay about growing up in the shadow of the Indian Point nuclear power plant and Dani Shapiro's masterfully terrifying essay "Plane Crash Theory." While the idea of home carries with it the notion of safety, or at least the hope of it, in reality home is also often the place where we were first afraid, as depicted in Catina Bacote's "We Carried Ourselves Like Villagers." Home can also be the place we were pushed past our limits, where we were betrayed, exposed, left in the cold, or, simply, left. As in Debra Gwartney's searing essay "Broken Home," home can also be mistaken for a safe harbor, until the day we realize that it is achingly impossible to keep any place truly safe, for ourselves, and sometimes, for those we love.

Like the rooms within a house, the essays in this collection inhabit the inner space: the thoughts, memories, emotions, questions, and meditations with which we envision and embody the idea of home. In this regard, it is not surprising that these essays connect to so many of the issues now at the forefront of our conversations: immigration, gender equality, sexual and family violence, homelessness, and poverty. It is no accident that we open the collection standing in the kitchen with Kate Lebo, "Here." Imagining home, creating home, staying home, and leaving home—whether to go to work every day, or leaving a household or homeland for good—are all political acts for women. We rejoice in this; it makes us powerful. We hope you feel the same.

—Margot Kahn & Kelly McMasters

Here

———

Kate Lebo

My personal, artistic, and professional lives are tangled most stubbornly where the kitchen table meets the kitchen wall and window. From there I can walk 72 inches to the sink to wash a mug, 48 inches to the stove to heat the percolator. Swivel 180 degrees to retrieve milk from the fridge, go on tiptoe to reach the microwave that heats my milk. Then turn back around and walk 12 inches to the table, pour coffee into milk, tease a skin of scalded protein off the top with a fingernail, and walk 24 inches to my kitchen chair. There I will eat, drink, talk on the phone, look out the window, resist the urge to check Facebook—which requires a 72-inch walk into another room—and write and write.

I have made my life, quite literally and with onions, in this kitchen. If every time I walked the kitchen I left a trail of silk like a spider, I could fall asleep between the stove and the fridge in a homespun hammock.

My neighborhood has become the sort of place *Sunset* magazine writes articles about, a land where 50 percent rent hikes are mean, but not crazy. If my landlord and I have one thing in common it's that we both need to make more money. That's why in thirty days I must leave this kitchen.

After I lose my apartment my friend says, "*This* is what thirty looks like?" She just lost her job. She's thinking about moving to New York.

When my mother was thirty, she moved for the fifth time in five years to follow my father to another job. She was pregnant. I was two. That was the year my friend's mother would move from Mexico City to Miami, where she would divorce her husband and raise two children alone.

"Apparently." I make a comparison to help us feel better: "Except for husbands and children, our mothers' lives looked like this too."

I have planted a garden. I have harvested rhubarb, herbs, and radishes. The rest of my seeds are start-sized, tender.

Here is where I stirred pots, moved pens, read poems, all without boyfriend or husband or children. I was lonely here, happy here, caught between cabin fever and deep peace. Here is where, as my neighbor once said, I was my own man.

———

Kate Lebo is the author of *Pie School* and *A Commonplace Book of Pie*, and co-editor (with Samuel Ligon) of *Pie & Whiskey*, an anthology of writers under the influence of butter and booze. Her work has appeared in *Best American Essays, Best New Poets, New England Review, Gettysburg Review*, and *Gastronomica*, among other places. Her new book of nonfiction, *The Book of Difficult Fruit*, is forthcoming from Farrar, Straus & Giroux. She lives in Spokane, Washington.

Away from Dangerous Things

Desiree Cooper

O ne night in 1942, when my mother, Bobbie, was only nine years old, the walls of her family's tiny, wood-frame house began to shudder. Her heart thrashing, she jumped up in the bed. Beside her on the bumpy, thin mattress lay her mother, deep under the spell of slumbered grief.

"Mommy?" Bobbie whispered. "Do you hear that?"

At first, the sound was like the rumble of the Norfolk Southern making its midnight run through Waverly, Virginia, a depot town of barely a thousand people. But then, it gathered into something more discrete—a furious pounding like a crew of carpenters at work. Hammer against nail. Saw against grain. Hinge against jamb. Anger against regret.

"Junious?" Her mother sat up in the bed, pulling Bobbie close. "What you doin' in the kitchen?"

Neither mother nor daughter stopped to question that it was anybody but Junious, now four days dead. Nor did they question

3

that he would be in the kitchen, in the thick of the night, raising holy hell.

Bobbie heard her father's disembodied voice rasping from the back of the house. "Stay in the bed!" he commanded. Terrified, she whimpered as her mother held her tight.

This was not Junious's first visitation. Since his death, he had come in the darkness and rocked their bed like a dinghy on the open sea. He had pulled fresh clothes off the line and strewn them across the backyard. He'd caused the naked light bulbs to blink off and on. Now he was in the kitchen, banging furiously on the back door.

Decades later, my mother would tell me this story like it was a testimony. By then, she was a long way from the little girl cowering in her mother's bed, listening to her father's ghost rage through the night. But she never lost her belief that her kin could visit from the other side, bringing with them signs and omens, protection and advice. The night that her dead father hammered in the kitchen was no exception. Later that day, they heard from the neighbors that there had been a thief on the prowl on the Rural Route 40. He had stolen corn from bins, the Stokleys' good ax, and hams from the Johnson's smokehouse. But no one had bothered the widow and her little girl, Bobbie, even though they had fallen asleep with their kitchen door unlocked.

My mother believed her father had come to hammer their door shut and keep them safe. The neighbors called it a miracle.

When Bobbie was twenty-one, she married my dad, Willie, in a civil ceremony in Connecticut. They had been neighbors in Waverly since they were six years old. Despite their deep roots in the sawmill town tucked in the Virginia Piedmont, neither ever doubted that they would one day escape its clutches. My dad's ticket came in the form of a football scholarship to North

Carolina A & T in 1952. When he was cut from the team after his second year, he joined the air force to continue his education. My mom did what many women did back then—she went to college to find a husband. But after two years, she ended up marrying the boy next door.

They say that fleas, when captured in a jar, will eventually stop trying to escape even after the lid is removed. I often think of this in contrast to the human spirit, which can continue to push against what appears to be an airtight reality, against all odds. To this day, I marvel that two young people who grew up under the oppression of the Jim Crow South would even imagine that they had a right to be citizens of the world. But my parents did. Within four years of my dad enlisting, they found themselves a black couple in post-war Japan, expecting their first child, far away from the comforts and terrors of their native Virginia.

It's not accurate to say that I was "homeless" most of my childhood, even though we lived in Japan (three different times), Texas, Colorado, Florida, New Mexico, and Virginia, all before my fourteenth birthday. Not even the word "nomad" works, since nomads often carry their homes with them. Perhaps we were more like immigrants who leave everything behind but their most prized possessions and their roots.

Like those immigrants, my parents knew that they didn't have to own a home to make one. Home is culture, tradition, and memory—not mortar. For my mother, that meant carving out a routine as reliable as an atomic clock, building a universe of belonging around my brother and me. With each move, she furiously stamped her imprimatur upon the cookie-cutter military base housing, making each place unmistakably ours. She adorned the walls with her framed needlework and hung my father's painting of Jesus—with long, dark hair, brown eyes and tanned skin—to bless our dining room table. She filled the air with the aromas of her Southern cooking, especially on Sundays, when the table was lavishly spread with roasts and potatoes, gravies and collards, pound cake and the sweetest tea on earth.

She was the Kool-Aid mom, and ours was the house where our friends were welcome. She was the Girl Scout leader and den mother; my father coached my brother's baseball teams. Long after we should have outgrown them, my brother and I are still partial to taking Sunday drives.

We were a team when we were traveling, like astronauts cocooned in a capsule, as we crisscrossed the country three times before I was ten. My dad always seemed to sit a bit taller when he was behind the wheel of his Buick (the only brand he'd ever drive), taking us sightseeing around the base or venturing off-base to the markets, or Shinto temples, or White Sands or ancient desert caverns or the Rocky Mountains or the Atlantic. He was always on the lookout for the mighty forces of man and nature, pointing to a suspension bridge or a fighter jet or water tumbling over shorn cliffs, and saying to us, "That's a dangerous thing!"

My brother delighted at the hint of threat. At an Okinawan festival, he'd watch a habu (a deadly Asian serpent) attack a weasely mongoose or gargantuan Sumo wrestlers face off on television and ask my dad, "Is that a dangerous thing?" My dad would laugh and nod. For us, dangerous things were strangely reassuring, as long as they loomed outside of the fortress of our family—the way listening to thunder as you snuggle beneath the covers can make you feel both lucky and safe.

Not counting Christmas, moving day was the most exciting day of the year. When the van would pull up into the driveway, my brother and I would be as giddy as ferrets. After school, we couldn't run home fast enough to push open the door and squeal through a completely empty house. The size of the rooms doubled in their emptiness, and the stripped walls threw back our voices.

As we got older, moving meant a time for reinvention, a chance to reset our lives. *When we move to Florida, I'm going to ask mom if I can do my own hair. I'm going to start a babysitting business in Virginia. When I get to the States, I'm going to learn how to dance.*

Of course, there was the grief of leaving behind all that had become familiar. My last day at school would be full of hugs and tears and signatures in slam books like "Stay sweet and crazy. Friends forever." But the sadness was always tempered by the extraordinary realization that I had best friends all over the world. I just hadn't met them yet.

Wherever we went, I knew it would be home in no time at all.

Now, I have resided in Michigan for thirty years. It's where I became a writer, a wife, a mother, and a grandmother. My children have lived their entire lives in the same town with their aunts, uncles, and grandparents just one house away. They are still in touch with their kindergarten best friends. They have roots. I guess that means that after all of my girlhood travels, I am finally rooted, too.

Yet, I still have a moment of hesitation when people ask me where I'm from. Am I from Japan, the country of my birth and the place I spent the bulk of my childhood? Am I from Detroit, which has been home to me for three decades? Or is it Virginia, where my lineage seeps down into the soil, and where my heart keeps migrating in my dreams?

Over the past six years I've moved four times, each time with fewer belongings in tow. At fifty-six, the moves have not been filled with the excitement that I felt when I was a little girl. They have been stressful and anxiety-ridden, precipitated by divorce, unemployment, foreclosure, and family demands. Each unmooring has felt more like amputation than opportunity. Now I think, I'm too old for this.

My parents, however, have stopped moving. For all of their desire to escape Virginia, they returned in 1974 when my dad retired from the air force. For the past forty years, they have lived just an hour from Waverly. They are salmon who, after battling upstream most of their lives, have returned to the river of their birth.

Now in their eighties, they are clinging to their independence. My father is making a go of it, but his short-term memory has trapped him in a constant loop of remembering and forgetting.

My mother is living, once again, with ghosts. She sees her mother's face come alive in pictures on the wall. Strange figures enter her room at night to loom over her bed. Children she doesn't recognize scale the steeples of pines in the backyard. As her life gets emptier, the spirits are crowding. This time, they haven't come to save her.

Dementia, it turns out, is the one dangerous thing that has finally penetrated the sanctum of their home.

I go to check on them often. During a recent visit, my mother suddenly gasped as we were watching TV. I gazed at her expectantly to see what she was going to say. These days, sudden memories and secrets tumble out as her mind wanders, uninhibited. I braced myself, but she said nothing as she looked around the den wide-eyed.

The room has remained pretty much unchanged since I was in high school. The elm coffee table and matching end tables came with them from Japan, replete with inlaid marble and three-dimensional carvings of feudal life. Over the sofa hangs my mother's framed needlework, a peacock with a fan of magnificent feathers. The fireplace is adorned with figurines, pottery, and silk flowers. Every other wall in the room is plastered with family pictures that go back as far as my great-grandmother's generation.

Only a couple of pictures survive from my mother's childhood. The largest is one of little Bobbie and her father Junious at the county fair the year he died. His eyes are wide and all-seeing, but his spirit is silent. There is no hammering at the back door, no furious warnings in the night.

As we sat there, my mother gazed at her ark of memories, all of her beloved tchotchkes. Then she turned to me, her eyes as scared and lonely as a lost child's.

"Whose place is this?" she asked. "When are we going home?"

Desiree Cooper is a former attorney, Pulitzer Prize–nominated journalist and Detroit community activist whose fiction dives unflinchingly into the intersection of racism and sexism. Her first book, *Know the Mother*, was published in 2016. Cooper was a founding board member of Cave Canem, a national residency for emerging black poets. She is currently a Kimbilio fellow, a national residency for African American fiction writers, and was a 2015 Kresge Artist Fellow.

A Family Business

——

Jane Wong

How to lob an egg into a parking lot: Wait until it's dark, settled-in dark, not sunset dark, say, 9 p.m. The sound of breaking is better when you can't see it happen. When your father isn't looking, go to the fridge and steal two eggs from the bottom of the carton stack and wrap them in a small towel, folding the towel like you would an origami cup. Sneak out through the back of the restaurant, mind the potholes, and circle around front to the parking lot. Unfold the towel and give your little brother one egg. When he says the egg is too cold and smells rotten like unbrushed teeth, tell him to shut up. Ground your heels into the gravel, as you imagine baseball pitchers do to gain traction. Give all your anger up to the egg. Breathe your hot breath on it. Hold it up to the sky like an offering, a sacrifice, this careful thing that could have grown into something else. Tell your brother there is nothing to be afraid of. Tell him to stop shaking. With your arm bent back at 45 degrees, hurl the egg high into the air, into an arch any city would welcome as a bridge. Hurl the egg and do not think about anything—not about how your father disappears for weeks to gamble in Atlantic City, not about how your mother crushes cockroaches with her fist—no, nothing at all. You must give the egg all of it. You can open your eyes or close them; it won't matter since you won't see it land. But, you will hear it. You will hear your brother squeal like a pig at mealtime. You will hear the splat—the crepuscular glob of the yolk spreading across the hood of a car. Poor car, you'll think, poor, stupid car.

How to lock your brother in the meat freezer: Say the following with love and intention:

> "You won't even last five minutes."
> "It's 100 degrees outside."
> "Mommy said you have to get the spareribs."
> "Look, I can see my breath in here. Huuuuh-huhhh."
> "I'll give you five dollars."
> "Let's go to Alaska."
> "You aren't afraid, are you?"

How to be in Alaska: You live on the other coast, the Jersey side, and the wildest thing you've ever seen was a goose eating chips at the beach. But in the velvet cold of winter, in sad February, you can escape anywhere. You can be transported to the other side of the country. To travel, you must wait until closing time, around 11 p.m. when the parking lot empties and your mother begins shaking the ants out of the MSG bin. Pull on your boots and grab two brooms from the supply closet and run outside. Ask your brother where he'd like to go. Alaska, he'll say, arms high in the air as if a puffin would adopt him any second. Earlier, at lonely 5 a.m., before you woke up, a snowplow's jaw pushed all the snow from the lot up against the street lamps. Take your brother's arm and give him a broom, bristle side-up. Don't ruin the expedition, you'll say, or I'll send you back to Jersey. As if Jersey was punishment enough. With the alien light of an Alaskan sun, dig the end of the broom into the hard snow— a mix of ice, gravel, and car oil. Climb up the mound, declaring coordinates along the way. 64.2008°N, 149.4937°W! At the top, sit with your little brother, your back against the street lamp, the bare warmth of electricity running through this conduit, this lifeline. Close your eyes, frost thickening along your lashes. Imagine what it feels like to be so far away from home. To leave this strip mall, this state, this way of life. Imagine traveling to places beyond Alaska—Hong Kong, Seoul, Cairo, St. Petersburg. Vow to leave Jersey the instant you graduate high school; link your two pinky fingers together and promise yourself to leave. As you fall asleep, surrounded by glaciers and your mother's sharp voice slicing through the ice, your brother declares everything he wants to see right now: sand, yak, mud, ice, caribou, polar bear, volcano, fox, rainbow fish, ants, ants, ants.

How to pretend to fall asleep so your mother picks you up: You've seen it on TV before—how children fall asleep in unlikely places and how parents look at them with pure wonder and affection. You've seen parents pick them up gently, kiss them, and tuck them in someplace safer. Don't worry; you have an upper hand in your ability to fall asleep in unlikely places. You have your choices: dining booth, supply closet, under the sink (if it's not leaking). To pretend to fall asleep, become a fat noodle— a floppy, waterlogged noodle. Leave a book or a can of orange soda on your chest so that, when it inevitably falls in fake-sleep, she will hear it fall and be compelled to come over. Slow down your breathing; become a hibernating bear, a top-notch sloth. Dream of the ways she will find you—not hours later when she is done with her shift and you actually fall into real-sleep, but when she is finished cutting strips of wonton, refilling the water pitcher, and carrying dirty plates stacked tightly like the layers of an onion. Dream of the kiss on the cheek. Dream of the real feeling of her real arms wrapped around your back. Dream of her picking you up like a sack of sugar, a wet bleach rag, a suitcase she packed diligently many years ago, in a country 7,186 miles away. Open up that suitcase and see what you can find.

How to read in the half-dark: Contrary to the advice of any decent optometrist, you won't need that much light. Your eyes are good at adjusting. You can think of yourself as a cat, if that helps. Head next door to the dry cleaners with your copy of *Matilda*; look in to see if anyone is there. The owner will be in the very back of the store, steaming a shirt—the smoke trailing like a campfire someone forgot to put out. Head straight for the changing room. Pull back the velvet curtain and settle in. Clean the space as you would clean your apartment—the apartment you imagine having when you are thirty-one and, to the disappointment of your grandparents, unmarried. Push the fallen pins to one corner. If there is lint, roll it up like a dung beetle—with purpose and slow precision. Your eyes should have adjusted by now. You should see light at the bottom of the curtain, intermittent waves of custard yellow. Start reading and when the owner opens the curtain ten minutes later, lower your eyes so that the light doesn't flood in too strongly and make you hiss. The owner will say hello to you in Korean because that is her language, and you'll say hello in Cantonese because you haven't forgotten your language yet. You'll look past her scoured, pink hands to see a customer behind her—a tall, impatient man who wants his suit measured correctly this time. You'll meet people like this later in life. The ones who will mark you as laborer, as not worthy of their time, and you will add them to your revenge list.

How to pass the time: Brush your hair fifty times; untangle hair from a wool blanket; shake up a can of orange soda; defrost shrimp; defrost your hands; chase the curly white dog who lives along the train tracks behind the restaurant; brew honey water; water the jade plant, covered in dust; scrub graffiti off the restaurant; hiss at boys; draw on the backs of menus; stick gum under the table and see how long it takes to fall; sweep up piles of your father's cigarettes on the back stoop; breathe in deeply; peel grapes over a red plastic bucket; scrape grease from the griddle; drop wonton wrappers into the fryer; roll grapes under the fryer and imagine them melting, days from now; punch a bag of flour; recite your revenge list; listen to the sound of gravel under tires; clean the muck out of the curly white dog's eyes; teach your grandpa to say "apple" in English (no, he says, teach me how to say "poverty").

How to carry dishes: Carry a pile of dirty dishes with both your hands first; you don't learn to shoot a basketball with one hand first, do you? Then, after a few weeks, carry the dishes in the crook of one arm like you carry your textbooks. When you feel bold, stack crushed soda cans on top of the dishes. Put one foot in front of the other—this rule of thumb can be applied to dancing with boys, which unfortunately won't be relevant to you during middle school or high school for that matter. Don't forget that you quit ballet after one day. When you naturally bump into the prep table and drop a dish, its porcelain center splintering in all directions like the sun's rays, do not listen when your mother laughs and says: "And who would marry you?" Instead, keep putting one foot in front of the other until you reach the kitchen sink, a wide, deep crater. Lay down the dishes, the refuse of others, the barely chewed pieces of beef fat and hard stems of broccoli. Raise your outrage—who is rich enough to leave food behind? Wash the oyster sauce trickling down your arm like squid ink. Add these customers to your revenge list, too, for making your family cook Chinese American food—sticky, sweet food your family had to learn to make. Food that is not your mother's, father's, grandfather's, or grandmother's. Never eat this fake, plastic food, the photos of which are oversaturated and laminated above the ordering counter; wait for the real Cantonese food that your mother makes during 20-minute lunch and dinner breaks. During dinner, help your mother carry your favorite Cantonese dish—whole tomatoes, ginger, soy sauce, egg, and rice. When your mother was pregnant with you, she grew tomatoes all around the small duplex your four uncles and grandparents lived in. Think of your mother at twenty-one, arranged to a complete stranger, your father, and sitting on a mattress in the duplex's attic, squirrels running across the beams. Imagine her eating a tomato like an apple, the juice trickling down to her knees. Think of the bright green vines wrapped around you as you eat your favorite dish, the tomatoes as sweet and tart and large as your heart. Forgive your mother for being so tough on you; you don't know what she will have to carry over the years—the bills, the food on the table, the disappearance of your father, the work. Yes, the work. Lest you forget and you mustn't forget: look at her hands, rough as canvas and trembling, wanting to be held.

How to write your revenge list: Start with the cruel ones. The neighborhood boys who threw rocks at you, who picked up smooth, flat rocks from their landscaped yard and threw rocks at your backpack as you walked home. Add the ones who ignore you, the ones who look at clouds more than they look at you. The ones who have low expectations. The guidance counselor who placed you in lower-level English, despite your test scores, despite your abilities, despite the stack of novels you read a week. Add the untrustworthy ones, the ones who smile too wide and compliment your hair while pointing out your too-large ears. Add the creepy white guys who always sit next to you on the bus, in the park, anywhere really, and ask if you are Chinese and if you can speak English. Imagine stabbing them like stabbing the foggy eye of a steamed fish. Add the popular girls, the rich kids, the customers who get frustrated and yell at your mother because they can't understand what she's saying, the kid who punched your little brother, the politicians, the racists. Add them, add them. Think about adding your father who will leave very soon and will always, somehow, be leaving. Think about how he gambled away your family's money and drank and smoked and lied and never spoke to you. How, when you were little, he didn't pick you up from band practice and you had to sit with the teacher for four hours until your mother came. How he decided to go to Atlantic City that day and kept going there like a moth drawn toward light—casino light, brash and blinding. Think about it, yes, give it a thorough evaluation, but please, do not add him. When he decides to leave your family and comes back after four months for your birthday and tries to give you a carton full of rice and chicken thighs, take the gift. Do not let him past the door, for forgiveness is difficult, but take the gift and allow the weight to leave his hands.

And what to do now, now that you're older and far away: There is not much to do now that the restaurant is gone; you'll find this idleness disconcerting and want to grab a broom to sweep or stomp or throw. You'll want to hiss for the sake of hissing. You'll want to chase raccoons just to find your likeness, your feral child-self. Instead: move to New York, to Hong Kong, to Iowa, to Montana, to Washington, to a place so close to Alaska you can smell the muddy toes of moose in mid-July. Call your brother, your mother, call them in apology, as in: sorry it's been so long and what did you eat today? Marvel over how your brother has grown exponentially taller than you, 6 feet tall, and how he stands like a pine tree, rooted, no longer shaking. Listen to your mother laugh like a bursting tomato, free and wild. Over a bowl of soup, forget your father; let the broth rise and soften your face. Forget and forgive your father. When buying groceries, open an egg carton and check if anything's broken. Let the eggs feel heavy and round in your hands and do not calculate the physics of projectile motion; you were never good at science anyway. Read and write in good light, in hovering white light, in egg light, in a bed you share with no one. Do not be afraid of loneliness; remember your teenage self and what your mother told you right after your father left, the both of you struck by the sting of salt and wind along the boardwalk: "If I was allowed to choose, I would choose to be alone." Allow yourself to make your own decisions. Become your own book, your own revenge in language struck with a cleaver. Repeat the little Cantonese you know to your grandparents: 我唔知道 and 食飯. When you return to the strip mall twenty years later, the restaurant will still be a restaurant and there will be a small black-haired girl from another family, another life. Do not look her in the eye. Do not tell her who you are. Do not ask her to draw you a picture on a menu or how long it takes for her to de-vein shrimp or if she falls asleep behind the fronds of potted plants. Does she stick gum along the ribs of bamboo? Don't ask her. It will be too close, too rotten, too down-to-the-bone honest to reach out and tell her everything you know.

———

Jane Wong's poems can be found in anthologies and journals such as *Best American Poetry 2015*, *Best New Poets 2012*, *Pleiades*, *Third Coast*, and others. A Kundiman fellow, she is the recipient of a Pushcart Prize and fellowships from the US Fulbright Program, the Fine Arts Work Center, Squaw Valley, and the Bread Loaf Writers' Conference. Along with three chapbooks, she is the author of *Overpour*. She is an assistant professor of creative writing at Western Washington University.

Freeing Thanksgiving from My Family

Jennifer Finney Boylan

It was a few hours before dawn, and the cartoon characters were in sad shape. There they lay, half inflated in the streets encircling New York City's Museum of Natural History: Snoopy and Hello Kitty and Kermit the Frog and Superman. They were tethered to the ground with giant nets, like something out of *Gulliver's Travels*.

"I'm not going to make it," I said to my friend Beck.

"Come on now," said Beck. "You just gotta dig deep."

It was 4:30 Thanksgiving morning, and sunrise was still a long way off. New York was mostly deserted, except for police officers, parade workers, and insomniacs.

And Beck and me. It was 1982. Our plan was to stay up all night, watch as the balloons were inflated, then go over to his apartment for Thanksgiving "on our own terms." I wasn't sure what this meant, but I suspected turkey wasn't going to be part of it. I was twenty-four, working in a bookstore, trying to finish a novel, determined to remake the world using the felicity of my own insufferable genius. Turns out, this was harder than you'd think.

It was my first Thanksgiving away from home. I'd been glad to get away from my parents, and what I considered their stifling view of the universe. Until that year, every Thanksgiving I'd ever experienced had been the same: my mother burning the marshmallows atop the sweet potato puff; my father silently staring into a fire that never quite lit; my grandmother rattling the ice cubes in her glass of vodka and, at a certain special moment, clearing her voice and asking, "Have I ever told you the story of the night your father was conceived?"

I'd left all that behind now, and struck out on my own. Henceforth I would celebrate Thanksgivings among my downtown peers. There would be writers and painters and people in berets reading Goethe in German. Somewhere in my heart, thinking of the life I had chosen, dwelt the phrase, "This will show them."

Beck, a friend since college, was the author of a play titled *Little Condo on the Prairie*. At the climax of this work, the skeleton of a dog was placed in front of a Victrola, just like the RCA Victor dog, except dead. Beck was known for wearing a chef's hat all the time, even though he did not cook.

The plan for our anti-Thanksgiving had seemed clever enough. We'd stay up all night and watch the balloons inflate.

The flaccid Superman would be a visible object lesson, we figured, on the failure of American culture.

But now, the thing that was failing was me. "I'm hungry," I said. "I'm sleepy."

"All right," he said. "Maybe what we need is a classic New York City coffee shop. Eggs over easy, bacon, home fries."

That, of course, was the solution. So we set out in search of a diner. I pictured us sitting in a booth, opening the little packages of grape jelly, steam rising up from the eggs. This, I thought, is a Thanksgiving for a writer.

But the first coffee shop we went to had a sign on the door: CLOSED FOR THANKSGIVING. We stood there, stunned. It had never occurred to me that diners in New York ever closed, Thanksgiving or no.

The next one had an identical sign. Every diner from 82nd Street to 99th was closed, in fact, as Beck and I learned as we walked up Broadway through the dark, deserted city. At last, Beck said, "Let's go to my mom's house. We can have breakfast there, plan our next move."

We walked over to West End Avenue and quietly opened the door so as not to wake Beck's mother or sister. He fried up some eggs and bacon, and I looked around the kitchen. Taped to the fridge, there was a picture of Beck in Little League. Another showed him as a one-year-old, a tiny pink pig in his mouth.

"My mom's had a hard time letting go," he noted.

After breakfast we left our dishes in the sink and flopped into his bed. Soon enough, he was snoring.

I lay awake, staring at the ceiling of Beck's childhood bedroom, at his high school trophies, and a semi-naked poster of the actress Karen Black.

I wasn't sleepy anymore.

In years to come, I would spend many Thanksgivings away from home. My father would pass away just four years later, followed in turn by my grandmother and all of my aunts and uncles, and at last, in 2011, at age ninety-four, my mother.

Now I have a family of my own, and my sons—college students—make the journey each year back to Maine to be with us. I do not know how many more Thanksgivings we all have together: many, I hope. But I do know that someday I'll get a call, or a text, telling me that this year they're not coming home. It makes me wonder how my mother felt when I told her, back in 1982, that I'd be spending the holiday with my friend the playwright, watching strangers blow up Superman in New York.

Except that things turned out differently that year. As Beck lay sleeping, I sneaked out of bed and put on my clothes. I left him a note: "I'm digging deep." Then I walked through the dawn and took the subway to Penn Station. A train was leaving. I got on it.

By lunchtime I was walking up the streets of my childhood toward my parents' house. I opened the door. It smelled like turkey. There was my mother, putting the marshmallows on top of the sweet potato puff. She looked up.

"You're home," she said.

———

Jennifer Finney Boylan is the author of fifteen books including the novel *Long Black Veil* and the memoir *She's Not There*. She is the inaugural Anna Quindlen Writer in Residence at Barnard College of Columbia University and serves as the co-chair of the board of directors of GLAAD.

Broken Home

————

Debra Gwartney

A month after I'd sold our house in Western Oregon, my third daughter called me to say her cats were missing. Our family cats, now in her charge. I drove over and she and I walked the streets of her new neighborhood, calling for Misty and calling for Norman. I'd seen the cats just a few mornings before, when I'd dropped by the house this eighteen-year-old daughter had rented with friends. Norman, black with a swipe of white moustache, was perched on the railing of the front porch that day, staring at me like she was the very symbol of our now disjointed family. Like she was wondering why I had let everything unravel.

After a few hours of searching, we walked back to her house, my daughter rubbing at her face as she tends to when she's upset, and rolling a cigarette, though she knew I hated that. I held her for a second before she pulled away and went inside and then I stood on the porch, certain she was wanting her old house, her real home, her room painted tomato red where she closed herself up to listen to Billy Joel when she'd had it with the rest of us. She'd insisted she was ready to be on her own, but I didn't believe it. Maybe I didn't want to believe it. Not of her or of the other three daughters who'd packed up and left too fast. But then, I'd left fast, too. I'd moved into a loft studio, no pets allowed, above an audiology center. People, mostly old ones, drifted into the office to discover how much they'd been missing, while I sat by the window upstairs, feeling old myself, and bewildered.

Of course there are many reasons the five of us dispersed as we did, and isn't this the way of things: children leave, mother grieves. Except I have come to blame the rush of it, the abrupt and jagged edge of it, on a man. A man who brought a taint into our house. He brought a poison. Maybe we could have eventually wiped our rooms clean of him, but I doubt it. In fact, one time a neighbor showed up with a smudge stick and I followed her, the children trailing us, while smoke did its filmy business, floating into corners and under bureaus and beds, soaking into curtains. I went so far as to light a stack of kindling and newspaper in our fireplace, adding logs until the flames were licking, so my kids could toss in every pair of their underwear. But it wasn't like we could burn the man up or smoke him out. We couldn't dump him in the street, a smoldering pile of ash.

The man's name is William Green.

First there was the clerk at the grocery store who noticed lewd photos of a child on a roll of film she was printing for a customer named William Green and called the police.

Then there was the officer who took extra time searching William Green's house so that he found a secret compartment in the garage that held dozens of videotapes.

There's the detective who, once he viewed the tapes himself, locked them away in his office so that no one else could. That same detective called me one afternoon to ask that I meet with him in person, so he could tell me that he'd counted, on William Green's tapes, the naked bodies of nearly one hundred girls from our town, four of whom were my daughters.

Here's how William Green did it. He hid outside girls' bedroom windows at night with his camera; he filmed them as they undressed for bed. Then the next day, or the day after that, he found a way to get in. Maybe he jimmied the lock with his contractor tools while everyone was gone, while I was at work, my daughters at school. He filmed himself masturbating on the girls' beds, their panties wadded in his hand. He spliced the footage together in his garage, film of the girl undressing, sliding under her covers; film of him on her bed, his head on her pillow. Against my will, I pictured him. I pictured him watching what he'd made in a sweaty corner of his own dank house.

I left the detective's office that day with a stake jammed in my side. Now I'd have to go home and tell my children what had been perpetrated upon them, which I did. Now I would have to make up a story to tell others about my lack of culpability, which I did—in fact, I recited it to anyone who'd listen. I mean, what could I have done about a hidden man and his hidden camera? Except here's the thing. My daughters no longer believed I could keep them safe. At least that was what I took from them as we went through grand jury hearings, the trial, the sentencing, the disclosures of what William Green had done to us and others. One at a time, the girls came to me: *I need to make my own way now.* How could any of us stay? That was their argument. How would any of us feel unwatched, uncontaminated in our house again?

When I first drove into our Oregon town in the early '90s, it was already dark. I parked under the lights at a Safeway to figure out where I was, a map of the city unfolded in my lap. The daughters and a single cat were asleep behind me. I knew no one here. No one to call if a child got sick, or if I couldn't start my car some morning. I was just divorced, far from their father. My new job would start in a few days. The plan was that we'd hole up in a two-bedroom apartment until I could find a better place for us to live. I had $150 in my bank account. What I wanted to give my daughters was stability, but there's nothing stable about a dry leaf tumbling down a sidewalk and that was me. Still, did that ex-husband of mine believe I'd fail now? I was thirty-four years old sitting in the parking lot that night, and no one was going to tell me I couldn't do it all—earn a paycheck, make Saturday morning doughnuts from scratch, transport the children on field trips to the coast where they could bend their bodies into the stiff wind. I would buy a house, too, as soon as I could, an address that would be stamped in my children as indelibly as it was on the front stoop.

Two years later, I found one, a house that had been a rental for years, with holes in the walls and cardboard boxes laid out on the bathroom's peeling linoleum, carpets soaked in dog piss. That could be cleaned up. And I could leave the children alone a few evenings a week so I could work longer hours to make house payments and afford to fix the leak in the roof and pay some guy to scrape the dead possum out of our crawl space. A sacrifice, is how I thought about it then, a little skin scraped off for the good of us all.

The day my offer was accepted, the girls and I headed over to walk around the vacant house we'd soon own. On the way, I waited behind a Ford van for the light to change. A daughter called out and pointed to a black and white kitten that wobbled, as we watched, off the road divider and climbed up the van's rear tire. Almost unreal that it happened that way, but it did. The girls, between the ages of six and twelve, started to scream. And I mean: scream. The kind of sound that dents the side of your head. I honked, we shouted out the window, but the light turned green and the van started to move.

The screaming, if possible, was louder now, with seatbelts strained to the breaking point, their bodies ready to hurl out the windows to rescue the cat. After the van turned left, onto the street where we'd soon live, and we followed, still honking and yelling, we watched as the kitten was catapulted from the tire well, landing hard on the side of the road. I pulled over and we jumped out. Girls on their hands and knees pawing through the grassy strip until I said we had to face the fact that the kitten was gone.

The next day after work, kitten turmoil somewhat abated, we tried again to go to the house. I thought I'd wedge open a window, slide one of the smaller girls through the opening so she could unlock the front door and let us in to rooms we hadn't yet seen clear of others' belongings. Once we arrived, the girls ran ahead to look into a box on the front porch. I was thinking only about getting in so I could convince myself to keep stretching thin, my thin money and my thin time.

I saw the oldest daughter stand up, holding a note she'd found in the towel-lined box. *I think this belongs to you,* it read. Inside was the kitten, unharmed save her tail, which was severed about an inch from the root. My first thought was, I can't afford a second cat. A hurt cat would be a chore, a nuisance. But before I could tell them so, my daughters stood as a wall of resolve in front of me. The cat's name was Norman, the oldest one said, and we were giving her a home.

At one point in the investigation, the detective let my daughters and me watch a single piece of film confiscated from the cupboard in William Green's garage, where police also found bags of girls' underwear and swimsuits, snarls of hair pulled from drains and out of garbage cans, as well as collages of photos he'd stolen from family albums, including ours. The footage wasn't of a daughter undressing or of William Green on her bed, and yet it was somehow more disturbing. I hadn't known, until I watched it, that he'd filmed at our living room window too. But here it is. The four girls sprawled on sofa and chairs, one daughter's legs entangled with another's. It's a hot night: they're wearing shorts. Their long blonde hair tied in loose knots on their heads. Norman is sitting next to her favorite lamp, until a daughter pulls the cat into her lap. Misty is there, too. Ghost television light flashes across the girls' faces and you can see me like a shadow down the hall, an apparition in the kitchen, puttering about, so ordinary, such an ordinary weekend evening, no threats, no fears. I leaned in to scan for any sign in that mother on the film that she must be vigilant now against the trouble seeping under our door and in through our windows, but I saw nothing.

The detective worried that the girls might cry when they saw the living room tape. But they didn't. There was nothing left to cry about. They'd already faced the shackled William Green who sat behind the defense table, maybe eight feet away from us. At the end of the last hearing, the judge said that, really, we were so very lucky that the girls hadn't been touched. This wasn't much of a crime after all: the only things stolen from us were a few pictures, a couple of pairs of underpants. Not one girl's body, he said, had been violated.

Then the judge dropped charges relating to taping and tres-
passing, the lesser charges, and sentenced William Green to
prison for fourteen years. William Green's name would not appear on the state's list of sexual predators. His access to cameras,
upon his release, would be limited but not denied. Schools and
neighbors would not be notified of his past behavior. I remember that the judge looked down at my daughters from his chair
and told them to count themselves fortunate for what had not
been done to them. It was his attempt to reassure, to comfort,
though I heard only dismissal. He told my children to leave the
courtroom and get on with their lives.

Which is what they did.

By the time our house sold, the oldest daughter had moved
out. The second was in college in Massachusetts. Number four
had gone to a boarding school in Colorado and the third daughter gathered up Norman and Misty and trundled away to the
house downtown. Our family house became a rental again,
packed with college boys who probably laid cardboard on the
bathroom floor and let their dogs pee on it. It's a simple beige
house on a busy street. But this is where I lived with my children for ten years. This is where I got so busy making the life I
thought we should have that I failed to notice. How had I failed
to notice? The rings dug into the soil under the girls' windows
from the bucket he stood on, the gaping holes in our photo albums. I remember folding laundry, annoyed at the missing pairs
of underwear. Where are they? Are you leaving them at school
after PE, at a friend's house? I said: go search your backpacks,
look under your beds. My daughters shrugged.

The tapes my children appear on span four years. Forty-
eight months of William Green. Let's say: enough footage for

a feature film, or two, all those dozens of times he was at their windows. All the times he was inside our house. I understand it is a particular torment of motherhood to believe in hindsight that you could have done better, that you should have done better by your children, or maybe I'm the only one who gives up a part of each night to poke pins in my personal map of wrong-doing. But, still, one question burns in me and I suppose it will keep on burning until the end of my days: when William Green was coming after your children, where the fuck were you?

A couple of months after the third daughter and I gave up trying to find the cats, someone showed up with Norman. That someone brought our cat to the door of her rental house. *I think this belongs to you.* I picked up my daughter, who held Norman limp on her lap while we drove to an emergency vet clinic. The doctor there said Norman had been hit by a car. Broken bones had healed poorly. She stank of rot, of death. She was alive, breathing, but there was nothing but panic in her eyes. Norman weighed less than five pounds.

The vet left the room and then came back with an estimate. Thousands of dollars to rebreak the bones, to put Norman into some odd cat-cast for weeks of healing. A high-protein diet to restore vitality. My daughter was the first to say it, *no,* and then I said it, too. No. I was done; this was finished. The vet got stiff, argued with us. I think she even said, *I can't let you do that.* She refused to produce the shot that would allow Norman to drift away, so we left with our cat. The next day the same vet called me at home, arguing, calling me cold, calling me callous. I was those things. Maybe I had to be those things now, though I wasn't going to explain it to her. Then the man who would later be my husband took over. He found another vet who promised he would bring Norman peace.

Norman spent her last night in the bathroom of my loft studio, with its shiny faucets and slick tile floor. We were alone, the two of us, in a place where neither quite fit, and where one of us was thinking she'd do about anything to go back and stand as a sentry at the windows of our house, alert, awake. Norman wouldn't let me touch her. She growled and snapped if my hand came near. She hunched in a ball in the corner of the box I'd made for her, packed with towels and bowls of food and water she didn't want. I leaned against the wall and stayed with her until morning, letting myself indulge in memories of my home, the ring of the girls' laughter, their fights, unfinished homework on the table, bread in the oven, and Norman staring at her favorite lamp in the living room. But now that was gone. If it ever truly existed in the first place, it was over, and this cat and I were tired. Both of us were wondering how it had come to this. Norman and I were together in a cold bathroom on a still night, sharing a single desire: we wanted one more chance to go home.

———

Debra Gwartney is the author of a memoir, *Live Through This*, and has had work appear in such journals and magazines as *Tin House*, *The Normal School*, *Creative Nonfiction*, *Prairie Schooner*, *American Scholar*, and others. Debra was co-editor, along with Barry Lopez, of *Home Ground: Language for an American Landscape*. She lives in Western Oregon and teaches in the MFA Program at Pacific University.

On Moving Home

Kirsten Sundberg Lunstrum

Whenever a new acquaintance asks where I live, I give only the barest details. "Not far from here," I might say. "Close enough to the beach to hear the ferry's horn!" I sometimes enthuse. I don't invite friends over, I schedule my kids' play dates for the park, and I keep the specifics of my address to myself. Why? Because I'm thirty-four, and just over a year ago my husband, my children, and I moved in with my parents.

For four years before my husband and I decided to move back to Washington—and into my parents' house—we lived in New York. I had a great job—a tenure-track teaching position in creative writing at a college not far from New York City—and my husband taught part-time at the same college and was a stay-at-home-dad the rest of the time. We rented a tiny apartment in a suburb north of New York City, and for the most part life was fine. Before New York we had lived in the Midwest, and before that in California, and life was mostly fine in those places, too; though through all of those years, we were both aware of a vague and distant homesickness, dropped like a shimmery veil over our new landscapes, only visible in the loneliest kinds of light. "Someday," we thought and even sometimes said aloud. "Someday we'll go home again."

We're both originally from Seattle (or, more honestly, we grew up near Seattle), and our parents and siblings are all still settled in the blue-green stretch of land that runs between Puget Sound and the Cascade Mountains. That land has always—for both of us—been the place we're talking about when we say the word "home." New York, no matter how we tried to root ourselves to it, was never home. In fact, the longer we were there, the less it felt like we belonged.

During our last year in New York, however, my homesickness became unbearable. While it had been a low-grade fever before, it was now a full-blown virus from which I could not recover. I thought of home at every turn. On my early morning runs, as I looked out over the pitched roofs of Tarrytown to the lights of the Tappan-Zee Bridge and the slubby brown water of the Hudson, I remembered the silver lights that outline the ferry docks on Puget Sound—the layered multi-blue wash of water-mountains-wide western sky—and I felt gutted by the memory. In the evenings, lodged in traffic on my way home from the college, horns blaring both ahead and behind, I felt a frantic, caged frustration and a sense of powerlessness that made my heart race and my stomach tilt. And nights, kissing my children's foreheads and tucking them in, I was flooded with a sudden and deep sorrow, a feeling that I was failing them. They were becoming New Yorkers. When they said home, they meant here: this foreign place with its endless, clustering buildings and sunsets made beautiful by smog. They meant this place in which we—their father and I—felt ourselves alone among strangers.

As the year progressed, my sickness only worsened. I was angry—inexplicably—almost all the time. I did not like myself in New York. I did not like my growing resentment of the place, my inability to fully invest myself in the present because the present was happening there. I didn't like how difficult gratitude was becoming for me, and joy, and ease. Instead of feeling those things, I was moving through my days tripped up by my own restless anxiety and the buzz of my generalized anger.

And then, one night in November, during the college's Thanksgiving break, it all finally broke open in me. I lay awake, my heart pounding out of rhythm and my breath drawing up short: a panic attack. I hadn't had one in years. I needed to go home. We needed to go home.

So we did. That spring I resigned from my teaching position. We let go of the lease on our apartment, sold what furniture we could, said our goodbyes. In June, just a week after school got out, we drove west.

To some, I suppose, the risks involved in our decision to leave steady employment and good benefits might seem too great. And it's true—they were great. We came west with no jobs waiting for us, no health insurance, no guarantee beyond our own intuitive certainty that our family would be happier in Seattle than we had been in New York. Looking at it from the outside, our move might seem impulsive and immature, an irresponsible leap of faith for the parents of two young children to make. We didn't see it that way. We saw our move as an investment in long-term happiness—both our own and our children's—and a chance to show our kids that sometimes, even when it's risky, you just have to jump toward what you want and believe that you will find a way to land safely.

The other truth, however, is that we could not have left New York if my parents had not been here, in Seattle, ready to welcome us home. And this brings me back to our domestic arrangement—our intergenerational household.

We've now been living with my parents for just over a year. When we first arrived, we had no sense of how long we'd be with them. We planned to stay until we had jobs, were grounded here, ready to buy a house of our own nearby. But how long would that take? We didn't know. Six months? Nine months? At that time, a year seemed impossibly far away. Now though, looking back, I see how quickly it slipped away. Since we unpacked our boxes last June, our son has grown a full clothing size, lost three teeth, become a proficient (and avid) reader, and completed his first year of school. Our daughter, who was just two when we moved—still in diapers, still speaking in broken sentences, still timid about the newness of this place—is solidly a preschooler today. She talks almost without cease, has climbed to the highest rung on the monkey bars at the playground near our house, and has grown into a personality that is at turns hilariously funny and wickedly independent. My parents have been present to witness those changes, and that is a gift we could not have given the children had we stayed in New York.

But the reality of living with my parents is that we get far more than just their presence for major events. We get the routine of daily family life. My father drives my daughter to preschool twice a week, a habit she treasures. Every morning, she and my mother have breakfast together and talk about their plans for the day, plans that last weekend included building a fairy garden together in an oversized pot in the garden, as well as filling the cherry tree's bird feeder with seed, and later baking a loaf of bread. While they were busy with that work, my father took my son to the public pool for Open Swim (and afterward, my father reported, they talked about sea creatures and Legos and friends). Most nights we all sit down for dinner together at the same big table my parents had when I was a kid, and then the children kiss "Amma" and "Papa" goodnight, and I usher them upstairs so that my husband can give them their baths and I can read them their bedtime stories.

We've also seen all of one another's imperfections. My parents have now witnessed my son raging with a temper that still sometimes shocks me. They have pried him off the floor mid-tantrum and carried him up to his room amid his wails to set him in time-out. They've tolerated my daughter's incessant, obnoxious whining on the days when she's missed a nap she really ought to have taken. They've shared the kids' viruses, helped clean up endless glasses of spilled milk, withstood our circus of noise. And we've seen them at their most fatigued, too; we've seen them weary with the exhaustions of work and physical pain, with the ordinary and particular strains of their lives. It would be dishonest to suggest that there have not been moments of discomfort in seeing so much of each other; but in the sweep of the year, most of those moments have been few and forgettable. Overwhelmingly, this has been a gift of a year—and not just for the children, but for all of us. I know my parents as adults now in a way I did not before moving home. My family has always been close, but our already tight bonds have strengthened in this year of joint living.

Beyond that, and apart from the family life we've found here, for me there is also the utter joy I daily feel about being back in this landscape that I have missed for so long. I can catch my breath here on the shore of Puget Sound. I can work and rest now without the hollow feeling of absence slowly carving me empty. Home, I've discovered, is not something that can be made anywhere; for me, at least, it is a definite and fixed point, a holy center, and I am more myself here in that center than I could be anywhere else in the world.

Even still, it feels risky to me to write this. I've put it off, actually, worrying about how I'll be perceived once it's known that at thirty-four, with two kids in tow, I shucked off a "successful" life that just didn't quite fit and moved back in with my parents. Living with your parents as an adult is a joke in our culture. It's a sign—perhaps *the* sign—of real failure, and I've fretted over being judged for it. I've fretted over having my parents judged for it (they are, after all, the people who raised me to think that happiness might be worth more than stability). Until now, in fact, I've not let many people know that we live with my parents. But I feel guilty about that reluctance, which seems to me a betrayal of my parents' generosity, a denial of how truly well this year has gone and of how grateful I think we all feel to have lived it together.

This internal conflict is particularly strong right now, as my family's multigenerational cohabitation is about to come to a bittersweet end. In another two months, I'll start working full-time again, reinventing myself as a high school English teacher. My husband will soon mark the first anniversary of his own major career change (he's left teaching completely and is training to work as an electrician), and we've begun the process of buying our own house. The house has a bedroom for each of our children—which, after our time in New York, still feels like a luxury—and a backyard big enough for a swing and a garden. The kids are excited, but they're also saddened by the prospect of leaving their grandparents' house. "We won't be far," I reassure them. Our new house is within walking distance of my parents' place. "We'll be Amma's and Papa's neighbors," I say. I mean to be comforting, but I can see the doubt on my children's faces, and though it sounds cruel to say so, their doubt makes me glad. It's a confirmation, you see, that we did the right thing in leaving New York to come west. It's a sign that, despite the risks and the fears and the losses, we've all found what we were hoping to find here—happiness and rootedness and home.

———

Kirsten Sundberg Lunstrum is the author of two collections of short stories, *This Life She's Chosen* and *Swimming with Strangers*. Her fiction and essays have appeared widely in journals, and her writing has been recognized with a PEN/O. Henry Prize and a Jack Straw Writers Program fellowship. She lives north of Seattle with her husband and two children, just down the road from her parents.

Between My Teeth

——

Naomi Jackson

On this trip to the Cape, I'm surprised and comforted by the Jamaican accents I hear all around me. My father jokes that you can find a Jamaican and a Nigerian everywhere. And true to Daddy's word, here are Jamaicans in the most unlikely place, although I wonder how this seaside town diverges from and resonates with their memories of home. These are the people who first loved me, West Indians with loud talk and patois filling their mouths, a raunchy, cutting sense of humor. There are women who work in the shops and then there are the men on the road. One catcalls to me as I walk the long, hot highway to Race Point Beach. "Beautiful," he calls out from the truck he's driving. I look up and smile, not because I enjoy being harassed on the street, or because I think this compliment bears any relationship to me, but because his voice takes me home. Home is the language you are loved in.

My story of home begins in my grandmothers' houses. I have a complicated family tree that extends in many directions, two moms—my biological mother and my stepmother, one father, three grandmothers. I learned how to make home from the women who made me. I've taken these lessons with me into the world, carrying them, as Maya Angelou once said, between my teeth, in these years when I've learned to call home anywhere I rest my head at night.

～

My paternal grandmother, Ruth, hails from Antigua. She raised her husband, six sons, and several of her sisters' and brother-in-law's children in a two-bedroom house in a neighborhood that was down at the heels for years before it was razed for tourism ventures—"down Fibrey" as my father and his brothers called it.

In the 1970s, just before they left to try their fortunes in the States, Ruth and my grandfather Herbert Jackson and their children built a house in Villa, a new development just outside of town. The new house was a serious upgrade: four bedrooms, a rose garden and a gallery in front, space to hang laundry and for her beloved dogs in back. As she began earning dollars at her job at a Queens nursing home, my grandmother made additions to the house. In the 1990s, she built a bathroom with hot water that none of her grandchildren were allowed to bathe in without her express permission. Every afternoon after her four o'clock tea, my grandmother took her evening bath, her sizeable frame creaking the wooden floorboards as she slowly, deliberately, made her way to her bathroom. I learned from my grandmother that rituals of self-care were sacred moments not to be interrupted by anyone, especially children, and that the benefit of years of hard work and sacrifice was making and enjoying, quite literally, a room of your own.

In the care that my grandmother took with her house, I found a model for making my own home and creating space for myself and my needs. Over the many summers I spent with my sister, cousins, and large extended family in the house down Villa, I came to appreciate how, in building this house by hand, my grandparents and uncles made a place to which we could always return and call our own. I also came to understand how it was possible to make a space for quiet solitude even in the context of a large, occasionally raucous family.

My second grandmother, my stepmother's mother, Lily, also built a house. She built her home in Jamaica's Windsor Forest, a tiny district high in the mountains of Portland. The house sits at the top of a potholed road where everyone peers into your car without shame when you arrive, staring and trying to sort out to whom you belong. Below the house is a shop that sells sundries for the people who want the convenience of buying batteries or rice or cigarettes without going all the way into town. There has been talk of turning it into a bed and breakfast, offering donkey rides to tourists.

During my only visit there, on a junior high spring break to Jamaica with my stepmother meant to cool the venom that had risen between us, I had the best sleep of my entire life. Something about the cool breeze and quiet melted away the worry that dogged me in Brooklyn. Experiencing tranquility for the first time in Jamaica, I began to understand the sacrifice my parents made to give themselves and their children better chances at life in the States. What they'd given up in leaving the Caribbean was not some abstract sense of home, but quite literally peace—the possibility of touching and knowing peace in a place that was yours. They forfeited the calm of rootedness that their ancestors knew, and a calm they knew they would never find elsewhere, for the uncertainty of life elsewhere.

As I slept in Jamaica, I pressed my hands and heart to the treasure they'd left behind and understood the gamble they'd made of our lives.

⁓

My mother's mother in Barbados, Oriel Loleta Brewster, lived the last ten years of her life before she passed in 2014 in a chattel house that she built with her own sweat and money. For years, my sister sent my grandmother money each month to supplement her pension from her work as a nursing assistant in England. Granny, whose thrifty ways I've inherited, used some of that money to support herself, but most of it went into building the house.

She enlisted her childhood friend and onetime sweetheart, now an architect, to draw up plans for the house, paid contractors, and bought materials. In the end, the house was humble—two bedrooms, a living room, and a kitchen nearly destroyed by a fire she set while trying to cook with wood fire on a gas stove because she could no longer afford cooking fuel.

Like my grandmother in Antigua, Oriel had a beautiful white rosebush in front of the house. On the side of the house, there was a small plot of okra, pigeon peas, tomatoes, and other staples she used to stretch her meals and money. Long before the artisanal and slow food movements that are so popular in America now, all my grandmother's meals included ingredients she'd grown with her own hands.

In the end, the house wasn't much. But it was hers. As is the tradition with homes in Barbados, above the threshold of the white clapboard house was its name, two words printed in blue cursive: "Why Worry?" When I find myself worked up about some existential, overwrought, and usually self-made crisis, I remember these two words and my grandmother's resilience in the face of a world that was at best indifferent to her survival. It anchors me when I am tempted to be led astray from my path, when I am led too far afield from myself.

Back on the Cape, later the same day as the cat-calling Jamaican, a white man offers me a ride to the center of town. I tell him I'm only going as far as the grocery store, and he asks me if I work there. I am offended but I also find myself comforted by his racism, which is a kind of home I've lived in for most of my life. As an American child of Caribbean immigrants who fears the distance that my life choices have taken me away from my family and the people I so love, I find solace in being recognized, even for the wrong reasons, as a Caribbean woman. Is it my gait, or my accent, or my clothes, or his racism, I wonder, but will never know.

That evening, sitting in the audience at a reading at the Work Center, I trouble a grain of sand from Herring Cove between my teeth and remember that I will soon be home, am just a few days from a trip to Barbados where my grandmother is no longer alive and troubling me with her eccentricity and her hot mouth. I will see her beneath the ground and sink my toes beneath that sand and know that we will never talk again, that she will never again press her hand to the formidable arm

I inherited from her to make a point as she tells me a story. But right now, the sand that I eat is the sand from Massachusetts, a place I will soon call home. It is not the sand of the beaches on the islands that made me. But it is what I have for right now. The sand from a place that will soon be home, and the knowledge that home for me will always be held just between my teeth.

———

Naomi Jackson is the author of *The Star Side of Bird Hill*, nominated for an NAACP Image Award and the Hurston/Wright Legacy Award in Debut Fiction and long-listed for the National Book Critics Circle's John Leonard Prize and the Center for Fiction's First Novel Prize. Jackson studied fiction at the Iowa Writers' Workshop. She traveled to South Africa on a Fulbright scholarship, where she received an MA in Creative Writing from the University of Cape Town. A graduate of Williams College, her work has appeared in literary journals and magazines in the United States and abroad. She has taught at the University of Iowa, University of Pennsylvania, City College of New York, Oberlin College, and Amherst College. Jackson lives in Brooklyn, where she was born and raised by West Indian parents.

Allá En La Fuente

Lina María Ferreira Cabeza-Vanegas

"Wait. Where you say you were from?" the man asks me from behind a screen.

"Um . . . Colombia," I reply, plugging in another donated laptop at the Iowa City's Shelter House.

"Seriously?" the man says, emerging from behind a screen.

"Yeah man, why? You know it?"

I sit down in front of one of the crumb-encrusted computers.

The room is small and nearly full—five others around the chipped-corner conference table we use to run the thrice-weekly job and house-hunting lab.

"Yeah," he replies, smiling wide. "I been there."

I left China, after a year and half, only a few months ago, and I'm still jetlagged.

Wenzhou, Shanghai, Frankfurt, Bogotá, Houston, Cincinnati, Cedar Rapids, Iowa City. From grad school in Iowa, to unemployment in Colombia, to a lectureship in China, to the

49

possibility of a visiting job somewhere in Ohio. Not a job, just the possibility. So now I'm here in Iowa City temporarily, volunteering twice a week at the local Shelter House. Helping other people find part-time jobs and part-time homes while I wait between interviews for maybe jobs and maybe visas to maybe see where I'll live next.

So I drive around in circles. I play video games and sit on sidewalks. And sometimes I ride my bike slowly through Iowa City and imagine it is the small town in Colombia where I spent the first seven years of my life. Pretend I never left, pretend it never let me go. I pedal through the pedestrian mall and imagine it is Chía's dirty cobblestone colonial town square and that the injure-proof jungle gym is the dry fountain at its center. I stand on the pedals of my bike, as tall as I'll ever be, and remember feeling my legs tremble as I sat on the back of my mother's bicycle. Five years old, wearing orthopedic shoes and fighting their weight to keep them from touching the spinning spokes and making us crash into a dry town-square fountain.

The man across from me is handsome and no older than twenty-three, broad shoulders, black skin, dreadlocks. He wears a sleeveless white shirt and sits beside a young woman with slick-black hair in a ponytail and features as if painted with a thin brush on tracing paper. He seems uninterested and she seems exhausted while a toddler pulls on her sleeve and wipes his nose with the back of his hand.

"No way!" I respond with what feels like an insincere amount of enthusiasm. "That's cool." I try to correct myself, as if tuning a radio with a broken dial.

The man nods slowly and stares at me intently, as if he were checking a counterfeit bill. So, I sit very still and smile, wondering if they know for sure they can stay here tonight—because it's a raffle after all, you can never know until you know, and most of it is waiting. The toddler rubs his eyes yawns.

I hope they know, hope they can stay. "Where are you from?" I ask.

The man first seems taken aback by the question and then disappointed as he slumps behind the screen.

"Chicago," he mumbles.

I'm trying to stay in the U.S., though I don't like to admit it. Don't like to mention how my parents thought I'd have a better shot at life if I lived far away from them, from everything I knew, from the machismo my mother was constantly crushed under and the self-cannibalizing brutality of an endless civil conflict. And I especially don't like to admit that I think they were right.

But it feels like a betrayal of the little dry fountain in the middle of a small town square, and the song my mother used to sing when we passed it on our way to the butcher shops.

"Chicago," I parrot clumsily. I have friends there, they live in a loft on a nice side of town, but that's not what I say. Instead I just say, "That's cool," partly because I don't know what else to say, mostly because I assume that he's not from that nice side of town. Then I cringe at how unfair it is to assume as much.

"Do you have family there?" I ask.

He seems disappointed once more. "Um . . . yeah," he says, "My mom."

"That's cool," I repeat, while the others in the room continue scrolling through pages and pages of mostly broken links. "It's not too far," I try again, "If you wanna visit."

He nods and scratches something on the plastic beside the keyboard while the toddler begins running circles around the conference table.

"It's like . . . what? Six hours on a bus, right?"

He nods again, keeps scratching whatever is stuck to the battered laptop.

"I don't get to see family that often."

After Chía I lived in Cali for three years. I chewed sugar cane through math class, popped the sun-made blisters on my shoulders with *guadua* splinters, and listened to the adults whisper about the cartel at the height of its control over the city. Some kids came to school with bodyguards and brand new clothes their fathers had just brought back from Miami. They threw the best birthday parties and had marble fountains on their front yards that remained filled even in the hottest days of a city in the throes of perpetual summer. And everyone agreed, "The Cali cartel is just better." At church, on the bus, on the street, "Not good, but better." Even those who hated the cartel on principle—the priests, the cops, the drivers, the soldiers—they all preferred the cartel that had not declared war on the entire Colombian state. "Let Pablo burn himself out trying to burn the country down," they said. "Let him make all the noise. Let 'em go deaf." Because the capos of the Cali cartel understood that so much violence draws so much attention, that there is no point in making a point, and no point ever worth making if you can't keep making a buck. The economy of bloodshed dictated by the banality of bookkeeping. So they let Pablo and his Medellín cartel set bombs all over the country, let him make the capital click and tick and shatter and weep, and they let their own city simmer in the quiet amassing of white-powder wealth, while Pablo paid two million pesos for every dead cop that any kid with a gun could take down.

I don't like to admit it, but it really was better in Cali. Chía was too close to Bogotá and Pablo's war. In Cali I liked listening to those classmates with bodyguards tell me in whispers about the spinning tea cups in Disney World and the limousines parked outside the Miami airport, while our teacher explained how in the trash dump a few miles down the road there were people living between heaps of plastics bags and towers of scrap metal, and she showed us how to double bag leftover rice so those people in their tinfoil homes could find it clean when they went digging through our trash. "That's how you can do your part," she said.

The man looks around as if for a distraction. His eyes bounce from spot to spot until finally he settles on the room's only window. But there are only cubicles on the other side, and the glass is broken anyway.

I'm glad the conversation is over. I look down at my own screen, my own list of obsolete links leading to filled positions and occupied apartments. It's my job to purge this list. Delete the broken links and leave only the paths that lead somewhere.

Soon, however, I can feel him looking back at me, even before he says, "So . . . where you from, exactly?"

"Oh . . ." I stumble. "Well, Bogotá," I say, "It's the capital." Speaking mechanically and clicking through the expired links of defunct pages, "It's up in the Andes, kinda cold weather but not really. It's . . ."

"I know." He smirks again, "I was just there." And suddenly, it seems, we are finally where he wants us to be.

After Cali it was Orem and then Provo, Utah, while my father earned an MBA. In Provo I didn't speak—not in English, not in Spanish—nothing for a whole month. I attended the wrong classes because I couldn't understand the student who gave me my schedule, and when a boy found out I was Colombian he pushed me against the lockers because, either, the boy's brother had gotten sick from drinking the water in Colombia, or had been shot near water in Colombia. Which one I will never be sure.

But after two years, I could speak, and we went home.

"Really?" I ask tentatively, "That's not usually where people go, like, for a holiday. It's usually Cartagena, or Medellín, or San Andrés. You know. Warmer weather. Less traffic." Bogotá sits well over a mile and half above sea level. It is, depending on the listing, either the third or fourth most populous city in South America—though it does not, by any means, compete with the square footage of the other cities on the list. It is densely packed, clotted jaundice-yellow with taxi traffic, and fresh-scab scarlet with red buses that feed one into the other into the other like a long chain of rusty-fanged snakes. It is high up on a shelf like something delicate or poisonous that children should not be able to reach, but it is no city upon a hill. It is built on a hollowed-out Andean plateau, built on the quicksand ground of a former lake, where I lived from ages twelve to seventeen and what I mean when I say that I want to go home.

"Yeah." He scratches the computer's dirty plastic panel with his fingernail, looking down at the keyboard and up at me intermittently like he has the script and is waiting for me to say the next line.

"There's plenty to do in Bogotá though," I say, trying to stay on topic though my mind is already wandering. When I lived in Chía my older sister used to call Bogotá "the place where bad things happen." I imagined she mainly meant the bombs, the mechanical ticking and nervous twitching of a sieged city waiting for the next explosion. But that's not fair either. There is no place on earth where bad things don't happen—more things, worse things—and that's never all that ever happens in that one place in that one time. Everything happens, everywhere, at once. It's not what Bogotá is now, anyway. "I hope you had a good guide."

"Yeah," he shrugs, and brushes one of his dreadlocks from his eyes, "I was with people."

"Did they take you to *La Candelaria*? Or the 93rd Street park? Or the salt cathedral?" I hear myself speak as if my city were a kid on picture day and I am combing furiously through knots with a fine-tooth comb. "There's nowhere on earth I'd rather be than a mile underground in the salt cathedral."

The man does not seem to hear me. He seems lost in his own thoughts as he continues to scratch at whatever dirt clings to the donated laptop and then, he finally looks up again. "Nah," he shakes his head, "I was only there a couple of days."

I pause.

If I've ever known anything in my life it is the price of a ticket to Bogotá. The price of a ticket, and the length of a trip. Eight hours, on the low end, $800 on average. But then there are taxes, extra charges, layovers, delays, and the minutes that an immigration line can alchemize into agonizing hours. *A couple of days in Bogotá*, he said. And slowly, I begin to understand. Which, maybe, shows on my face because he meets my eyes and seems excited once more.

"I didn't really leave the hotel that much." He speaks calmly and emphatically, and then he pauses, as if he'd just thrown a pebble into a well to see how deep it goes.

"Oh," I reply, feeling his words grind like sand between my clockwork organs. "I see." And what I see is this young man behind a donated computer screen not quite smiling, not quite winking, but something in between.

I've always thought that extremists had a philosophical advantage in this one point and no other. One could be entirely, irrefutably wrong in one's conviction, in one's choice, one's faith, one's belief, but to die in belief, for belief, any belief—even a completely twisted, misplaced notion of nobility, nationality, or ideology—has always seemed to me better than to have died to simply liven up someone else's party.

I know this is unfair. But recognizing that it's unfair makes no difference.

I still hate Studio 54, hate the '80s. Hate the music, the hair, the videos of people dancing all night covered in sequin scales and oil-slick sweat. The lingo, the retrospectives and the nostalgia for wilder days of purer unbridled humanity. I hate the men who come up to me at parties and repeat their own variation of a familiar theme, "I was crazy then. Unstoppable-crazy. With what I did, *how much I did!* Whew. Doctors have told me I should be dead."

But they're never dead, they want me to know. "I could be, but I'm not. It's my constitution." They want me to see in their imagined bruises and chapped lips how close they came, and I never want to know, and I always hate them. I know it's unfair, I know. I do. But I hate the bored bankers and the tired moguls. I hate the fringe artists, the outsiders, the sensitive musicians and activists who have struggled, who *really know* what it's *really like*. Who buy free range, and free trade, and who speak up for all the filthy-winged third-worlders gathered voicelessly around dry fountains, while simultaneously inhaling expensive white dust.

I hate Elton John flying over the Alps and thinking to himself, "That's like all the cocaine I've sniffed."

I understand the narrowness of my hate, the oversimplification and generalization. I do—I like "Rocket Man" too. But knowing doesn't seem to make a difference. I still hate it, I still hate them.

"There are some amazing things in Bogotá," I say, with a quiver in my voice while trying to maintain the same smile. "It's a shame you didn't really get to see them."

"Hm . . ." he replies, slumping down again. "Well . . . I saw a little," he says, feeling the growth of his beard with his fingers. "It's really real man. Like . . . I'm from Chicago, so I know, right?" I nod, though shouldn't. I'm not from Chicago, I don't know. "We think we have it rough out here, but you guys down there . . . whew."

I continue to smile but I don't know why, because I don't know what he means. But still, "Right," I say, "Well," feeling the sides of my smile cut into my cheeks, "It's like everywhere else."

I am not included in that "*You.*" That "*You*" is not me. Though I'm not sure he knows that, though I'm not sure how to tell him. I come from a long line of albeit frequently destructive and occasionally tragic, always educated, middle-class Colombians who mostly got by. And though my father has since lost nearly everything he saved and made, he did very well for a time. I went to a good Catholic high school in Bogotá. I got good grades, wore knee-high socks and a plaid skirt, and I washed my shoe laces dutifully when the former priest turned disciplinary director yelled at me after mass, because, "Where exactly do you think you are going with brown shoelaces? What exactly do you think people will think of you, of us, if they see you like this?"

I imagine a dilapidated airport hotel. Sheets made impermeable from wear, and sweat, and spilt coffee, and semen. Yellow lightbulbs flickering, dead flies on the windowsill, and the chill of Bogotá nights slipping through cracks in the glass. I've gone past these hotels more times than I can count and never before imagined that inside there would be a man like the one before me now.

He's too tall for Colombia, even sitting down, I can tell. And he's not dressed right either. Doesn't carry himself like we do, like they do. Like *those people* would. I think.

I try to speak, but nothing comes out, nothing comes up. I wonder if he was scared in that hotel room, if it was fun. I want to know where they took him, what he saw, and why. And I want to know for whom he feels so much pity, because there's insult and compassion in the sentiment and in this alone I think I understand him.

I've hated this man for such a long time, I'm paralyzed. Not this-this man across the table, but *this man, these men*, across the street, across town, across the border. Crisscrossing the Colombian countryside and financing its eternal war.

When I was a child I used to think that an enormous snake lived deep in the heart of the jungle. It had a long and bloated body covered in fine brown fur and black-tar pus, and it stretched out for miles into the mist, so far and so twisted that no man really knew how long it really was. In my mind I saw its body wrap itself around trees, saw it eat and eat and eat, and grow so fat it crushed those trees to splinters, chewed and chewed and chewed on bullet-riddled limbs and skulls like cracked goblets until it wore its fangs down to dull points. And then I imagined men would show up hauling bodies in wheelbarrows and, just as the creature began groaning for more, they would fill the creature's belly, file its teeth to points and gather the white-fang dust into little bags to sell up north.

It was a disturbingly comforting image that I sometimes long for now.

I watch the toddler pull out a beat-up book from the donated toy chest, I click on a few links and watch error messages pop up, one after another after another. It's like ringing doorbells and peering through darkened windows. *Error 404, no one home, don't come back.* The toddler hits a button on the side of the book and a little MIDI tune plays out. I delete a link from the list. *Where did this man go while he was there?* I wonder, *Where did they take him?* And then, *Where would I take him to explain this better?* To the anise-scented clubs and the gastropubs, to a *fútbol* match? To the sharp edges of the city where the children sit in sewers listening to *fútbol* on the radio and lighting up co-caine paste cigars? To the dry fountain of Chía's colonial town square where filthy pigeons flutter and flock? *What am I trying to explain?*

"Really real," he repeats under his breath and I think I hear pity in his voice. *That's not fair.* I think of Elton John, I think of the Alps and the Andes, and I feel my fist clench under the table. But then, I have a bed to in sleep in tonight, and a job interview in Ohio. I see the toddler press his backward-bendy fingers on the book's buttons and the tune slips out again, and again, and again. I hear my mother in my head, singing about a mostly dry fountain on a wholly hot day and I want to leave some broken links up on the page. A few paths that lead nowhere, just because.

Then I think of one of the many boys who took Pablo up on his offer. How he must have gotten a friend to drive him to the nearest station so he could take out a *tombo* with a bor-rowed gun. He would have never heard of Elton John, he would have never been to an airport. He would have been angry, or he would have been numb, or else, he would have been bored. Most likely he would have planned to buy his mom a brand new television when he got paid, and planned to get very drunk that night. He would have probably had a family, though he could have, just as likely, been related only to the street. He would have been, almost unfailingly, young. Regardless, he would have been

Colombian, and he would have been poor. Just like the cop he felled with a single shot, as if god himself lived inside the barrel of his gun.

Silence.

I hold my smile as if with meat hooks. Like I'm still worried about what people might think about me, about my country, if they see how dirty I've allowed my shoelaces to become.

The man speaks again. "So . . ." He starts tentatively while the woman tilts the screen toward herself, giving up, I imagine, on whatever attention he might pay to their joint search.

"Do you know anyone in the trade?" He smiles again.

Silence.

The feeling of a heel driven straight into my abdomen like light through a windowpane. A stomach made wind tunnel, no pain, no impact, only absence. A freshly dug well were my organs would be, and I find myself waiting just like him, for the pebble to tell me how deep it really goes.

"The trade." I've never heard it called precisely that. "The trade." *The* trade. *El narcotráfico.*

I raise my eyebrows. The woman beside him shakes her head at the screen.

The trade, the trade, the trade.

Then I hear myself laugh.

Because it's funny. Right? If only a little.

I look at the woman beside him, *nineteen*, I decide, which judging by the toddler playing with a torn book, must have meant she was really very young when she had him.

"Are you serious?" I ask.

"Well," the man shrugs, "You do, don't you. You know someone."

"I . . ." I stutter. "I don't think so."

He cocks his head, "Really?" And narrows his eyes. "You sure about that."

"No, man. I'm not connected like that." And I think about the first time I ever saw a "Colombian necktie." Five years old, pressing my face against a seventeen-inch screen. Staring at a bloodless body on the news, at this murky stare and an open mouth like an empty grave. At a dry blood trail down his chin that I followed with my eyes like bread crumbs up into a deep, carnivorous-plant gash above the collarbones from which his tongue had been pulled out like a thread through the eye of a needle. *Not at necktie at all*, I realized, but a message: *this is what happens when you talk.*

"Not like a cousin, or an uncle, or someone?" He leans forward and examines my expressions closely. "No one at all? For real?"

I can feel my smile begin to slip. I want to go home, I want to stay here. I want to stay angry forever, because it's right to be, because someone should be, because that feels more like home than anything else anymore. But that's not fair either. "If I did," I say to the man as pebbles finally strike the rock bottom of my dry well, "Do you think I would tell you?"

————

Lina María Ferreira Cabeza-Vanegas is the author of *Don't Come Back*, a collection of essays, short stories, and translations that navigates the Colombian civil conflict with a personal investigation into her own life, family, and mixed heritage. Ms. Ferreira received her BA from Brigham Young University and MFAs in literary translation and creative nonfiction from the University of Iowa. Her essays have appeared in *The Sunday Rumpus*, *The LA Review of Books*, and *Fourth Genre*, among others. She is currently a visiting assistant professor of creative nonfiction at Virginia Commonwealth University and the executive nonfiction editor of *Anomaly*, an international journal of literature and the arts. She is working on a novel about the devil and a second nonfiction book titled *The Former New Kingdom of Granada*. She lives in Richmond, Virginia.

Home in Four Acts

————

Akiko Busch

The Living Room

When my sister and I were kids, my family lived in Southeast Asia. In the summer of 1958, when I was five, we moved to America. We spent that first summer on Cape Cod, at our grandparent's shingled ranch house. In subsequent years, that house became a year-round residence. Additions were built, a master bedroom suite constructed, a deck added. But that summer, it was little more than a fifties ranch.

The room I remember most, where my sister and I spent the most time, was the living room. My mother had lovingly brought with us our carved Siamese desks, tiny bamboo chairs, a small teak table, but it was our grandfather's revolving chair that gave us the greatest comfort. Squat, square, upholstered in some synthetic fabric the color of dust, the chair was positioned on a fully rotational base, enabling its occupant to turn a full 360 degrees.

In retrospect, it was a feat of postwar engineering, physical representation of the marvelous idea that the fifties might be a time when one's perspective on the world knew no limit. But for my sister and me, such a chair was a carnival ride, and we spent hours spinning one another around and around. It was the ultimate in human-engineered furniture. For kids who had just come halfway around the world, the spinning of the chair was a giddy relocation that made us happy, that thrilled us, that we could handle.

The room was also equipped with another staple of fifties design: a huge plate glass window. The view stretched from the intimate to the grand, from the patio and my grandfather's rose garden to the marsh of sea grass beyond, to the sliver of beach beyond that, and then to the bay where all manner of sailboats drifted by all day long. This was a picture window in every sense; even a kid knows that a view of the ocean is a view to infinite possibilities. Much later in my life, a designer told me—in respect to having a desk near a window—that it is healthy "to look at infinity." His statement took me back to that summer and my grandparents' plate glass window.

There were plenty of other things in that room—armchairs, a chinoiserie desk, big chunky glass ashtrays, stacks of magazines and *Reader's Digest* condensed books. But it is the chair and window that I most remember. One of them could spin me around until I was dizzy. The other provided a view that was nearly endless. And I know now that whether it is furniture or something else completely, whatever offers such experiences are enough to furnish a room.

The Blue Sofa

From the beginning, the blue sofa was too large for the room. A monstrosity upholstered in crushed velvet, it had been left by a previous tenant in an apartment that was far too small for its huge cushions and its massive arms. I wanted to think the color was a deep Mediterranean blue, but in fact, it was an ordinary dark navy. It seemed to consume the space, and somewhere in the first few weeks I lived there, its monumental presence and immense weight came to represent all those other troubles that seem to persist.

I couldn't move the thing myself, so I asked the Salvation Army to come and take the sofa away. The man I spoke with gave me a seven-hour window of time during which the moving truck would come for it, and I agreed to be there for every minute of that time. But when I arrived home that afternoon to wait, the truck had come and gone twenty minutes earlier than the time stated. A few days later, a friend of mine told me he would take it away but he had to find someone to help him, and he didn't know how long that would take. The sofa wasn't going anywhere and continued to squat there with all its acquired malevolence. That the inanimate world has a tenacity all its own was not news to me.

And then one afternoon several weeks later, I walked into the apartment. In the first few seconds I knew that something essential had happened, but I didn't know what. The air in the room had changed. And then I realized. My friend had found someone to help and had let himself in. The sofa was gone. Where it had been were only a few scratches on the floor, some dust, a few spectral vestiges of its vast presence. Suddenly, it was a memory.

And I remembered how I had once been on West 25th Street in Manhattan when a forty-ton piece of sculpture by Richard Serra was being moved out of a gallery. A crane was lifting the gigantic hunk of elliptical steel. People had gathered on the sidewalk to watch. "It's like going to the moon," said a man standing beside me. And I thought also of the artist Michael Heizer, who made arrangements to have a two-story rock weighing 340 tons trucked 110 miles from the desert in Riverside, California, to a museum in Los Angeles. The truck had 176 wheels and a bed that was 300 feet long and it traveled that distance between 5 and 8 miles an hour for 11 nights.

And I realized that in some funny way, accommodating a massive shift in the weight of things seems to happen both instantaneously and last over a long period of time. I thought there must be some psychological corollary and I asked a friend of mine who is a therapist if there is a word for this. You mean breakthrough, she said.

And I realized, too, this is how things so often exit our lives. We beg for them to be gone, have fantasies of that empty space and how we will put that to use. And then when it finally happens, neither the eye nor brain can quite fathom the absence. It takes a moment or two to register the empty space. And I can't say now which is more important, acquiring things or getting rid of them. I know that comfort and how we furnish a room has something to do with how objects come into our lives. But I am certain that the way things leave us matters just as much.

Signs

Some friends of mine came to dinner last week. As they arrived, they handed me a narrow, white paper bag, inside of which was

an expensive bottle of white balsamic vinegar. I was happy to
have it, but the paper bag was what caught my eye. It was white,
with a logo in the center, a circle outlined in dark forest green,
and inside the circle, an intertwined G and C, letters surrounded
by the words, "Williams-Sonoma Grande Cuisine."

I knew this logo well. I lived in San Francisco once, decades
ago, when the company that came up with this brand was just
starting out in a small store full of exotic and expensive kitchen-
ware, shining toasters, and beautiful white French country
tableware. My boyfriend and I lived in a small apartment. We
weren't able to afford any of those things, yet somehow I had
managed to have a little white canvas tote bag with the same
logo from that store.

I used the tote bag a lot, but I remember it being most in-
dispensable during that time I broke up with my boyfriend,
suddenly and quickly one night. I stuffed some things in the bag—
a blue shirt, a green sweater, a book, a cassette tape, a few other
things—and I left the apartment. I didn't quite know where I
was going and spent the next few weeks on the sofas and in the
spare bedrooms of friends. Eventually, I found a new place to
live, got some furniture, kitchen things, but I remember those
weeks, then months, as one of those times when nearly everything I did seemed like a colossal mistake.

And now, even all these years later, when I see that little
green intertwined G and C on some bag or appliance, I don't
recognize the logo as some little insignia of the good life. My reaction has nothing to do with elegant dinners or perfectly set tables with chic striped placemats. I do not think of shining pasta
makers and blenders, Le Creuset pots, or virgin olive oils from
Italy with lovely hand-drawn labels. Instead, I think of sleepless-
ness and hangovers, aspirin, loneliness, the fog in North Beach

during a cold summer, the worry in my mother's voice on the telephone three thousand miles away in New York, and all manners of uncertainty of the worst order.

I understand about branding. I understand about that practice of arranging letters and signs and little shapes to have them construct an entirely new meaning that has to do with beauty or speed or efficiency or luxury, or whatever else it happens to be. But what I don't understand at all is why the people who make these logos and then apply them to bags and appliances and household goods and clothes and everything else are so certain we will attach that same meaning to them.

Because, of course, we don't. My kitchen now is a room I love. The ash cabinets were built by my husband, the same man I left that night in San Francisco all those years ago. We have the imported olive oil now, and a blue Creuset stewpot and a little Italian espresso maker. This room is a place of sufficiency in every sense of the word. In an effusive moment, I might even imagine it as Grande Cuisine. But even today, when I happen to glance at the green circle and letters on the white paper bag that the vinegar came in and that is hanging on a doorknob in the kitchen now, what I think of most is not having any of this at all.

Exile

My friend and I are sitting across from each other in the museum café. We have just looked at an exhibition of paintings by the English artist John Constable, clouds and trees and rolling fields of the English countryside. According to a placard, the artist once said: "The sound of water escaping from mill-dams, willows, old rotten planks, slimy posts, and brickwork, I love such things."

My friend and I have known each other for over thirty-five years, and we are telling each other stories. We are talking about the paintings, our lives, books, people we know. And she says to me that she awoke that morning thinking about three houses: a house where she was once a caretaker; a friend's house in Massachusetts; and the house in which she lived in Vermont for three years with her husband to whom she is longer married.

I don't know why it is that I remember these rooms so well, she tells me. *But I remember them viscerally, physically. I remember how it felt to stand at the sink running the water, or to pull open the drawer of a desk, or the angle of the sunlight as it fell across the kitchen floor in the house in Vermont. I remember the feel of these rooms much more than I even remember the people in them. I can just recall their faces, but it is the rooms that I remember with the most detail.*

And I suggest to her that it is possibly because remembering the people associated with those rooms may be so difficult, so painful. A friend who is no longer a friend, a lover with whom intimacy has passed. And she says, *Maybe that's it. But I'm not sure it is. I think I remember those places,* she says, *because they are the rooms that are forbidden to me now. I know these rooms continue to exist, but I will never be in them again.*

And this is something that perplexes me. We spend our time and money trying to make the places in which we live accommodating, open, and gracious. We desire the rooms we live in to be hospitable and human, and we do what we can to make them so. But in the end, it may be the ones that remain forbidden to us that we remember most clearly. And it is the rooms from which we are exiled that may fasten themselves most tenaciously to our memory and imagination.

———

Akiko Busch is the author of *Geography of Home, The Uncommon Life of Common Objects,* and *Nine Ways to Cross a River. The Incidental Steward,* her essays about citizen science and stewardship, was awarded an Honorable Mention in the Natural History Literature category of the 2013 National Outdoor Book Awards. She was a contributing editor at *Metropolis* magazine for twenty years, and her essays have appeared in numerous national magazines, newspapers, and exhibition catalogues. She is on the faculty of the MA Design Research program at the School of Visual Arts and is currently a visiting teacher at Bennington College. Her work has been recognized by grants from the Furthermore Foundation, NYFA, and Civitella Ranieri. She lives in the Hudson Valley.

Plane Crash Theory

Dani Shapiro

These are the first words I've written since J. fell down the stairs, unless you count lists. I have lists in my pockets, lists tacked to the bulletin board above my desk. Small lists on Post-its ruffle like feathers against walls and bureaus. Chunky baby food, milk, Cheerios. Diaper Genie refills. Huggies overnight diapers. This is what I do now. I cross things off lists. The more items I cross off, the better I can breathe.

J. was just seven weeks old when we moved from Manhattan across the river to Brooklyn. We bought an old four-story brick townhouse with a dogwood out front. A green-painted front door with glass panels led into a foyer with a pale pink chandelier dangling overhead. An antique cherry banister curved in one fluid line up two steep flights of stairs. The staircase itself was polished, with creaky, uneven steps.

My husband and I looked at a lot of places before we decided to live in Brooklyn. Manhattan was out of the question—we

needed four bedrooms—so we explored Montclair, South Orange, Hastings-on-Hudson. We considered the country. Litchfield, Sag Harbor. During a trip to Seattle, on a sunny day when
we could see the mountains, we thought about moving out west.
We kept reminding ourselves that we're writers, and writers can
work from anywhere. But Brooklyn won us over—so close to
our friends, to everything we knew. And then, after a parade of
realtors showed us dozens of narrow, dark Victorians, we fell in
love with the brick house. The night after I first walked through
the house, it filled my dreams. I was in my eighth month of pregnancy, and my dreams had become colorful, baroque. I floated
through each room, focusing on the wide-planked orange pine
floors, the intricate, crumbling moldings.

We ran out of money shortly after J. was born. It was
my fault. I was giddy, on a postnatal, hormonal high. I was a
mother! I wanted everything to be just right for my little family.
The parlor needed an armoire for Michael's record collection.
The baby's nursery had navy-blue curtains hanging to the floor
and a hand-loomed rag rug. We had thousands of books, so we
found a carpenter to build in shelves. And as long as he was already there, we had him install library lights, extra electrical
outlets. You never know when you'll need them. I pored over
"shelter magazines": *House & Garden*, *Metropolitan Home*. I
looked at photographs of other people's shelters. A shelter with a
small Mondrian above the mantel. A shelter with an eighteenth-
century writing desk in a child's room. We relined the fireplaces,
built closets, installed an alarm system, and before I knew it, we
were broke.

Eighteen steps lead from our front hall to the second floor,
to J.'s nursery and our bedroom. They are steep and creaky.
Along the curve of the wall, near the top of the staircase, there

is an indentation in the wall shaped like a tablet, like half of the Ten Commandments. I am told it's called a coffin.

Things don't go wrong all at once. There are small things—invisible things—that constantly go wrong. Wires fray inside a wall. A van speeds through a yellow light. Someone leaves a Q-Tip in the baby's crib. These small things almost always just scatter and disappear. Big wind comes along, and—poof!—they're gone. But once in a while, they start sticking to each other. If this happens, you find yourself with a big thing on your hands.

Whenever we're on an airplane taxiing down the runway, I ask Michael to explain this to me. He calls it Plane Crash Theory. I know he wonders why I need to hear it again and again. But I do. His theory is simple, scientific: in order for a commercial airliner to crash, many things have to go wrong in sequence. Many unlikely things. No single event causes an accident. It is the sheer coincidental accrual and velocity of these failures that sends two hundred people plummeting into the ocean. This makes Michael feel better. He finds comfort in these odds as he settles into his seat and cracks open a newspaper as the jet takes off. Me, I think it's as likely as not that I'll be on that particular plane.

Michael and I have always lived hand to mouth, though from the outside it doesn't look that way. We occasionally get a big check, then go months—sometimes years—without any money to speak of coming in. We bought the house with the expectation that a big check was on its way from Hollywood. It was a done deal. What we didn't realize was that done deal, in the language of Hollywood, does not, in fact, signify a deal that is done. The producers are on vacation in Hawaii. Larry (who's Larry?) is on the golf course and can't be reached.

Here are the things we didn't do when we moved to Brooklyn, because the check didn't come. I still have the list tacked to the refrigerator: fireplace screens, seed garden, repair roof hatch, basement beam. Last on the list was runner for staircase.

J.! He was perfect, with a burly little body. Late at night, while Brooklyn slept, he burrowed into my soft belly as he nursed, and I watched him with bewilderment and joy. Where had he come from? He seemed to have inherited a temperament that didn't exist in either my husband's family or my own. From a grumpy, depressed bunch of people comes this smiling boy. In the darkness of his nursery, I stared out the window at the glowing red face of a clock tower in the distance, and thought obsessive thoughts of all the things I had read about in the baby books. He could choke on a button, or the eye of a stuffed animal. He could suffocate in his own crib sheet. He could strangle himself with the cord of his purple elephant pull toy.

This is what I do with happiness. *Kayn aynhoreh*, my grandmother used to say, repeating this magical Yiddish phrase to ward off evil. *Kayn aynhoreh*. I need to think of the worst-case scenario. If I think about it hard enough, it won't happen.

There is a cage in our basement. I've never gone down there. The stairs are dark and rickety; the third step from the top is loose. The cage is made of rotting wood poles and chicken wire. It was built earlier in the house's history, a less affluent time. Maybe it was once a rooming house. When we moved in, Michael found an axe propped in a corner of the basement. He's not in the least spooked by it. This is one of the reasons I married him. He's been using the axe to tear the cage down. Sometimes, I hear the crash of metal, and he emerges, covered with dust.

We come from money, my husband and I. Not huge family fortunes, but from first- and second-generation Jewish parents who made good, who have more than one house and drive the cars they swore they would never drive (those Nazi-mobiles) and take first-class round-the-world trips. Parents who wish we had become doctors or lawyers instead of writers. I'm saying this because we could have put our pride aside and asked. We could have said, Mom, Dad, we're short on cash. We need a couple of thousand. The staircase is slippery. We should do something about it. Put up a runner.

We settled into the new house over the long, hot summer. I rarely left. I was captivated by J. and spent hours doing nothing but singing the Winnie-the-Pooh song to him. Saturdays, we had a routine: We walked with J. in his stroller to a farmers' market at Grand Army Plaza; I circled the market buying goat cheese, banana muffins, and grape juice, while Michael and J. played in the shade. It was the first time in my adult life I had a full refrigerator. I kept the grapes in a Provençal bowl we had brought back from our honeymoon.

One day during that summer, Michael and I were driving through the city, heading home after visiting friends who had just given birth to a premature baby. Michael turned right from 34th onto Broadway, and drove straight into a swarm of police officers. They had set up a trap and were pulling cars over for making an apparently illegal turn. Michael, usually a calm guy, lost his temper. He screeched to the curb, and got out of the car. Maybe it was sleep deprivation, or the heat, or visiting a three-and-a-half-pound baby in the neonatal intensive care unit. I saw him waving his hands at the traffic cop, who didn't meet his eye, shrugged, and began to write a ticket. Michael opened the car door, grabbed a camera we happened to have handy, and began snapping photos. The corner of 34th with no sign. The traffic cop himself. He got back in the car. "I'm going to fight this," he said. I wondered if he'd bother, or just forget about it.

That coffin, that empty space, bothered me. Broke as we were, I decided that something belonged there. But what? Fresh flowers? An empty vase? I gave it a lot of thought. Then, I bought an arrangement of dried sprigs of herbs, baby roses, big bulbous things that I didn't know the name of that drooped from the edges of a cracked white urn. I placed it in the coffin, and it filled the space nicely, with some of the dried arrangement pushing out into the stairwell in a burst of color. A bit precarious, perhaps: but hell, it looked so good that way. I could picture it in one of those shelter magazines.

September. Back-to-school time for me. Leaving for my teaching job in the city was impossible. I would walk down the front steps of the house while Michael and J. waved bye-bye from the door. I could barely breathe, but I didn't say anything. Just waved at them, blew kisses at J., and wondered if I would ever see them again.

On the subway, I would hang on to the pole and stare out the smudged window at the graffiti on the tunnel walls. I thought of J., of Michael, of anything safe and good, anything to pull me back, but thinking of them only made it worse. I was underground, with no way out. Moving farther away from them by the minute. Was this what having a family meant?

Of course, J. needed a babysitter. We interviewed fourteen women for the job. Who do you trust? We talked to cousins, sisters, best friends of babysitters of friends, and friends of friends. Finally we chose Marsha. She was young and pretty, with a Louise Brooks bob and big brown eyes. She was so gentle, so sweet, that her eyes seemed to be constantly brimming with tears. She had a little girl of her own. She pulled a photo from her wallet; I liked how proud she was of her child. Marsha would never be one of those babysitters I saw in the park, talking to her friends with her back turned to my baby.

One morning, when the train pulled into the station, I stood on the platform, paralyzed, watching as the doors opened, the rush-hour crowd pushed its way in, and the doors slid shut again. This had never happened to me before. I climbed back upstairs and stood on the street. I wondered if I should just walk the two blocks home. Call in sick. Give up for the rest of the semester. It was too hard. I didn't know what was wrong with me. An off-duty cab was approaching, and, impulsively, I flagged it. The driver stopped for me. As we rolled down Flatbush, we got to talking. He said his name was Tony. He came from Nigeria. He lived nearby, and was on his way into the city to begin his shift. By the time he dropped me off at school, he had given me his number. I told him I'd call him the following week to pick me up on his way in. Maybe that would make it easier.

On her first morning working for us, Marsha put too much detergent in the wash while she was doing the baby's laundry. The water flooded my office and dripped through the old floorboards to my bedroom closet below. As we frantically mopped up the mess, I tried to comfort her. I told her it was just an accident. Nothing was ruined. It could have happened to anybody.

That afternoon, Marsha and I pushed J. in his stroller to the park. I wanted to give her my guided tour of the neighborhood. The health food store, the pizza place, the Key Food. It was a warm day, just past Halloween, and the playground was full of moms and kids and babysitters. I lowered J. into the baby swing, and he laughed and laughed as I pushed him. He has the most unusual laugh I've ever heard in a baby. It's like he cracks himself up. Everything was funny that day. The leaves falling off the trees were funny. The little girl with her orange plastic pumpkin was funny. Mommy making her silly faces was very, very funny. He was wearing a Red Sox baseball cap and a blue denim jacket. Already, at six months old, he wanted to go higher and higher.

On the morning of Marsha's second day, we take a family nap together before she arrives. J. falls asleep between us, his little mouth open, his eyelashes blond and long. We hold hands across his sleeping body.

It is a teaching day. I dress in black cargo pants, a black turtleneck sweater, black boots. Tony will pick me up at nine o'clock. I feel pretty pleased with myself at this arrangement. Marsha arrives a few minutes late. Michael is going to catch a ride into the city with me; today is his court date to fight that traffic ticket, and he seems strangely energized by it. J. is in his high chair, being fed strained plums. I take the dog out for a quick walk, rounding the corner by the bodega. A truck honks. You look beautiful! the driver yells. I'm in such a good mood— I've figured out my life!—that I yell back, Thanks!

We cross the Brooklyn Bridge, and for once I feel at peace on my way to school. Michael is in the back of the taxi next to me. Tony is an excellent driver. And Marsha is at home with J., feeding him strained plums in his safe, ergonomically designed high chair. It's a perfect day. The city is a jagged, sparkling cliff along the East River and I notice things I don't notice on the D train when it crosses the bridge. The small boats, the abandoned Brooklyn Navy Yard, the faint outline of the Statue of Liberty off to the left in the distance. I feel, for a moment, lucky.

We drop Michael off somewhere near the courthouse. He gets out of the taxi, a manila envelope containing proof of his innocence—photos of the corner of 34th and Broadway—in his hand. He has graying hair and a mostly gray goatee, and he's put on some weight since the baby was born. He's wearing his usual blue jeans, black T-shirt, green army jacket. We pull away from the corner, and, as I always do, I turn and watch as he walks away. In our marriage, I am the one who turns around and watches. He is the one who walks deliberately, in the direction of wherever it is he's going.

This is the first morning since J. was born that we have both been out of the house at the same time.

As I speed farther and farther away from my neat and well-appointed house (the bookshelves, the sheer white bathroom curtains, the ficus thriving in the south-facing window, the dried flowers bursting forth from the coffin in the stairwell), up the West Side Highway past terrain more familiar to me than my Brooklyn neighborhood, where even the silence and the birds chirping and the car alarms in the middle of the night still feel strange and new, I close my eyes.

When my cell phone rings, it surprises me. It rings from deep inside my briefcase, which is a bag I use only once a week, when I teach. I unsnap the briefcase and pull the phone out from its own special little pocket inside. I'm thinking, It's Michael. He's forgotten something. We are speeding towards the 79th Street boat basin. The traffic is light. I flip the phone open.

Even when I hear the screams on the other end of the phone, I don't get it. Marsha is screaming, J. is screaming. There's static on the line, I can barely hear anything but the screaming, and I'm thinking, We just left twenty minutes ago. Nothing terrible could happen in twenty minutes. Her voice is shaking so hard all I can hear is, I fell, and stairs, and He hit his head, and I'm sorry, I'm sorry, I'm sorry.

I notice that Tony has wordlessly turned off the West Side Highway and is heading downtown, back towards Brooklyn, pedal to the floor. I tell Marsha to call 911. She's crying so hard, hyperventilating, that I have to keep my voice gentle, ask, Can you do that? Can you do that for me? I tell her I will call her back in three minutes.

I try to think. The world shrinks around me. I call J.'s pediatrician. I can practically see her office from where I am right now, in the back of Tony's car. We haven't switched to a local pediatrician, believing irrationally in Manhattan doctors over Brooklyn doctors. While I'm on hold, I try to catch my breath, because I can't think clearly, and my heart is going to explode, I'm going to have a heart attack right here in the back of a taxi, and that won't do anybody any good, will it?

Kids hit their heads all the time, J.'s doctor tells me in a professional, soothing tone, like she's talking someone off a ledge. Tell the babysitter to put some ice on it. Is he crying? Well, that's a good thing. It's when they're not crying that you worry.

I call Michael's cell phone. He's at a diner, just about to go into the courthouse. And I say there's been an accident, that it's going to be okay, but that it appears that Marsha has slipped and fallen down the stairs while holding J., and EMS is coming, and I'm on my way home. Michael is halfway out the diner door before I've finished the first sentence, and is sprinting in his green army jacket to the subway. And I am somewhere on lower Broadway. Tony is weaving in and out of traffic.

The stairs. There are eighteen. Have I mentioned eighteen? Maybe she fell near the bottom. If she fell near the bottom, on the last few steps, and landed on the small rug in the foyer, that wouldn't be so bad. What part of his head? Babies have soft spots. All I can think about as we pass the Tower Records building and make a few quick turns and speed down the Bowery is, Please, not the curve at the top of the stairs, the place where it would be most likely to fall, the place where the steps are narrow and the dried flowers make the passage even narrower, and it's a long, long way down. Please, not that.

He was screaming. Screaming is good. Screaming is the best thing. That's what you want to hear. Big, loud, shrieking sounds.

I call my home, and a stranger answers the phone. A strange man. A strange police sergeant man. He asks me who I am. I say I am the mother. How's my baby? He says, Ma'am, your baby has quite a bump on his head. I melt for this man, I want to collapse into his big, blue chest. His voice is not shaking, he is calm, he is imparting information to me, information I need. Quite a bump. We can deal with quite a bump.

I call the school. I won't be able to teach my class. Baby fell down stairs. Baby fell down stairs trumps all. Trumps viruses and flus and the dog ate my student's homework. I call back the doctor. They're taking him to the hospital, I tell her. She seems annoyed. After all, she's certain that I'm a hysterical mother, that this is only a minor bump. And it occurs to me, not for the first time, that this doctor is younger than I am. When I was in second grade, she was in kindergarten. What is she doing, taking care of my son?

I grew up in a home where prayer was where you turned in moments like these. But I have never been in a moment like this, and I do not know how to pray.

I catch Tony's eyes in the rearview mirror, and then notice for the first time a yellow plastic taxi, dangling there. It looks like it's flying, floating against the pale blue sky. I keep staring at the cheerful taxi, imbuing it with supernatural powers. Nothing bad will happen if I just don't take my eyes off the taxi and keep repeating Please God over and over again.

We pull up to the emergency room of a hospital somewhere in downtown Brooklyn. All I have in my wallet is a twenty, and the meter is much more than that, but I hand Tony the twenty with an apology, and he turns around and looks at me like the father of four children that he is. He says, I'm not leaving until you come out and tell me about the baby.

There were eight of us, friends and acquaintances, who were pregnant at the same time with our first babies. Something about the age thirty-six. Thirty-six means, Get serious. Thirty-six, at least in New York City, means that you're still young enough to do it, with any luck, without fertility doctors and injections and in vitro and all the stuff of middle-aged motherhood. Thirty-six is still normal. And so I would think, sometimes, about my pregnant friends, and then I would think about statistics. Most of us would be fine: a little morning sickness, indigestion, varicose veins. Half of us would end up with C-sections. One or two would have some serious complications during pregnancy: gestational diabetes, preeclampsia. The sort of thing our mothers didn't even know about but that we, with our shelves of pregnancy books, our middle-of-the-night online surfing, know only too well. I would think about the odds. Then, the woman whose due date was just before mine developed severely high blood pressure during her birth, and she very nearly died. I felt, in a completely unscientific way, that she had taken the fall for all of us.

J. is on a tiny bed in a tiny curtained-off area in a tiny ER, and he is not crying. He is not shrieking. His eyes are closed, and he is just lying there. Why isn't anybody doing anything? Marsha is sitting on a plastic chair by the window, a tissue pressed to her nose. Her eyes are red, and she looks like her life is over. Two police officers are standing near the door. Sit down, Mommy, one of the nurses tells me.

I pick up my baby. He is unconscious. But he was screaming just a little while ago! Screaming is good. What happened?

I don't want to shake him. Shaking is bad, I know. I clutch him to my chest, feel his breath, whisper in his ear, "Mommy's here. It's going to be all right. Mommy's here." His eyes flutter open slightly, and he lets out a pathetic little whimper. "Look at me," I command him, my six-month-old whose entire vocabulary consists of "Ga."

Michael rushes in. His face is white, his eyes are huge. He hugs me and J. together, he turns to the doctor, a Pakistani named Noah, and asks what's going on. "We've ordered a CT scan," says the doctor. "Does your baby have any allergies?"

While J. is sedated and taken in for his CT scan, two men in suits approach me. They introduce themselves as police detectives. They are lumbering, uncomfortable. Ma'am? Can we just ask you a few questions? Your babysitter. How long has she worked for you? Two days, I say. They exchange a glance. Ma'am? You don't think . . . well, you don't think she did anything.

Our pediatrician calls the Brooklyn hospital. She wants J. transferred to the Upper East Side hospital where she works, the hospital with the best neonatal intensive care unit in the city. Suddenly, she is no longer calling this a minor bump. She is no longer sounding annoyed. She says she's sending an ambulance, a team.

I don't want to hurt Dr. Noah's feelings. I don't want him to think that we believe his hospital to be inferior to the Manhattan hospital where we are about to transfer our baby. Our pediatrician wants to see him, I shrug apologetically, marveling at my own ability, even in a moment like this, to be polite at all costs. It's my nature. I have a nice surface. Dinner party, emergency room, it really makes no difference. Can I get you something to drink? You look tired. Here, put your feet up.

Marsha gets up from her plastic chair by the window where she has been interrogated by two detectives from the 77th

Precinct and walks towards me. Her whole face has crumbled, and she looks like a completely different woman. Not young. Not pretty. Her arms are outstretched, and I realize that she wants me to hug her. And so I do. I wrap my arms around this trembling woman who fell down the stairs, who doesn't know how it happened, who was wearing socks on the slippery, slippery wood. Who let go of my baby so that he tumbled by himself from the sixteenth or seventeenth step down who knows how many steps before she grabbed onto his arm and caught him. Are you okay? I ask her.

Tony waits outside. At least an hour has gone by, and he's sitting there in his taxi, meter turned off.

This is how they transport a baby in the back of an ambulance: I lie on a stretcher, and they tie me down. Then they hand me J., bundled up in the pajamas he was wearing this morning. Blue pajamas the color of the sky, printed with clouds shaped like white sheep. I cradle him in my arms, his head resting against my breast. His hair is tangled, his upper lip is rubbed raw from crying. The bump is getting bigger. The team—a driver, a paramedic, a nurse, and a doctor—lifts us into the back of the ambulance. I watch through the window as we are driven away from the Brooklyn hospital, siren going, through the congested streets of downtown Brooklyn, over the bridge once more, and up the East River Drive. The doctor, a lanky, dark-haired woman with a big diamond on her finger, keeps checking J.'s vitals, while I keep myself sane by asking her where she went to medical school, how long she's been out, what she wants to specialize in.

I don't want to be a writer anymore. I want to be her.

Hellooooo! coos the pediatrician as she parts the curtain in the ICU. Her face is scrunched into her practiced, good-with-babies grin. Let's see that bump. Oooh, that's a nasty bump.

J. is in a hospital crib, and I have lowered the rail and crawled in there with him. If I tuck myself into the fetal position, it's not such a bad fit. The pediatrician opens her wallet and passes around a photo of her own six-month-old daughter. The nurses coo, then hand me the photo. She's not a cute baby, not cute at all, and she's sitting up against one of those department-store backdrops of lollipops and balloons. I keep looking at the doctor, J.'s doctor, wishing I were the kind of person who would say, Excuse me, but what the fuck are you thinking?

At night, friends bring bagels and lox. Chocolate bread. Cheeses, a cheese board, a knife. We have a party in J.'s room. He's coming to, coming out of that gray place he went to. He gives everybody a weak little smile.

The phone rings. It's Tony, checking on the baby.

The pediatric step-down ICU is festooned with photos of its long-term patients. Birthday parties, staged plays, tired-looking nurses wearing clowns hats. In some of the rooms there are special video monitors, so that parents and children can hook up to say goodnight. I sleep curled up with J., waking every hour as a nurse comes in to lift his lids, check his pupils, take his blood pressure and pulse. Michael wanders the corridors, talking to the children. An eleven-year-old who has lived in the hospital for nearly the past year, waiting for a heart and a liver, tells him about her seven-year-old friend down the hall, who she feels sorry for, because she's only seven, and she hasn't had a chance to live yet.

J. has had a normal CT scan, but they decide to do an MRI as well. That's why we're here, with the big guns, isn't it? My husband goes in with J., into the noisy, noisy room where we get three-dimensional color pictures of his brain. My husband is instructed to remove all metal from his body: watch, coins, belt buckle, wedding band. I put his ring on my thumb, twirling it around and around as I wait.

The MRI shows a contusion on J.'s brain, just below the nasty, nasty bump. Wait a minute. Contusion is a fancy word for bruise, right? And bruises bleed. Bruise on his brain?

We're talking fractions, here. I was never good at math. We're talking an infinitesimal distance between healthy baby and dead baby. That's what we're talking.

Kayn aynhoreh.

In the morning, we check out of the hospital. We are wheeled, J. and I, down the long white corridor. I've pulled a striped knit cap over his misshapen head, and he's grinning, flirting with the nurses who wave and call out, There he goes! There goes our boy! like he's on a float and this is a parade. The two transplant girls wave goodbye, too, in their robes and slippers. The head nurse gives him a kiss. They are all so happy, so happy to see him go.

When we pull up to our house and bring the baby inside, I feel as though I'm walking into a crime scene. The police officer left his card on the kitchen table, under that jar of strained plums with a plastic spoon still stuck inside. The kitchen tap is dripping. Yesterday's newspaper is open to the metro news. I carry J. upstairs. The steps are so old, so creaky and uneven. And the dried flowers look like tumors, like malignant growths on an X-ray, egg-shaped and prickly. I watch J.'s eyes for any flicker of fear, but he's focused on the ceiling.

Marsha called that night to ask how J. was doing. Michael said he was fine. He didn't want her to worry. Then he fired her. It wasn't easy. We felt bad about it. When she asked why, her voice gentle and resigned, the only answer—you almost killed our baby—seemed like more than could be said.

The socks, the stairs, the dried flowers, Michael's traffic ticket, our empty bank account, the strained plums, my subway panic. It all adds up to something. Doesn't it? It adds up to almost died.

Kayn aynhoreh.

The Hollywood check finally arrived. The first thing we did was buy a very nice runner for the staircase. It's a pale brown the shelter magazines might call "sand" or "birch," and there are pastel stripes running up the sides. I yanked out the brown, bulbous things that hung over the edge of the cracked white urn, and pulled out some of the roses until there was nothing pushing its way out of the coffin.

I stay pretty close to home these days. Downstairs, J. is laughing. Have I mentioned that he has the most unusual laugh? The sun is streaming through the tall parlor windows. It's early afternoon, almost time for his nap. I can picture his sleepy eyes, the way he bangs on his plastic butterfly when he gets tired. I can't write anyway, so I go downstairs to see him.

I rock my baby while he sucks down his bottle. The bump is gone. Sometimes, I think I can still see a bluish stain on his forehead. This is what I do, every single time I put him to sleep: I sing him three rounds of "Hush Little Baby," four rounds of "Twinkle, Twinkle, Little Star." Then I count backwards from fifty. When I get to one, I finish by saying, Thank you, God. Please keep this baby safe. Please watch over him and keep him safe. I repeat it over and over again while I rock. I can't alter the routine, and if it's interrupted, I have to start all over again. I imagine an invisible hand cupping my baby's head, softening the blow by a fraction as he smashed into the corner of a stair. Whose hand? What grace?

The house is quiet. Outside, birds are chirping, pecking at the grass seeds we've scattered in the backyard. I'm not sure where Michael is. He's around here somewhere. He's always doing something practical around the house. Maybe he's in the basement, taking down the last of the cage I have never seen.

———

Dani Shapiro is the author of the memoirs *Hourglass, Still Writing, Devotion*, and *Slow Motion*, and five novels including *Black & White* and *Family History*. Her work has appeared in the *New Yorker, Granta, Tin House, One Story, Elle*, the *New York Times Book Review*, the op-ed pages of the *New York Times* and the *Los Angeles Times*, and has been broadcast on *This American Life*. She has taught in the writing programs at Columbia, NYU, The New School, and Wesleyan University; she is co-founder of the Sirenland Writers Conference in Positano, Italy. A contributing editor at Condé Nast Traveler, Dani lives with her family in Litchfield County, Connecticut.

Mother Tongue

Jennifer De Leon

Early one morning, a few minutes past six, I stumbled into my two-year-old son's bedroom and as I lifted him out of his crib he announced, "I want meatballs." This was just after I had said, "Good morning, mi amor." Had he not heard me? "You want meatballs?" I asked, just to be sure I heard him right. He was wearing his favorite monkey pajamas. "Sí," he said. At that moment, like any moment where he speaks Spanish, where a Spanish word instead of an English one escapes his little mouth, I instantly feel a fierce floating happiness, that all is right in the world and in my life and his life or at least in that sentence, Sí. In those moments, he could ask for anything and I would probably give it to him. Meatballs at 6 a.m. Why not?

My first language was Spanish. Or, so I've been told. When I was a young child, my family and I only spoke Spanish at home. It was my older sister who brought English to our two-bedroom apartment in Boston. She was the one who diligently did her worksheets and packets of homework while seated on the plastic-covered couch. Once, I asked my mother why she didn't know the answer to one of the worksheet questions, but my sister did. You're old, I said, as if old people knew everything there ever was to know, as if learning stopped at a certain point, like growing in height. My mother laughs when she tells this story.

After English invaded our home, displacing Spanish word after Spanish word—first through those photocopied packets and later through television and eventually my own crinkly-covered library books—Spanish became the stepchild language. I didn't want to play with her anymore. She was weird. Cartoons were in English. Movies, too. We heard English at the mall and the doctor's office. So my sister and I spoke mostly in English. When my parents talked to us, which was always in Spanish, we replied in English. Then, we moved to a town twenty miles west of Boston where my parents bought their first house. My dad built a fence, painted it white. Bit by bit, episode after colorful cartoon episode, grade after grade in my sunny suburban elementary school, where it seemed everyone spoke in English, even the mailman, my world continued to be eclipsed with the sounds and songs and sayings of English.

The summer I was nine years old, my parents took us—by then there were three of us, all girls—to visit Guatemala, their homeland. I can practically sip those sensory details through a straw. Thin cucumber slices sliding in bowls of lime juice and salt. The smoke-filled streets as we squatted in the back of an uncle's pick-up truck and swished past the city and onto dirt roads bumpy as logs. The sound of iron gates opening and closing, people everywhere, in and out, hola, adiós. Then, a sudden longing on my part: how I wished to move between two languages! But my Spanish was nearly lost by then. So in Guatemala I used

English whenever I could and when I was absolutely forced to speak in Spanish—say, to my thousand-year-old tías—I would do so with hunched shoulders, a lowered chin, furrowed brows. Painfully, the words would crumble out and with them my aunts would giggle like girls. I clumsily chopped verbs, failed to use the subjunctive properly, addressed elders with a casual tú instead of usted. So I began using Spanglish. And I can't say I ever really stopped.

On that first trip to Guatemala, to the land my father still longs to return to someday, to the home my mother carries in her heart but vows never to inhabit again, I found other ways to communicate. I used gestures or made up words like *watchear* and *la ketchup*. Or, I begged my older sister to translate. She had a tighter grip on Spanish, perhaps because she was the first born and had more time to absorb the sounds and rhythms of the language, before I came along. During our visit to Guatemala my parents, it seemed, were around but not available. Either they remained plugged into hushed conversations around the table at night, adults sipping black coffee in which they dipped torn pieces of pan dulce, or they were totally unreachable in the midst of back-slapping laughter with neighbors and relatives they hadn't seen in over a decade. So I was left to fend for my own words in which to express what it was I wanted.

What I really wanted was to start fresh, to learn a language that was mostly my own, and not to subject myself to the burning humiliation of getting a word wrong in Spanish. So in sixth grade, when students were asked to select one language elective—French or Spanish—I imagined myself grabbing fistfuls of French words like a gambler extending his arms across a felt-covered blackjack table to collect his winning chips. I was greedy. I wanted three languages, I said. I wasn't yet aware that

I would always mourn the days when I only reached for words in Spanish, for the nights when I dreamed effortlessly in Spanish. Back then, though, I rationalized, it wouldn't matter—I was learning French!

In college, like in high school, I excelled in French and I ended up double majoring in International Relations and French Studies. I could easily write a five-page academic paper in French and pass an oral exam. And during my junior year when I lived with a host family in the 15th arrondissement of Paris, I could argue with my six-year-old host-brother, in French. He liked to jump on the mustard-yellow leather couch in the high-ceiling formal living room. Arrête! Arrête maintenant! I'd say, without trying, without making those mini-bridges of translation in my mind before my lips moved. French came easier to me than Spanish.

Sometime in my twenties I read on a magnet: What would you do if you just gave yourself permission? The question throbbed in my subconscious, or my brain, or my heart, or wherever these questions live and feed and eventually demand your attention. What would I do if I could just give myself permission? I had never gone to Guatemala by myself, alone. So I gave myself permission to learn, or perhaps relearn, Spanish. I read, wrote, listened, spoke, and yes, eventually dreamed in Spanish.

During the immediate years that followed, I would return to Guatemala again and again, even getting married in the old cobblestoned capital of Antigua, surrounded by friends and family, in English and Spanish and of course, those languages that transcend words—food, music, dance. By virtue of being fluent in Spanish, particularly as an adult, I experienced my surroundings differently. No one giggled at me. Instead I found I was able to speak of politics, women's rights, and the cost of chicken. I held this new relationship to Spanish so tight, gripped it in my palm, my fingers curled around it. I belonged.

Later, back in the States when I was pregnant with my son, like many expectant mothers I read everything I could about the "growing life inside me." Blogs, websites, articles, books. This was my first pregnancy and I was deeply aware of its biology, and its magic. I had read about the benefits of expecting mothers singing to their babies in the womb, talking to them, reading to them. My own mother urged me to speak to the baby in Spanish. And I did, but with skepticism that the short phrases and occasional conversations wouldn't be enough, that eventually, English would swallow any crumbs in Spanish whole, like it did me. I gave up before I had even tried.

Once my son was born, and I mean the second the midwife thrust my son's slimy body onto my chest, I cried. That was the first language, my animal language. Then I said, "Yo te quiero." I love you. My first words to him needed to be in Spanish. I didn't plan this. I didn't know in advance what I was going to say, not say. But then, after dunking him ever so briefly onto my chest, the midwife passed him like a football to a nurse who whisked him across the room where a team of doctors poked him and tapped him and used a suction thing to eliminate the liquid in his mouth, lungs. I yelled to my husband, who was hunched over our baby, "Talk to him!" I watched all this from my delivery bed in the hospital, never doubting that my baby would live. Instead, what I worried about in those first minutes of his life, had to do with words, sounds. The nurse's Boston accent, "Come on, honey, you gotta push!" The doctor's doctory language. The voice on the intercom paging a surgeon. The sound of the air-conditioner buzzing. The early morning birds cawing in the distance before the metal and rubber of traffic were muting the sounds of nature. It was all wrong. My husband *needed* to speak to our son. My son *needed* to hear him, us. And he did. And our baby woke up, mad and wet, crying and wailing. Animal sounds.

A few weeks after he was born, after the foggy, hormonal, timeless stretches where I traded the ability to sleep, eat, pee, or shower for those indescribable nose-kisses with my newborn, I could finally think again. One thought: he is growing so fast. The next: he needs to learn Spanish right now, while his brain is a sponge or what not. Hurry, hurry! We have to download nursery rhymes in Spanish, I told my husband. And where are all those picture books in Spanish? The ones we had put on the baby shower registry? I know! I said, remembering a chapter I had read in some baby book. You speak to him in English and I will speak to him in Spanish, okay? Okay!

That didn't happen.

We played a few songs, though.

During these early months when my son was an infant I attended a group for new mothers inside an old church on a one-way hilly street in Jamaica Plain. The group met once a week. Mothers sat in a circle as we held our babies in our arms or placed these warm cooing bundles onto baby blankets that we had stretched out onto the circle-shaped rug.

One particular Wednesday, I asked the facilitator to hold my son while I ran downstairs to use the bathroom. Sure, this is why I'm here, she said. So I reveled in the weightless journey down the hall and down the stairs, nothing in my hands, no bag digging into my shoulder, no need for a wobbly balancing act over the toilet where I always feared dropping my baby. No. I used the bathroom, took my time. I washed my hands! As I began to make my way back upstairs I noticed a bulletin board—yellow and blue fish, pececitos, painted onto white paper plates. Numbers, letters, shapes, colors, all in Spanish. A Spanish immersion preschool. I took an informational folder with me back upstairs, collected my baby, and hugged him tight the rest of the class.

I didn't read through the folder immediately. To be honest, at the time I couldn't imagine leaving my baby with strangers, not then, not in a year, two years, not ever. But even long before my son turned one, I felt the buzz of the preschool waitlist hysteria like an annoying mosquito in my ear. Sign up my son for preschool now? He can't even keep his own head up. I wasn't going to be one of those parents.

I filled out the forms. Better to be safe. But then I blinked and it was September. Time to go back to work. My son spent that first year with my cousin and my mother, and yes, she spoke to my son in Spanish and yes, this made me feel less guilty for not speaking consistently to him in Spanish. Soon it was summer again. September. This time my now one-and-a-half-year-old boy would start school. Spanish immersion.

I admit, many days I wonder if he is too young to spend stretches of time away from his mama. The guilt is a cement cloak I wear most mornings when I drop him off and swallow the question: Will he be okay? That he is hearing Spanish all day from his teachers (native Spanish speakers), that the songs they sing and the books they read and the games they play are all in Spanish, this is what soothes me.

Still, there were two things I wasn't prepared for: the expensive tuition, and the fact that most of the other kids are white.

My family and I live in one of the most expensive cities in the country. I get that. Yet, what I truly didn't anticipate was that while learning Spanish day after day, my son would do so beside blonde and red-haired children who don't look like him, whose parents don't look like me. Does it matter? For me, the experience of speaking Spanish was always grounded in family, place. For my son, it will likely be associated with art, music, early friendships, and discovery. What will this mean for him later? For his identity? Will my son learn the kind of Spanish that sticks close to the bone, his core being? The way it does for me? When I lift him out of his crib and he asks for meatballs, is he coming off of a dream dreamt in Spanish?

I don't know.

The truth is, I want to protect him. Yes, I want to empower him with fluency in Spanish, his mother's mother tongue. But I want more. I want for him to be able to open and click that gate between languages with total confidence, never hunching his shoulders to embarrassment, shame, for forgetting where he started. I want him to keep this tradition alive for his kids and their kids. For all of us. And yes, I want him to sit between the blonde and red-haired children and feel at home in both languages. He is lucky to be learning in a time and space where Spanish is treated—mostly—like an asset, and not a disability he must conquer, like testing out of an English as a Second Language track at school. For instance.

I want him to understand that Spanish is part of us, our family and our bond. I want him to feel that the words in Spanish are more than just an extra warm blanket piled on him at night, but that they are an extension of my love for him, for who he is and who he will become.

By the time my now two-year-old son and I make it downstairs, into the kitchen on this overcast spring morning, and I prepare to take meatballs out of the freezer, he suddenly announces that he doesn't want meatballs, he wants yogurt. Okay,

I say. Yogurt it is. Then, between yawns, I let the dog out. Fill her silver bowl with food that makes a clang when it hits the bottom of the dish. Reach for a mug. Grind the coffee beans. Above the noise, I hear a small, sugary voice that requests, "Más please." My son. Mi amor. And I give myself permission to leave words behind momentarily, think not of the day and its many tasks ahead, and instead I listen in the distance for the birds that fly in wind that has no language.

———

Jennifer De Leon is the editor of *Wise Latinas: Writers on Higher Education* and a current City of Boston Artist in Residence. Her short story "Home Movie," originally published in the *Briar Cliff Review*, was chosen as the *One City, One Story* pick for the 2015 Boston Book Festival. Named the 2015–2016 Writer-in-Residence by the Associates of the Boston Public Library, De Leon is now an Assistant Professor of Creative Writing at Framingham State University and a GrubStreet instructor and board member. She is working on a YA novel, *Don't Ask Me Where I'm From,* which received a Walter Dean Myers Grant from We Need Diverse Books.

The Privilege Button

———

Maya Jewell Zeller

Fairwood Park II HOA, Article II—Protective Cove-
nants, Section 2.04—Temporary Structures: No trailer,
basement, tent, shack, garage, barn, camper or other out-
building or any structure of temporary character erected
or placed on the property shall at any time be used as a
residence.

For nine years my husband and I lived in a beautiful
turn-of-the-century four-bedroom house on North Jefferson
Street, near West Central Spokane. We pulled as many weeds
as we could work out of the cracks between the rocks, planted
perennials—lilacs, phlox. We put plastic on our windows to help
keep out the cold in winter, and when the temperature dropped
into the negatives for over a week, we used a hair dryer to thaw
the pipes that ran too close to the un-insulated wall in the basement. We tried wrapping them, too, but it seemed their freezing

was a condition of their location, of the old foundation. There were things about the house that we couldn't fix, and we loved it for its imperfection, for its charm.

I always felt rich in this house, the first I'd owned. When we took out a loan for $100,000 in 2005, I thought we'd spent a fortune. We were *homeowners!* Or, at least, our payments each month went toward something we might get to keep. When I was growing up, my parents were renters, even squatters; sometimes, we lived in a garage. Sometimes, we lived in a van. When I repeated this to my husband, years into marriage, he shook his head and said, with a realization I hadn't reached, "Maya, you were homeless."

I had never thought of myself as homeless. *Itinerant*, maybe, *gypsy*, sure—I didn't yet know the term's problematic usage. Not homeless. More like a mouse after a flood, finding a new place for its nest.

No; our friend Joe was homeless; he tracked us down each Thanksgiving and gorged himself on the salmon my brother caught. He bummed a joint from my dad, took a shower if we had one. Joe was homeless—sometimes he had a car, sometimes he didn't. When he did, it was full of his stuff. But *we* always had a roof, of some sort. We always had access to natural spaces (a benefit often ignored as a privilege of those in rural poverty). We didn't always have a bathroom, or running water, but we always had a roof, a basin, a wood stove. We went to school (usually). I don't remember being hungry for more than a few days at a time.

My mother used to sing Cher's "Gypsies, Tramps, and Thieves" while she darned our socks, and my father hummed "King of the Road" when he was only two beers into the night and still feeling jolly. When my father occasionally took up driving a tow truck, our homes were surrounded by cars in the bushes, treasure troves where we might find free cassette tapes, T-shirts. They were playhouses, magic passageways to other lives and times. We weren't homeless.

Fairwood Park II HOA, Article II—Protective Covenants, Section 2.05—Minimum Dwelling Cost: No single family dwelling shall be permitted on any lot at a cost of less than $100,000 exclusive of land.

When I began college in 1997, the socioeconomic privilege of my peer cohort was often taken for granted by my instructors, who would say things like, "Well, *we* can't really understand, being middle class." They used words like *cul-de-sac* and *IRA,* and sometimes made cultural references from TV shows like *Seinfeld* and stations like CNN. They said *The Dow is down two points*; I kept my eyes low. I didn't really know what middle class meant, though I'd been passing so far, and I spent a few years revamping my understanding. When I took a course in the culture of poverty as it related to education and language register, I finally understood: I grew up "in poverty," "in a family of addiction." But I knew how to move between formal and informal language register, so no one picked up on my past. Still, *I* was what we were studying: how to move from a culture of poverty into a culture of education. How to serve an "at risk" population. In my teaching practicums, my "at risk" students had family lives like mine: cycles of addiction, impermanent addresses, free and reduced lunches. During these discussions, my classmates often said things like "I had no idea so many people lived without blank and blank," or "I realize now how lucky I was that both my parents went to all my soccer games," or

"I always thought of poverty as something that happened because of your choices, but it turns out it can be beyond your control."

I kept quiet; I was not interested in being a lab rat. I was not interested in changing, in their view, from the competent, assertive person I'd worked hard to be known as, into an anomaly of class transcendence. How many questions would follow? They were questions I did not feel comfortable answering. I still don't.

～

Two years ago, my husband and I were browsing Zillow and came across a home, a 4 bed/3 bath, with a beautiful treed yard near a partially protected wildlife area, outside the city, in the suburbs, on a quiet cul-de-sac.

I'd always thought of suburbs with some measure of disdain. Suburbs were those places where children had bicycles from the time they were small, where fathers never came home drunk or yelled at the moon, where there were Christmas lights and where Santa always brought gifts, and where people believed it *was* Santa—those places so many of my peers in college imagined just meant *America*.

As I grew into my identity as part of the working middle class, I held less disdain, but I never coveted that world. Materially, I felt comfortable in our first home—it felt like enough. I was with the people, *my* people. There were renters among us; people who didn't water their lawns; people who didn't shovel their sidewalks; cars on blocks; tiny homes with large gardens; the occasional woman walking down the street with her garbage bag of clothes—I'd go out and see if she needed a ride to the shelter or a bus ticket to somewhere better than she'd been, a relative, maybe, a friend. I stood at my fence with my baby on my hip and I talked with Richard from across the street; he reminded me of my father: he said *shit* a lot, even in front of my little one, and when he developed an infection and abscess in his foot, we drove to Walgreens to buy his iodine ointment, kept watch over his place while he was in the hospital hitting on Wendy, his nurse. And there was a recent trend to have block parties; our neighbor Dave was starting a community garden, a farmers' market. The neighborhood had a sense of community, of a little dirt in the cracks.

Lately, though, we'd had nightly break-ins to our car, and the sirens screaming by all hours of the day made me constantly anxious. I'd never acclimated fully to city living. I couldn't adjust to how close we were to major roads; our house was viewable by Google satellites, the tree cover too thin. We joked that we probably should not grow pot in our garden among the tomatoes, even if we wanted to. Outside our oasis of a yard, our children would grow up mostly playing on pavement, with the neighborhood kids who roamed freely, like quail, down the block. Would our children miss the fields they didn't know? Could we bring the woods to their door?

We calculated the economic reality. We weren't debt-free, but we were frugal, and we both had decent, working-class jobs. I was teaching as a part-time professor; my husband coached cross country and track. After nine years, we didn't owe much on our house; we'd paid down our loan quickly. So we *could* afford to move to this beautiful home outside of town. I had never dreamed of living in a suburb, but suddenly, after five years teaching at a university, I wanted to, and a small part of me, the part of which I was ashamed, felt I was entitled to live away from daily crime. Did my entitlement grow out of the privilege I'd managed to sustain?

Fairwood Park II HOA, Article II—Protective Covenants, Section 2.06—Minimum Dwelling Specifications: The ground floor area of the main structure, exclusive of open porches, and garages, shall not be less than one thousand (1,000) square feet for a one-story dwelling, no less than eight hundred (800) square feet for the ground floor area of a dwelling of more than one story. . . .

All dwellings shall have enclosed garages of at least 20 feet by 22 feet, with completely sealed interior, walls and ceilings, and with fully paved driveways to the street.

My husband and I discussed. Should we move from one perfectly acceptable home to another? To say I was torn would be understatement. Wallace Stevens would say I was "of two minds": part of me still hated money, hated to think of myself as the person who had it. The other part of me dreamed of quiet, the illusion of safety, a yard where my children could roam, naked. Was that too much to ask? Should any one person have that when everyone else cannot? I spent nights agonizing; I had metaphoric narrative nightmares; I woke sure I was a sellout. I thought of how, just a few years ago, I'd applied for unemployment. Though we were homeowners, we lived in an area of town where everyone struggled; I realized that struggle was part of my identity; poverty was part of my identity, and moving would mean admitting finally that I'd shifted in social class.

E. D. Hirsch, conservative educational theorist who influenced national policies during the Reagan Administration, writes in his book *Cultural Literacy* about "combating the social determinism that . . . condemns [children] to remain in the same social and educational condition as their parents." I'd mastered a good degree of cultural literacy; my membership had shifted, leaving behind the identity of my "disadvantaged" and "at risk" youth. I realized this with a degree of bitterness: many of the most positive aspects of my childhood, the things that had shaped me, were due to those less-than-acculturated circumstances. Days of unsupervised play, roaming the fields and forests; a dependent reliance on the public library (which afforded me a range of literary tastes, and, admittedly, some degree of American culture awareness); the ability to create a meal from scratch using limited ingredients; knowing what wild plants were edible (surely not in Hirsch's *Dictionary of Cultural Literacy*?); a sense of empathy for others who had less; and a realization that you have to work hard for what you have, and take care of it. I wondered: could a person sustain a working-class sensibility of the world, and—more importantly—instill it not as theory but as practice in her children, if they lived in a social bubble?

Plus there was the commute factor. The move would change my commute from two miles to twelve; that was just for my work, not to mention my husband's job, and our involvement as literary and athletic citizens in the downtown community. Moving would increase our carbon footprint, decrease our leisure time.

And the house was unnecessarily large—four bedrooms, a *third* bathroom (laughable to me, still, how unnecessary it is, how convenient). And a sprinkler system! And a doorbell! Two ovens! A two-car garage, with automatic opener! Some of the common areas between houses even had their own pools. All of these frivolities!

Still, I wanted it. We wanted it. We were tired of the city. My husband had grown up in the suburbs; I in rural places. The neighborhood of the new home was close to Fish & Wildlife land, with bald eagles and moose and a river. Our children could have nature—access to the kinds of places my siblings and I spent our formative years.

In town, we'd kept an urban garden, but now I imagined our long walks through the crumbled homestead and defunct dairy farm that made up part of the valley adjacent to the neighborhood. We might find an old apple tree, a field full of edible plants. When I was a child, I sometimes roamed all day, eating what was edible when I was hungry, coming home only when I was tired, my clothes stained with plums or salmonberry, my pockets full of fossils from the riverbeds, of petrified chunks of wood from the clay banks in the forest beyond. My siblings and I had memorized the maps to treasures only a rural roaming child can find: not Barbies but blackberries, not piano lessons but the steady beat of rain on a tin shed roof, the glinting rhythm of salmon fins fighting their way upstream.

My husband, ever practical, saw moving as the next step in our forward progress. He grew up middle class, to parents with a working-class upbringing, who are generous and kind, and whose expression of security sometimes means acquiring new material possessions. So after the fantasizing and the agonizing and the measured discussions, we agreed to move from one dream to another, and we promised each other that we would remain frugal, not fall into materialism, not take comfort for granted. We promised each other we'd remain grateful for our privilege. It was like another kind of marriage: admitting the merge we'd become, his youth-group-president with an eye for justice upbringing with my feral youth.

In January 2014, we moved into our 1970s house in a well-planned suburb with an HOA (Home Owner's Association). The HOA has a list of rules that govern how we interact with our neighbors, how we live in our homes.

At the annual HOA meeting, we introduced ourselves: I teach at one university, my husband coaches for another university, we moved to the neighborhood for the access to nature and for the "good schools"—the same district where my husband attended fourth through twelfth grade.

People were warm, welcoming. But some were furious about the Smiths, converting their home into a shared living space for their parents and elderly friends ("Three families in one house? Who heard of such a thing? There'll be cars coming and going all hours of the day!"). And they also talked about the apartments down the street, just beyond our HOA boundary, transitioning to low-income, government-supplemented housing. It's the beginning of this conversation, and an undertone I picked up: do not, under any circumstances, tell us you grew up in poverty. This breaks *Section 2.08, Exterior Maintenance*, which stipulates, among other things, all neighbors must keep a clean curb.

∽

Where I teach part-time is a private liberal arts institution, a school known for its basketball teams and its Jesuit tradition. A school known for its students' nearly consistently uniform privilege. (There are students on full scholarship, though, from apple country, from urban areas, from small Montana towns, who I'm sure are navigating a sense of culture shock and socioeconomic gap even wider than the one I charted at a state school.) In my first year, I approached the topic by teaching a section of Barbara Ehrenreich's *Nickel and Dimed*, the one in which she works as a Merry Maid. When some of my students found themselves appalled at the working conditions, of the meager American Dream offered to someone who worked full-time, or when some made statements about how a person could pull themselves out of it if they "just get a degree," I asked my students how many of their families employed maids growing up; half the class raised their hands. There were some awkward glances and equivocations, and then I told them how I worked as a custodian every summer during college, changing sheets and cleaning dorm showers of high school football campers somewhat oblivious to who picked up and replaced their towels (but who, sometimes, as a prank, would shit in the shower or behind the beds). Often I spend time in my classes talking about how we each need to clean up after ourselves, about individual responsibility; we're a university with a social justice mission, so this is naturally a part of our curriculum. But sometimes it's difficult to help these sweet young people, many of whom owned their own cars at sixteen (a car they did not live in), understand how hard work does not necessarily equal a fair shot.

I feel an inexplicable deep measure of guilt writing about my new social class, something I no longer have to worry about in the same way I once did, in the same way many of my readers do or will. I don't admit this guilt to my students. I also don't tell my students that Barbara Ehrenreich makes me angry, pretending at poverty as some sort of social experiment. The entire time she was undercover as a journalist, she had a bank account on which she could fall back, health insurance she could access. She did not have to make any hard choices; there was a clear end for her. I understand what she was doing, though: passing. Playing a role.

Fairwood Park II HOA, Article II—Protective Cove-
nants Section 2.15—Animals: No animal, livestock or
poultry of any kind may be raised, bred, or kept on any lot.

In Spokane, as in many cities across the nation, urban chickens are a large part of the neighborhood experience. Within the
last several years, our city passed an ordinance that increased
fowl allotment from three hens to five (no roosters). But in Fairwood Park II, the covenants forbid this use of your land.

We want chickens, but we've decided to wait it out.

This year, there was an opening on the HOA board and
my husband became default president. He and another at-large
member (whose wife is an artist; she grew up on twenty acres,
unschooled) talk about infiltrating the ranks and working toward modifying that covenant to allow people to keep birds.

We all know we're mostly joking, though. It would take a
quorum of 75 percent to change a covenant, and those opposed
have been here since the beginning; they've built their little
suburban utopia, and nothing is going to take it from them.
Frankly, we're not even sure how to begin this conversation,
among the talk of blocking off the end of our neighborhood so
"those low-income apartments don't have access" and the big
to-do over one woman's "garden art" that other residents find
offensive.

Fairwood Park II HOA, Article II—Protective Cove-
nants, Section 2.11—Fences: Fences shall be well con-
structed of suitable fencing materials and shall be artistic
in design and shall not detract from the appearance of the
dwelling house located upon the adjacent lots or building
sites or be offensive to the owners or occupants thereof.

My navigation of this world is still tenuous, and probably always will be. I'm trying not to project, but I make a lot of generalizations based on my social class growing up. Sometimes, it's unkind. But people who grow up with money don't understand they have money. (My children will be these people, no matter how much I ask them to reflect, to exist in gratitude.)

During my undergrad experience, I had a kind of poverty complex. After getting over some of my initial shyness about my upbringing, I sometimes made snarky statements to people about their swimming pools, piano lessons. I judged my housemate James by the fact that once he told me he had "1K extra dollars" and that he "wondered what to do with it." I grew red and fumed, "you should put it in the bank!" (and I thought, *you should shut up!*). I was living, at the time, on $250 a month. He was living on $1,000. As college renters, we shared a house. His father was a doctor. Mine sold tires.

Now, I drive home from work in my car, a twelve-year-old Subaru with kayak racks, turn into my quiet street, drive past the deer grazing in my neighbors' yards, and push the automatic garage door opener I keep on my sun visor, above my head. Like magic, the garage door glides up; I drive in. I call the garage door opener "the privilege button," and every time I push it, I have a private giggle with myself.

Living in a neighborhood where people all push buttons to enter their attached garages, where the outdoor plants will be watered by a preset sprinkler system, where there are signs that say "No Soliciting" at each neighborhood entrance, is still strange for me. I know I still need to work on my daily actions, work through my hypocrisies—we all do. But I want to believe that if we try to communicate across our intersectional ad- and dis-advantages, we might bridge some of these boundaries—those we can control, and those we cannot.

Driving down Fairwood Drive, one has to look out for deer. I go slowly, my eyes darting to the sides of the road. I turn right onto my street, and when I'm close enough, I lift my hand above my head, push the button. The door glides up to reveal the mess: our kayaks stacked on cement blocks, bicycles and scooters piled on a lawn mower, tires still in their bags, an unplugged refrigerator, a workbench with a few files scattered across it, some crates of books that never found a shelf.

My children open the door from the garage to the house, their faces sticky with melon juice. They've been practicing piano, or building worlds that lead to Narnia. They don't know yet what code switching means, but when they're old enough, I'll teach them, and I'll teach them too that they must practice kindness, they must always be mindful when they push the privilege buttons. They'll have more confidence, I think, and their roads will be roads I never drove. For now they can just be a bit feral, I think, as they run, grinning and barefoot, out to meet me.

———

Maya Jewell Zeller has received grants from the Sustainable Arts Foundation and the H.J. Andrews Experimental Forest. She is author of the books *Rust Fish, Yesterday, the Bees*, and the forthcoming collaboration, with visual artist Carrie DeBacker, *Alchemy for Cells & Other Beasts*. Maya teaches for Central Washington University's Professional and Creative Writing Programs and lives in the Inland Northwest with her family.

Some Notes on Our Cyclical Nature

Sarah Viren

Returning to Iowa everything is the same, but also everything isn't. It's still summer and the car is still packed. There is still that "Fields of Opportunity" billboard along with the Iowa border on Highway 218. There is still the sense of having made the right decision. We left the rain behind in Missouri. Now Marta is driving while I sit in the back seat beside our daughter trying to entertain her on the final stretch of this three-day road trip from Texas, where we live now, to Iowa, where we'll live again, if only for the summer.

"This is where you were born," I tell our daughter. "This is your real home."

But she's three so instead of responding she asks, "What's that?" A bowling alley beside an open field. And, "What's that?" The Iowa River streaming past a power plant. And, "Are we in Lubbock?"

When I first drove here, I was alone—alone with my dog Finn. In those days—before having a wife, then a child, and another child growing inside me—I talked to Finn. There is a certain confidence you develop with those who can never respond.

That day it was late summer and I also saw that billboard about Iowa's fields of opportunity, which made me laugh.

"Maybe it's a sign," I told Finn.

I had left behind a lot on that trip north: a well-paying job in Houston, a steady relationship with a kind woman I could nonetheless never seem to love, and, also, all my furniture and most of my belongings, save some rugs and blankets wrapped around framed pictures and maps of other places I'd lived and left.

I was moving to Iowa because I thought I needed a change—and in Houston I felt stuck. Finn was in the front seat beside me, his sleek black head reaching out the window to pant as we reached the last stop sign before our new home: a blue two-story house I had found on Craigslist, a house I would share with three roommates I had also found on Craigslist: a musician, a playwright, and a sculptor.

My plan was to rebuild a life just like that: via the Internet and thrift stores. I would build myself a bed out of foam core doors I found at a construction resale shop. I would buy a new bike at a garage sale and find new pots and pans at the auction. I would move my online dating profile from Texas to Iowa and mark myself single, add that I listen to a lot of Tom Waits and have an unusually long neck.

When we pulled up that day and I opened the door, Finn dashed out in a streak of black and bounded up on to the front porch, sniffing the corners and doorstop with the dutiful confidence of the newly arrived. After declaring it satisfactory, he looked back, still panting, and waited for me to climb the steps and join him.

The house we're staying in this summer belongs to one of those Craigslist roommates, the sculptor, a woman named Erica who just got married, who is now one of my best friends. She and her boyfriend, now husband, bought this house when it was condemned. They spent four years rebuilding it: carpeting the rooms upstairs, rewiring cables, planting a garden, hanging a front porch.

And when they were done, they got married and went on a honeymoon road trip. While they're gone, they're letting us stay here. And while we're here in Iowa City, where Marta and I met and fell in love and had our daughter, we're going to pretend we actually live in this town again, where we both still feel at home.

In the mornings, after I drop our daughter off at a farm daycare, Marta and I work at our respective desks, writing and reading. In the afternoons, we go to the farmers' market or the pool or the public library. At night we invite over old friends for dinner. We've started playing Memory at the kitchen table, and usually Marta wins. When the sun goes down, we read our daughter books until she falls asleep and, if we have the energy, Marta and I watch something together on Netflix or, even more rarely, we might make love.

We know this is not like it used to be, even though we are back where we were before. Because neither of us is who we were before. But we're still happy to be here. And within a few weeks it begins to feel like this house and this life we're inhabiting for the summer are ours for keeps. Except that our daughter keeps asking from the backseat when we drive around, "Are we in Lubbock?" Or less often, "Is this Iowa City?"

My first time in Iowa City, I spent my mornings alone, drinking coffee and reading through the postings from a listserve called Freecycle, an online group made up of people giving stuff away and others willing—or hoping—to take things for free.

I was searching for offers of furniture, of winter clothes, of a desk. But I only ever found things I didn't need: a stamp collection kit, a Tupperware Jell-O mold, three red-eyed tetra fish, a pearly pink conch shell listed beside the query: "Feeling the need to call Poseidon?"

The morning I arrived in Iowa, a woman named Candace was giving away a nearly full bag of Purina diabetic cat food, a post she concluded with three exclamation points, and by that afternoon she had returned, offering a jumbo pack of Pampers and coupons for Enfamil baby formula, this time with just one exclamation point.

In the days that followed, I unpacked, bought Finn some new chew toys, and went to get my new university ID. Meanwhile, Candace offered up one baby stroller, an almost-full container of Herbalife Cookies and Cream shake mix, and a George Foreman Grill. In return, she asked if anyone had the Weight Watchers Complete Food and Dining Out book, confiding that she planned to start dieting that week.

I was fascinated by the way her posts could construct a life, or, I now realize, how I convinced myself I could construe a life based on this stranger's posts. I knew almost no one in town then and Candace felt like a way in, a way to understand the landscape and understand myself within it. I pictured her in her mid-thirties, hair bleached to the sheen of corn silk, just a few pounds plump of shapely with feet that turned out slightly penguin style when she walked. She seemed stable in a way I didn't feel then. And for a little while, she was frozen like that: this caricature of a self-sufficient Midwestern mother I had invented to fill this flat, Midwestern landscape I was coming to know.

But then two days before my classes began, Candace posted again, and her offer this time was for "Ashley," her six-year-old, loyal, and mostly house-broken Jack Russell–Rat Terrier mix.

"We have a 6-month old son that is allergic to both our cat (which we are also trying to get rid of) and our dog!" she wrote. "I am extremely upset that I have to post this ad . . . but I have to for the sake of my little boy."

That same week, I lost Finn for the first time. I was in a new graduate student teacher training—learning how best to teach Iowa students Shakespeare, how exactly to handle their Midwestern tendency to avoid dissension—when I got a call from a stranger who said he'd found my dog wandering the streets and that he was taking him to the pound. When I arrived for him an hour later, Finn's muzzle was wet with nervous drool and he had a temporary pink leash around his neck. I distracted myself from crying on the drive back by lecturing Finn about the importance of staying close to home. But that afternoon, back at the training session, I cried despite myself when another graduate student showed a clip from a cheesy movie called *In Her Shoes* in which Cameron Diaz reads Elizabeth Bishop's poem "One Art" to a blind man.

"The art of losing's not too hard to master," Diaz read Bishop. "Though it may look like (*Write* it!) like disaster."

Finn was a mix-breed, just like Ashley, only he had the lithe body of a pointer and the energy of a black Lab. He'd found me while I was running through the streets of Houston one morning and followed me a mile back to my house, then waited patiently outside my door for an hour when I told him that, No, I couldn't take care of a dog, not even one as sweet as he was. But eventually, of course, I let him in. And he'd been mine ever since.

After I took Finn in, he began running with me. We ran through Houston's smog, in and out of Iowa City's forested parks, and, then, back in Texas, we kept running through the flat, crosshatched neighborhoods of Lubbock.

But in Iowa this time, I no longer run. Pregnancy stole my energy in the early months, and, now that I have my stamina back, my body feels too rounded and off-center to run, so I walk instead. Every morning while Marta and our daughter eat breakfast, I go out alone to walk through Iowa City's neighborhoods and, though I don't tell anyone, it's my favorite part of the day. Just like running with Finn used to be my favorite part.

It's been raining a lot this summer—a lot more than when we lived here before—and so often I pass over small bridges spanning swollen creeks and I love the way our movement intersects at that point, me walking across their running waters. I like, too, when chance takes me past someone else walking or running a dog.

I've never been good at approaching strangers, so usually I don't pet these dogs, but I want to with my whole body. This is another change that's come with pregnancy. When I want something, my desire doesn't stem from a small concentrated spot in my heart or stomach or groin; instead it overtakes me. And when I see dogs walking with their owners, I want to pet them with such an intensity that, when in the end I don't, I walk away feeling bowed with loss.

The desire began recently while we were having dinner with some friends here that Marta knew from before. They're a younger couple with two daughters, just like we will soon have two daughters, and they also now have a small black puppy who looks a lot like Finn did a long time ago.

I should have been playing with the kids or talking to Marta's friends that night, but I spent most of the evening wrestling and then snuggling their new puppy. When it was time to go, I kept making excuses to stay just a little longer, to pet her furry wriggling body just one more time. She was so soft and eager to be loved.

I knew why I was doing that, of course. But it was still surprising. It's been seven months since Finn died, six months since I got pregnant—again—after losing a previous pregnancy to miscarriage two months before that. I had thought I'd come to accept the exchange by now: a loss for a gain. But, of course, it's never that simple.

I wondered sometimes why I grew so attached to Candace in my first few months in Iowa, except that: latching on to the lives of strangers and using them to try to understand my own life and the changes to come. I watch people in airports, I read the classifieds, I eavesdrop when the opportunity arises. In some ways, Candace felt to me like a parallel life. Like she was who I could have been, if only I would stay put.

Even after I had all the stuff I needed, I kept checking Freecycle those first few weeks and months in Iowa because I wanted to know what would happen to her—to her pets, her son, her stuff.

A couple days after she posted about Ashley, the dog, Candace returned with an ad for her cat, Chooey, who she was also giving away because of her baby boy's allergies. She repeated her story for those, unlike me, who hadn't been reading since the beginning.

"She is a very good cat and has never given us any reason to get rid of her," Candace told us. "Which is why we are upset!"

The leaves began to turn. I started a supper club with new friends, and Candace posted asking if anyone had an aquarium for her family's new pet salamander—which she called the "perfect replacement pet." A week later, she offered up the baby bathtub her son had just outgrown and asked if anyone had a toddler bath chair.

A few weeks later, Candace posted about Ashley again. She said her dog had found a new home, though not through Freecycle. Her parents had agreed to take in the Terrier mix, which was good news, she wrote, because now her son would grow up knowing the dog that could have been his.

Winter fell, my first in Iowa, and I finally decided to write Candace. I couldn't know then that within six months I would meet Marta or that, less than three years later, we would marry and Marta give birth to our first child or that, three months after that, we would move away from Iowa for good.

What I knew then was that after so much investment in a stranger's life, I wanted closure—or maybe contact. I wanted to know how this would all end.

"I know this is a little late," I wrote to Candace. "But I wondered if you found a home for Chooey the cat? I have a friend who isn't on Freecycle but is thinking about adopting a cat and wants to take one that really needs a home."

It was a lie, of course. I had no such friend, but it was the only excuse I could think of to write and ask this stranger about her life. When Candace finally replied, her message was short and, as always, upbeat.

"Chooey found a new, loving home a couple of months ago," she gushed before, always considerate, adding: "Good luck in your search!"

Rebecca Solnit once wrote that places are more constant than people can ever be. Friedrich Nietzsche proposed the idea of eternal return: that time cycles rather than runs straight toward the horizon. Milan Kundera claimed that dogs link us to paradise.

I think about this baby growing inside me sometimes and the place she's in now. They say that after birth, we're left with the constant desire to return. That in utero is our only paradise, the only moment when every need is met and nothing has yet been lost.

With Finn, I was most at home on the road. We probably took a dozen road trips in our time together. We slept in a rest stop in my Subaru outside a Louisiana swamp. We stayed in a cabin beside the grave of Bonnie and Clyde. We drove up to see my sister after she got out of rehab and down to see my mom soon after her mom died. And, of course, wherever we went, we ran.

For our final trip, when I took Finn to the vet to be put down, Marta offered to go with me, but I wanted to be alone. He'd been sick for at least a year by then. I was pregnant for the first time, not yet aware that the fetus's heartbeat was about to stop.

On the drive to the vet's office, I talked to Finn the whole way. I told him that I loved him and that he would always be my best friend. He was in the back, lying on my daughter's duck towel, which I'd put there to soak up the urine he could no longer keep from leaking out of him.

The woman at the front desk checked us in, and while we waited to be called, I pet his soft ears and told him how glad I was to have found him, that he found me.

After they injected him with liquid that would make his heart stop, they left me alone with him, and I watched as his eyes turned blue and then, slowly, became glass. I felt his chest and his heart was still there, moving like a small baby inside him. Until it wasn't, and I left.

We were walking to an old friend's house for dinner last night and there was a woman walking her dog in front of us. It had finally stopped raining here and Iowa City looked just like it used to, even though I knew it wasn't. My daughter asked about the dog in front of us and then added, "Where is our dog?"

"Don't you remember?" I said. "Finn got old and he was sick and sometimes when animals get old and sick, they die. He's not ours anymore."

We've told her this story before, probably a dozen times. But she never seems to remember, or at least she doesn't remember what it means.

Three-year-olds see the world like that. We are in both Lubbock and Iowa City. Today is yesterday and tomorrow could be next summer. We once had a dog named Finn and we still have him. He's just not ours anymore.

————

Sarah Viren is the author of *Mine*, winner of the River Teeth Literary Nonfiction Book Prize, and translator of the Argentine novella *Córdoba Skies* by Federico Falco. Her poetry and prose have appeared in *AGNI, Iowa Review, Gettysburg Review, TriQuarterly,* and other magazines. She holds an MFA from the University of Iowa and a PhD from Texas Tech University. She is an assistant professor of creative writing and literature at Arizona State University.

Subjunctive

——

Naima Coster

Let's say your name is Brian. We met at college, a very good
one, near my hometown. And let's say we decided early on
that we wanted very much of each other, for as long as either of
us would allow. Let's say we got married. Let's say there was a
dog. Let's say you found a job, and we left my hometown for the
South. We found a blue house that we don't own but that feels
ours, especially when you rake the leaves, or we set out a pot of
mums in the garden even though it's autumn and growing cold,
or I call the gas company, and the truck comes, and they fill our
tank. To live in the woods, down a gravel road, to call the gas
man and say how many gallons of propane we need, makes us
believe we are much older than we are. We aren't. We made our
gambles on each other young.

Let's say we are happy with one another. Let's say this happiness is new. It contradicts all we have learned about what it
means to be alive. Our not-happiness was old, familiar, fibrillar,

123

as much a part of us as the color of your eyes, the kink in my hair, my mother, your mother, the generations we cannot name. Our way of living is obscene, but we go on with our sweetness, our quiet that may last.

You are beautiful—this is not a metaphor—and you grew up in a sun-filled place. Let's say you still learned darkness. Let's say your father drank, and once you broke down the door to the bathroom, where your father lay, so you could wrest the bottle away. Let's say it was your mother who called you to push. Let's say you were ten.

I was not beautiful, and I spent time in the bathroom, too, but no one came knocking for me. I was small, and I shut myself away so that the only harm came to me would be by my own hand, and by metal—safety pins, single-edged blades, pretty carbon steel.

Let's say we are not who we were. Let's say those days are behind us, up north. No one knows us in our country town; we left no address. Here we go for walks through mud and trees. We dirty our boots, find spider webs netted in our hair. In the summer we get too much rain; we learn to drive through the thunder. We talk about travel—there is a highway we could ride straight to the ocean; there is another that pulls west toward the mountains. Let's say there is no need to weep here, unless we are talking about how much we know, or seem to know now, and how little we knew.

There are daily blunders in our daily love. You say my socks smell funny, and I hear *Dirty*. You keep me waiting in the car, and I remember, *Waste*. You say you want to go for a drive on your own to see the changing colors of the leaves, and I am pursued: *Leech*.

Let's say I am still that girl in the bathroom. Let's say you still knock down the door.

When we plot about our children, we overlook the combined misfortune of our DNA, the nuclear not-happiness to which we did not consent. We wonder instead what it is like to be born into a little blue house, at the bottom of a gravel road. Their luck occurs to us when we are laughing in the car, or drying the dishes, making another pot of coffee, turning out the lights. We string a tree with secondhand ornaments, and kiss, listen to the usual songs. We put our arms around each other and ask: *Will we hate them for their joy?*

We talk too about dying, about leaving our kids too soon. Our cells must be very old, and there's no telling, Brian, whose mitochondria look worse. We'll explain it to the children with science. It's what history does to the brain, we will say. And the lungs. The heart. My old hometown, your sun-filled place. Our two bathrooms. We would like to go on, in our blue house, with our imaginary children, and the dog, long after the twelve months of our fixed-term lease. But there is nothing the body does not remember. A skinny shoulder shoved against a door. The tip of a needle pressed into tender skin. It is science, we will tell them. It is our cells.

A diagram—

My mother bloodied her fists on the face of every girl who called her father a murderer. She fought and learned how bloodied fists could quiet a child.

Your great-grandfather had his picture in the paper because he was struck dead by a bus. Someone in the crowd took a photograph, and your mother carried the clipping with her to the orphanage, after her own father died, at thirty-five. (His cells must have been very old.)

An indigenous woman gave birth in the mountains, driven out of the city by the white man for whom she worked. Her baby bore his green eyes, his way of seeing folded into your genetic code—

My mother's mother sold stolen jewelry to her neighbors; she worshipped pale-skinned statues of the saints. She wore lipstick and boiled rice, danced in the living room of her railroad apartment in a new country, unaware of the tumors filling her uterus. Only the saints knew she would soon be dead—

An uncle who drank himself to death in a hotel room—

A grandfather who carved his name into a prison wall, and the son who followed after him and found his father's name etched in the stone—

A little sister split open by a child, and then another, and another; two of them survive—

A bottle and dirt under your father's fingernails—

A man who cheated and a man who cheated and a man who cheated, and all the women who stayed—

The grubby tile and my pretty carbon steel—

The radishes you grew in a garden in your sun-filled place.

Let's say we get tattoos to tally our losses so that our skins can carry them instead of us. Ink numbers on our forearms. Anyone can live with a four, a five, a six. Let's say there is a bridge from your number to mine.

The bottom of our road is lonesome, and the trees are tall. The sounds of the forest grant us cover—the deer chewing sticks on the lawn; the wave of wind in the trees; the clattering of pine-cones; the scrape of a car across gravel. Let's say that only we can hear if I am weeping, if you are knocking on the door. Marriage is an ear pressed to the door.

We rake the leaves, and fill the tank, and we believe that they won't ever come. Let's say there is an end. Let's say that we have reached it. There are too many rocks; the hedges too thick. They will not find us here. This is the South, and our windows are shuttered. We have changed our faces, installed new locks. Even now the dog is in the yard, running circles in the mud.

———

Naima Coster is the author of *Halsey Street*, a novel about gentrifi-cation, family, and memory in Brooklyn, New York. She is a gradu-ate of the Columbia University MFA program and also holds degrees in English and Creative Writing from Yale University and Fordham University. Her stories and essays have appeared in the *New York Times*, *Arts & Letters*, *Kweli*, *The Rumpus*, and *Guernica*, among other places. Naima has taught writing in a range of settings, from prison to after-school programs, summer camps, and universities. She lives in Durham, North Carolina, with her husband and their dog.

Cold, Comfort

———

Miranda Weiss

When I originally moved to Alaska, twenty-four years old and with a boyfriend I had no specific long-term plans with, my mother didn't try to stop me. She wouldn't have had much of an argument, having left her native England to move across the ocean with my father at roughly the same age, but she had experience enough to warn me.

My mother grew up cold. At least that's what all her stories lead me to believe. She grew up in England in the 1940s, and her parents heated the house with coal or, more precisely, they heated one room in the house and even then, not very well. She went to Catholic boarding school where nasty nuns popped her pimples and she woke up winter mornings in her dormitory room with the washbasin water frozen solid. The school uniform in the coldest months was an above-the-knee wool skirt that chafed my mother's thighs. The cold brought on painful swellings in her

hands and feet called chilblains, which seem like a relic from another time, like trench foot or romantic train rides.

At eighteen, and recently graduated from the Sixth Form,
my mother was slender with high cheekbones and long blond-
streaked hair. She moved to London where she rented an under-
heated basement flat with five other girls and a single bath. She
worked at the Royal Brompton Hospital as a secretary, saving for
weeks to buy a £10 winter coat and eating a hardboiled egg for
dinner. Those were the days when poverty made you thin.

Sometimes I imagine that cold played a role in my mother's
decision to move to the States to marry my father. They met in
the Brompton where my father, a medical student, was taking
an elective. My father was a handsome and easy-going young
man, a guy with a sunny disposition. They say opposites attract.
He had grown up in an overheated Brooklyn apartment. As if
to conjure the warmth he was used to during his six months
abroad, my father had ordered a sunny yellow Triumph TR-6
before he had left the States. He zoomed my mother around England's narrow country roads. No doubt riding in the car was
a freezing experience, but life with a doctor promised financial
security, and financial security promised warmth.

My parents settled in the mild suburbs of Maryland just
outside Washington, DC, where our big brick colonial had central air conditioning and heat that kept the indoor temperature
a steady 70 degrees year-round. My mother is happy to have her
cold years behind her—some days I know she thinks I'm crazy.
Where I live now, we often wake up on winter days with the
house at a chilly 55. Even on summer mornings, I trudge around
the house in a heavy terrycloth robe.

For fifteen years now, I have lived in Homer, Alaska, a small
coastal town with a local economy fueled by summer tourists

and commercial fishing. Although Homer is in Alaska's "banana belt," winters last for six months and summers are always
cool and damp. We wear wool sweaters and down jackets year-
round, and on summer's sunniest days, a sharp wind whips off
the 50-degree bay on which I live and finds me everywhere.

I wasn't consciously seeking cold when I decided to move
to Alaska a few years after graduating from college, instead I
sought the things that cold so often brings: vast stretches of wilderness, undeveloped coastlines, rich ocean waters you can eat
out of, and dark starry skies. I took my decision to move lightly,
even as I mailed change of address postcards to friends and
family, indicating I was relocating to nearly the farthest point
I could while still within in the U.S., and began amassing the
kinds of possessions I would need in Alaska: heavy down parka,
rubber boots, field guides to western birds. I was too young to
see the ways in which a single decision can lead to the next and
to the next until the course of your life has been shifted without
you really understanding how or why.

What is it to live in such a cold place? It means that the
world around you is drowned for half a year under a sea of snow
and ice. You won't see your backyard for months. It means a
winter so cold it's devoid of smells and even of color. Nothing
is blooming, the leaves have dropped, all of the colorful birds
have flown south, and the spruce trees—blue-green during the
summer months—seem to turn black against the snowy drop
cloth. On the most frigid days, the fabric of your jacket becomes
stiff and noisy. Skis squeak across snow so cold and dry it has
no glide. In the middle of winter, the sun—if it appears at all—is
barely higher than eye level above the horizon. Even at noon,
the light is lean, casting long shadows across the frozen ground.
And during our few midwinter thaws, each a brief respite from

the regular deep freeze, we are not warm. Rain pelts the snow, partially melting the entire town until everything is lacquered in ice. Broken collarbones, fractured arms, cracked pelvises—these are some of the side effects of this warmth.

To live in a cold place like this, you forget what real warmth is. We often have to turn on the heat inside the house during the summer to take away the chill. We lose muscle memory of the wonderful full-body ease that true warm weather brings. Until we travel elsewhere, we forget the feeling of walking outside in a T-shirt and shorts and feeling absolutely, profoundly, just right.

Before I moved here, I didn't realize that the cold—preparing for it, insulating from it, warding it off, and reacting to it—would be the focus of life. Fall is the season of gearing up for winter, and spring the season of cleaning up after it. Summer—those light-drenched months that pass in the blink of an eye—is the season when you can finally coax green things out of the garden that are winter crops for people in the rest of the country: cabbage, broccoli, kale.

Paradoxically, summer is what brought many Alaska residents here, but winter is why so many of us have stayed. People who don't live here think winter must shut Alaskans inside for half the year. But it is the time of ice and snow when this—and other cold parts of the world—are their most accessible. A blanket of snow in the hills behind town smoothes out miles of tangled willow shrubs and untraversible hummocks, creating limitless skiing and snowmobiling terrain. In the northern part of Alaska, frozen rivers become marked highways connecting remote villages otherwise only reachable by slow-going boat or bush plane. Winter there means that cab service to a village of three hundred people is possible, as is pizza delivery. And since much of the state is sliced by rivers, bogged down in wetlands, and serrated by frilled coastline, the freeze turns the soggy expanse solid, making it navigable. Thank goodness, because we have to get out—to work, to eat, to play.

Unlike scurvy, cabin fever can't be cured by a daily pill. A few winters ago, when I was pregnant with my second daughter, a cold front plunged us into a spell of frigid weather for weeks, and the temperature rarely broke five degrees. I bundled my toddler to go out anyway. First the inside clothing, then fleece overalls and a fleece jacket, a heavy-duty snowsuit over that, thick mittens, thick socks, a hat, hood, and boots. Even then, we could only stay out for half an hour—twenty-five minutes to be safer. An extra five minutes and she'd be bawling, hands and feet cold and red beneath her layers and unable to get warm.

Cold kills far more people in Alaska each year than bears, wolves, and bush planes combined. Winter here plucks people from life, by avalanche, car accident, broken-down snowmobile far from help, or errant wave across the deck of a Bering Sea crab boat. Living here can sometimes feel like a list of "don'ts": don't tip your kayak into the bay; don't drop your car keys in the snow; don't go boating, hiking, or skiing without telling friends of your plan; don't go snowmobiling alone.

Even in summer, a simple afternoon fishing trip gone awry can mean drowning in frigid water within the first five minutes of being immersed. In whatever form, too much cold can make you lose your mind. You stumble, mumble, and lose your connection to reality. This is why people suffering from hypothermia often take off their clothes, insisting that they're hot.

Most of the time, I forget about the cold and about what it takes to live here. Then I'll recount a morning spent outside with my kids to my mother on the phone and remember: yes, we are tough here. We take our newborns outside in the middle of winter, our toddlers out to play when the wind is howling and the temperatures are in the single digits. While I complain about the fact that my daughters wear snowsuits for at least six months out of the year, I think the cold is, ultimately, good for them, making them tougher to adverse conditions and more adaptable. And I cannot deny I take pride in my own resilience to the cold and my stamina in the face of blowing snow, ice-slicked roads, and cold rain.

My own smugness aside, the greatness of our nation, some have argued, was born from the cold. Many early American colonists believed that New England's harsh winters helped breed a people of tougher constitution and greater resourcefulness than the ones they left behind. Surviving severe winters in the New World required not just fortitude, but vigilance and foresight. The cold provided a test of character, they believed, and those who prevailed proved their physical and moral superiority. This spirit of exceptionalism lives on in our politics here and in the myths of self-reliance that serve as mantras in our lives.

People assume that to choose to live in a cold place is to choose austerity and a life without comfort. Because, of course, to escape the cold—to winter in the tropics, retire under the sun, take off for the islands at Christmas—has always meant you had achieved a certain level of success. But a cold life is not without its own riches. There are clear winter days when the surface of the snow glitters like diamonds. We have access to silence, one of the rarest commodities. And cold ocean waters make for extravagant dinners: salmon hooked minutes before, clams and mussels gathered into buckets by cold hands, oysters slurped raw so that you can feel the ocean dribbling deliciously down your throat.

Living here means we have the opportunity to see how cold can shape a place. The terrain out my living room windows was under ice until about ten thousand years ago, and the land-scape—a mash-up of rounded hills, sharp mountains, steep fjords, and a four-and-a-half-mile gravel spit that pokes out into the middle of the bay—are remnants the ice left behind. Relatively low tree line makes for not only endless hiking opportunities and vast expanses of low-growing blueberries, but a tundra landscape that blazes red in autumn.

The cold is beautiful, and it has produced some of Earth's most elegant and enchanting species: polar bears, penguins, walrus, and the largest animal ever to have inhabited our planet, the blue whale. And cold is a critical element in the natural world, a condition many organisms need. Cold waters—in rivers, streams, and oceans—contain more life-supporting oxygen than warm waters and can thus support biologically richer animal and plant communities. Even in Alaska, scientists are working on ways to keep our rivers and streams cold as the climate warms and urban development flattens forests that would otherwise shade these waters. Their efforts are likely too little too late, as climate change is already transforming the world out our windows. Even so, when the news programs from the Lower 48 report record droughts, ravaging wildfires, and lethal summer heat, in Alaska we feel relieved to be escaping that mess. Cold starts to feel like a valuable commodity, something we should be sure not to take for granted. The cold may just be our salvation in a dramatically warming world.

But perhaps what is richest about the cold is the way it makes light and warmth feel so extraordinary. There is nothing like arriving at a friend's dinner party—hot food coming out of the oven, wine going down all around, light spilling out the windows onto the snow—after a headlamp-lit ski through a frigid winter evening. Nor nothing as festive as traipsing along neighborhood streets through an icy night carrying lanterns with a handful of neighbors as we progress between houses for the next of a many-course meal, as a friend plays a terrible rendition of "If I Were a Rich Man" on the accordion. Cloaked by cold, we feel closer to each other; we are lights in the dark night, savoring kinship in a big world.

Even so, the benefits of the cold can be hard to remember in the face of ice cleats, May snowstorms and frozen pipes. Not to mention our cultural bias against the cold. There's no comfort in cold comfort, no welcoming from a cold shoulder. A killer is made even worse by being cold-blooded, an enemy by being cold-hearted. There is nothing cathartic or healthful about breaking a cold sweat, and a cold fish is not attractive as entrée or lover.

In spite of it all, being cold makes me feel alive. I'm not sure who I would be if I moved back to the comfortable life—if I swapped rubber boots that are always getting mucky for sleek sandals that knew only pavement. How would I fill all of the hours I now spend with my children, dressing and undressing them? Whom would I relate to if I could no longer commiserate with those around me about the cold?

And yet, between our frequent laments about the cold, my friends and I breezily discuss our half-formed plans to leave: one considers moving back to her small, Iowan hometown near her parents, where you can bike everywhere year-round, and the kids can spend the summer in the local pool. Another friend applied for a school counselor job elsewhere—where summers promise tank top weather and extended family is only a two-hour drive away. I scan online want ads from towns within a day's road trip of my parents. But beneath the seemingly flippant exchanges among my friends, there is something tender and vulnerable: Are our friends going to abandon us in this cold place? If we left, would we realize that we've been wrong about everything all along, wrong about the correlations between proximity and intimacy, isolation and connection, cold and contentment?

I am more than three thousand miles from where I grew up and where my parents still live in suburban Maryland. We are four time zones, three airplanes, and more than a day of travel apart. My husband and I take our girls to visit my parents at least twice a year—I can't imagine seeing them any less. But for my parents, coming to visit us is like traveling to Japan. They don't need their passports or a foreign language pocket dictionary, but the hours of travel and the tricky airplane itineraries, the necessity to pack for a climate not their own—forcing them to drag winter clothes up from the basement even when they come in the middle of summer—and the brain-addling time change make the journey particularly arduous and the destination feel foreign to them. Without the ability to fly, call, email and video chat, I would never live here, so far away.

There are days when the cold issue is the throbbing heart to all of my questions about who I am and who I want to become. Am I an Alaskan? Am I tough enough to ignore the comforts and conveniences of warmer climes to fully immerse myself in—and cherish—life here? Am I to be the mother of two Alaskan girls? Do I have it in me to chart the course of my own life, or just wait until necessity dictates where I should go?

At other times, I think the cold question is just a distraction. The real issue feels harder, hotter, painful: Can I bear to live so far from my mother?

"Do you like all of that snow and ice?" my mother asks me every time I visit her. It's a funny question to try to answer.

"No," I often say, "I hate it." Or, No, but I put up with it. No, I sometimes want to say, but it is attached to certain things I do like, things I even love, things I may now not just desire in my life, but need. It's too long an answer to describe empty cross-country ski trails a ten-minute drive from my house. Or how we feel that the stars have magically aligned when the lakes freeze with solid, clear ice and we can skate across them, marveling at the silver, dinner-plate-sized bubbles trapped inches below our blades. Or the thrill of seeing the tracks of wild animals in the snow—moose, hare, lynx, wolves—and the way they are tangible proof of the beautiful, unruined landscape in which we live. "I could never live there. I could never stand all of that snow and ice," she says.

I cannot help but take my mother's indictment of the cold personally. And yet, these days, it is the cold that often brings my mother and me together. When my first daughter was born—two days before the darkest day of winter and in the middle of a snowstorm—my parents came to Alaska to help. I spent the first two weeks of their visit lying on the couch, doing little more than nursing my baby while my mother brought me glasses of water to quench my superhuman thirst. On the third week, when my father had flown home to return to work and I felt well enough to get up, my mother and I borrowed snowshoes and drove to a tree-cloaked nature center in the snowy hills behind our town. I put my newborn in a sling under my jacket, and I helped my mother put on the awkward footwear, her first time on snowshoes. Then we lumbered across snowy meadows and through the trees until we came to a clearing with a view of the bay. The scene was spectacular—the sun's light low and subtle, the mountains decked in snow, clouds braiding and unbraiding across their peaks. At that moment I felt my mother understood why I live here—so far away from her—and what it is about this cold, cold place that pulls me so.

My mother came up again after the birth of my second daughter, who was born in the summer, when the days are so long it seems there's two packed into every one, and the nights aren't even dark enough to see stars. A few days after she arrived, on an unusually warm June day, we hiked down a switchback trail to a remote stretch of beach. My newborn was strapped to my chest in a pea-green fleece suit, and my husband, toddler, and blue heeler trailed behind. The sky was a flawless blue and the mountains on the far side of the water shot sharp, snow-streaked peaks out of the sea.

Once on the beach, my hot-blooded toddler began taking off her clothes. One sandal at a time, then her pink leggings and minute underwear, which my husband slung over our dog's head to the toddler's thrill. My mother got down on her hands and knees then on the cobble beach and conjured elaborate made-up worlds with my daughter—whole families and houses out of rocks—while I sat on a driftwood log and nursed my newborn. Then my mother set off on a brisk walk. As her figure shrank down the beach, I watched my husband chase after the toddler. There was no wind and the tide was out, leaving a wide expanse of sand for her to run around on. The warmth was an odd feeling; the absence of cold wind felt like a strange presence, no rushing in our ears, no hair to pull out of our eyes and mouth. The sun warmed my face and bare arms wonderfully.

My newborn slept in my arms as my mother turned into a black speck down the beach, and thoughts played an exhausting tug-of-war in my head: How could I live so far away from my mother, a get-down-on-her-hands-and-knees nana, the kind who really talks to my children, and listens? But the empty beach, the beautiful gray cobbles, the mountains glistening with wind-shined snow, my toddler barefoot, naked, free . . . how could I live anywhere else? Still, there was my mother, the woman who raised me, held me, nursed me, who talked me through the heartache of lost friendships and collapsed romances—how could I choose to live so far away, where I cannot help her if something comes up, where I cannot even have dinner with her without months of planning and thousands of dollars of expense? They were the same thoughts my mind had turned over again and again.

"I have to go in," my mother said breathlessly when she returned. She was already scanning the beach for a good spot to leave her clothes. My mother is like me: when the thought flashes into the mind to get into cold water, it cannot be extinguished. This was the only way to fully experience the unusually warm, windless day. The tide had turned, and little waves rolled in. Already my mother was moving like someone cold, taking short, quick steps, a certain giddy nervousness overcoming her. We hurried up the beach to a driftwood tree trunk as if the opportunity to get in the sea might pass, or the will to immerse in water so cold it takes your breath away would soon expire. My mother yanked off her shoes and socks and the rest of her clothes. Then, with arms flapping at her sides, she stepped gingerly across the rocks, letting out a shriek when the first cold wave smacked her shins. She continued into the frigid, murky water, laughing and gasping, her body disappearing under the surface as her arms hovered above. And then she pushed off and swam out, up to her neck in the gray water with her arms swirling rapidly around her. For a moment she was unattached to anything—to the shore, to me, my still-new family, the past, the future. I stood watching her on the beach, chuckling at her jerking strokes and her constant shrieking, feeling something inside me quicken.

And then I did the only thing I could do. I put my sleeping baby down on the cobble beach and followed my mother into the cold sea.

———

Miranda Weiss is the author of *Tide, Feather, Snow: A Life in Alaska.* Her writing has appeared in the *Washington Post, American Scholar, Alaska Magazine,* and elsewhere. She lives in Homer with her family.

Vesica Piscis

———

Leigh Newman

There are places that feel like home and places that feel like where you live. The home-feeling ones ruin you for life. I have had the good fortune of a few of these. I grew up in Alaska. Even as a sullen teenager, I thought there was nowhere I'd rather be than my family's crappy plywood cabin on Shell Lake. The place was surrounded by shoulder-high alders and bears. The only way in or out was by floatplane or snow machine (in the winter), and if you wanted excitement, you could either wait for the flag on an ice-fishing rig to pop up or canoe down to the river's mouth for trout. At night, the sky was a live astronomy of stars.

In my twenties, I lived in the Lower East Side of Manhattan and, though my block was run by Dominican heroin dealers whose customers—mostly white, dreadlocked squatters—slumped like a parade of deflated human balloons along the steps to my door, I loved the six-kid families who lived to every side of me and my ramshackle apartment with rogue, smoke-infused wiring. I loved the wild, music-soaked neighborhood where empty lots were filled in with cornfields, sunflowers, and casitas. When the wind blew, you could smell the fishy brine off the East River through the smoke and hustle of the street.

Another time—and only for six months—I had a room in Paris with a sink and cot and window overlooking the city's rippling terracotta rooftops. The steeples. The moody gray sky. The smell of sewer and fresh bread. Every day I kissed the dusty tile floor with a sense of joy and belonging—even if I realized I was just another American so enamored with France, I thought I could wish myself into another nationality.

For the rest of my forty-odd years, however—and most especially now—I have not felt at home in my home. By home I mean the structure in which I live, the land, the vista from the window, the foliage, the flowers, the language, the customs and quirks and character of the environment that either dovetail with your soul—or don't.

Home, for many people, means family, friends, pets. And though I think these are part of the equation, they aren't enough to sustain the feeling on their own. Home, to me, is a place. A physical one. This definition probably has something to do with my spending much of my childhood in the wilderness, bored out of my mind at the time, staring at mountains, digging around in the mud until I lost a boot. There is a fingerprint early landscapes can leave on your inner life. Sometimes it hides for a while, drowned out by the clutter of other, more adult concerns. But when it surfaces, it's like a bubble of oxygen you didn't know you were gasping for in the middle of the night.

Only recently have I realized this. I live in Brooklyn. I have two kids. I am a writer. I bicycle and recycle and speak a few

languages and enjoy the occasional artisanal mayonnaise, if I
can force myself to part with the six bucks for the jar. All around
me are people that blow my mind with their kindness, their in-
telligence, their jobs resolving conflict in the Sudan or in documentary film, shooting outsider artists. My life is rife with poets
and activists and painters and jazz violinists and stay-at-home
parents who are also in a band and do stained glass. By any ex-
ternal measure, this 71-square-mile borough is a perfect fit. I like
the people. I like the people and learn from them. On any given
Sunday, I can go to an avant-garde puppet show I actually enjoy.

And yet, despite all this, I am not at home. Constantly.

It all started with my pregnancy at age thirty-three, when
the smell of Manhattan garbage made me vomit with such
vigor outside a Popeye's Chicken in Times Square I had to be
hospitalized. Around this time, the empty warehouse across
the street from my house had an alarm malfunction—hourly.
Then there were the perpetually operating jackhammers, as
the luxury condo crowd moved into their still unfinished glass
towers. Everyone around me told me how beautiful the neighborhood was. And it was: I could see it! The cobblestones! The
merry-go-round!

I just felt—unhappy.

My husband is an understanding man and went along with
me when I asked to move us to another neighborhood—one
deeper in Brooklyn, where we still live. The apartment there was
cheaper. It came with the miracle of a parking space. We had a
wonderful public school and a park with a sprinkler. And yet I
walked down the street and felt acutely, like a rash, as if the cement were trying to eat my skin.

For the first six months, I obsessed about the litter. It was the
same litter I had lived with in my twenties, but now it haunted

me so that I spent whole Saturdays going up and down our block with a garbage bag picking up bottles and flyers and mashed-up take-out food containers. At the end of our street is a huge gray wall that supports the subway track. I daydreamed of painting it green and began to put this plan into action, buying a ladder and rollers, until my husband informed me that I would be arrested for graffiti. Even if I painted it at night, using a headlight I had bought expressly for this purpose.

Do you see where these eccentricities were taking me? I didn't. Because I didn't want to. Where I was going was leaving New York. I had this struggle earlier in my life, but had told myself the same things I told myself now: (1) My husband loved New York, (2) My husband could only do his job—running a New York engineering and architecture firm—in New York, (3) My kids loved their school and their friends and we had just gotten them settled, (4) I couldn't support all four of us on my salary if I did move us—to Montana or Alaska or some place with enough natural splendor to silence the angry, trapped-feeling person I had become.

There were my feelings. And then there was everybody else's feelings. And then there was the cost of food, heat, and rent. Plus, it wasn't like I didn't like where I lived. I just did not—and do not—love it and love, I suppose, is the single prerequisite for feeling at home. You must love your home for it to be a home. You might also hate it, resent it, fear it, or fear leaving it at certain low points. But you also, always, love it.

There were two options left, and I pursued both. The first was depression—and all the self-loathing and exhaustion that accompanies that condition. The second was our backyard. Backyards are a luxury in Brooklyn. Our apartment came with a roach issue, an ant issue, a mice issue, tile floors, and a faux-brick wall that made you think of a 1960s cocktail smashed against the wall during a marital fight. And yet—outside the door in the kitchen was 20-by-40 feet of cement.

When we took the apartment—thanks to a generous friend—the area had been teeming with vines and weeds and rebellious daisies. Before we moved in, the Polish landlord had razed every tatter of green down to the ground. As a gift, he said. For you. Leaves bring mosquitoes.

I smiled at him that day. I thanked him. I stood out there on the smoking gray moonscape of my life and listened to the F train thunder by. Every seven fucking minutes. I can't, I thought. And I meant it. I can't.

The yard was edged in chain link on one side and scalloped wire on the other—the opposite side of which lay more cement. I took the jade plant from our old apartment outside and placed it haphazardly on a low wall made of even more cement. A friend who had been evicted from his place showed up with ten odd pots of mystery plants, some of them scallions from a long-eaten salad. My kids added carrot tops and lemon seeds. I threw around some wildflower mix and said, "Let's see what happens."

Three weeks later, I arrived at what my family calls my tunnel of happy insanity—a kind of total, maniacal focus that is my perverse notion of joy. A local preschool had put a rabbit hutch on the corner for the garbage man to pick up and I brought it back, planning to raise rabbits for the meat. (This didn't happen.) I invested in a dogwood, strawberry plants, tomato vines, watermelon seedlings. There was a concrete Madonna sculpture at the end of our yard with a long-dried fountain and I dug her out and filled the pool and watched as the water seeped out into the ground. I lined the pool and watched the water seep out all over again.

Still, I clung to the idea of pet turtles. And floating lilies.

An old man often leaned over the fence between our yards. The left side of his face was missing from the ear down, giving his jaw at torqued look. He was short and wizened and enthusiastically gesturing, wearing a beater T-shirt and ripped canvas shorts. The yard he was standing in was not his, but he had adopted it with the permission of the owners, to grow tomatoes. His yard, the next over, had twenty years of grapevines, a meat-smoking shed, a knife-sharpening station, and a hunting spaniel who bayed at the various squirrels and raccoons that jumped off the subway tracks.

My kids, my husband, my other neighbors—not a single one of them understood him when he yelled over the fence. Mostly because his partly missing jawbone distorted his speech. I would like to think that I was savant for deciphering his messages except that I suspect I had isolated myself so (see: depression) and was so intent on growing any kind of greenery that I paid extra-special attentions to his broken commands: "What are you doing! Don't water now, it burns. Don't do dat. Take this pretty, put it over there. See? The soil here is gold."

I worked at home and gardened for a half hour at 9 am, noon, and five. Plus all day on weekends. He was there at every hour, every day. For a year and half, I didn't know his name and he didn't know mine. But when he harvested his own grapes and made wine, he gave me multiple bottles. When I tried to give him some of my tomatoes, he said, "Are you kidding?" and handed me four more baskets of firm, perfectly round tomatoes.

When I got a tiny hunting spaniel and yelled at her for pooping in the house, he would remind me, "She's just a baby." When he left his dog out at night, I would bring her over to my yard and feed her treats. He dug up snapdragons from Sicily and left them on my picnic table. I went to Alaska and brought him back a whole salmon—which he refused, saying, with not a little affection, "We talked about this! Italians have their own food!"

We sharpened our knives together. He had a place upstate and showed up on Easter Sunday with a trash bag of freshly killed pheasants as a gift. Immediately, I turned around, skinned and processed the birds—which involved a mess of guts and feathers. My writer friends, there for brunch, thought it was wonderful but . . . uh . . . a little gross. My kids agreed.

Sal—which was his name, as I finally found out—had grown up in Sicily and done his best to re-create it in his backyard, from the snapdragons to the mini-vineyard. I couldn't re-create much of my Alaska due to the warm climate of Brooklyn. But I did plant Alaskan raspberries, Alaskan currants, and native northern daisies. I got a smoker for salmon, like the one I grew up with, and a grill. I set up a fire pit and sat out in the winter around the "campfire" with the kids. I bought plans to make my own kayak in the shed in back (this is still in the works).

My happiness was connected less to what I was doing and more to the act of doing. My childhood had been spent building outhouses, putting together woodstoves, hauling wood into the house. Sal's had been similar on his farm, he told me. What we both could not get enough of was that feeling of worth and hands and dirt, the brute self-enforced labor with which we had grown up.

This year, in June, I was walking home—from the wine store, of course—and Sal was standing in his front yard, tormenting his peach tree. This was a common discussion point between us—me telling him to let the thing free, him laughing as he roped up the branches and winched them tight into perfectly shaped boughs. This day, however, he got off the ladder. The rag shirt. The jack-o-lantern face. He had the cancer again. I did not know he had had cancer before—but, of course—his jaw.

This time it was in his lungs, his stomach, his intestines. Then he did something I never expected and will never forget. He broke down in sobs and hugged me and said, "I'm not ready."

I suggested we drink. A lot.

He said he couldn't. The chemo, plus his daughter.

His daughter was right behind him. A little older. Very nice. We nodded. And we all went home—to whatever we thought that term meant for those few weeks. Every day, I went into my backyard. Every day, Sal tossed over plants. Snapdragons. Tomatoes. Tools. He was giving me his garden—though I didn't realize it. I had this idea that when you had terminal cancer, it took a year. Or more. I went to Alaska for three weeks and lived in my friend's cabin nine miles from humanity, which was another way I was trying to get happy—short, choice stints in the wilderness.

The day I came back, the sink had clogged and I called the super. He came and yanked out the hair in the drain. Then yelled at me that he had a lot going on, he had all kind of jobs to do and the guy next door had died. He'd had to go to the funeral and everything last week! It took a lot of time!

I stood there blinking. My super's mouth moved—expressing, I like to think, grief as rage. I waited for him to finish, and when finally he did, I went into the backyard. And cried by myself. Then the kids came out and cried.

One week later, the owner of the backyard between us—where Sal had grown his tomatoes—came out with cement mixer and poured concrete over the whole yard. He didn't want the maintenance. While he was at it, he did the front yard too.

As soon as the cement truck left, I went over to Sal's. His daughter was there on a ladder with a garbage bag. The peach tree was loaded with small yellowish-whitish-green fruit. She was knocking peaches into the bag with a mop handle. I leaned against the wrought iron grate while my dog pulled against the leash, looking for Sal's dog, who had been sent away to another relative in the country. "Look," I said. "I miss your dad."

"You know," she said. "I tell people how I grew up in this neighborhood. In Brooklyn. How it was like a farm in Sicily, with the chickens, the rabbits, the crops Pop put in. How great it was. And nobody understood what I meant. Nobody believed me."

She handed me a garbage bag—the big kind—of peaches.

"I'll make a pie," I said.

"I know you will," she says. "That's why I'm giving them to you."

About three years ago, wrestling with the same problems, I went to a therapist. "You have a problem with reality," she said. She was very smart and she was right. I avoid the basic, practical things that end up making your life much easier if you pay attention, such as paying bills on time, defining goals, discussing problems instead of waiting for them to go away. This was why I ended up in messes and morasses and often felt as if my life was happening to me via the decisions of my husband, the needs of my kids, my own up and downs, instead of directing where it was going on my own.

And yet, I couldn't help but think—as I still think—that having a problem with reality is also a good thing. Not because reality is so gruesome, but because if you have a problem with it, you're forced to find solutions that just don't exist. You might write a book or lose a few days in a novel or build an ark or try to build an opera house in a jungle. Looking back I couldn't see that my backyard in Brooklyn was a home. It wasn't. It wasn't for Sal either. But where our dream worlds intersected, that real-life vesica piscis constructed out of plants, lumber, sunshine, and labor—was a comforting place, a place as homelike as I had felt in a long, long while.

Now that Sal is gone, my half of the world will go on. I have one of his grapevines going crazy on the chainlink below the subway and, eventually, I will make my own wine. I'm processing Atlantic salmon from Chinatown into Alaskan jerky in my new smoker. I'm still contemplating the rabbits, kayak, and pond. These are chores and fantasies I look forward to. I try to think more about them than about the fact that Sal is not yelling instructions to me from next door. There is no tidy reconciliation to losing him, I suppose, except for the fact that in any real home—even a dream one—there is always some feel of the person who built it, some ghost that is just too alive to be memory.

——————

Leigh Newman's memoir about Alaska, *Still Points North*, was a finalist for the National Book Critics Circle John Leonard Prize. Her fiction, essays, and book reviews have appeared in *One Story*, *Tin House*, the *New York Times*, *Fiction*, *New York Tyrant*, *Vogue*, *O: The Oprah Magazine*, *Bookforum*, and others. She has received fellowships from Bread Loaf Writers' Conference and the Corporation of Yaddo. She currently serves as Books Editor of Oprah.com and editor-at-large at Catapult Publishing. She teaches in the MFA program at Sarah Lawrence College.

The Explorer

———

Tara Conklin

You spend forty years saying that you never felt at home there. You tell people it's a small town, claustrophobic, provincial. Three hours from New York City, two hours from Boston, stuck in a minor mountain range at the tail end of the Massachusetts turnpike. The summers are too hot, the winters too cold. Only autumn, those brief days of gold and blue, seem worth the fuss.

You grow up in a house that is 250 years old. It is painted red with blue trim. Often, the toilet does not flush properly. The hot water demands short showers, a careful hand on the tap. Every winter, you huddle before the wood stove and claim you are freezing. The house is small but contains snaking crawl spaces and cavernous closets inside which you often hide with a flashlight and a book. Mysterious indentations mark the wood floor around the upstairs toilet. *From the old woman's cane*, your father says. *She'd knock when she was done so her servant would*

come and get her. When your father refinishes the floors downstairs, he finds a large dark liquid stain soaked into the wood.
From the school children, he says. *Someone must have spilled a
pot of ink.* Your mother believes that within the house lives a
ghost who finds lost objects and leaves them helpfully in plain
view. The ghost comforts your mother, she explains, because it is
evidence that ours is the kind of house that provokes an enduring attachment.

You have two parents and two sisters. You are the oldest.
For much of your childhood, your parents fight about money
and each other and your mother's depression. One night your
mother throws a plate of spaghetti and it cracks and splatters
against the wall. One afternoon your sister locks you out of
the house and you break a window with your palm. The cut is
not deep but it bleeds dramatically onto the floor and the window sill, all over your shirt and the snow on the ground. Every
Christmas, you hang stockings over the mantelpiece with push
pins. One year you notice dozens of little holes in the wood and
you are unsure if your family has made them all or if they belong
to other families, other stockings. That night, you crawl deep inside a closet with a flashlight and a pen and secretively, carefully
you write your name on the wall in your childish curving script.

Every day, you walk to school. Most of the children in your
classes are second- and third-generation residents of the town.
Their surnames adorn businesses and street signs; they are
cousins, friends since infancy, known to the same teachers who
once taught their parents. In the fall, boys are released early to
hunt deer with their fathers. In the winter, half the class empties
out to take ski lessons at the local resort. It is now, as a young
child, that you begin to see yourself as an outsider. Here are people who have chosen this small pretty place, this bucolic way of

life. To ski, to hunt, to claim this place for themselves as their parents did and grandparents too. You decide that the town and the people do not fit you; you do not fit them. There is no wrong or right. It is simply a bad match, like putting on a sweater that is too tight at the neck. It itches and pulls. You feel as though you cannot breathe.

After high school, you decide to travel. You work two waitressing jobs to earn enough for airfare and then you go. Your parents permit you—what else can they do?—and they say: you can always come home. Home? You realize that for you there is no enduring attachment. You spend a summer riding the trains in Europe. The next year, it is New Zealand, then Costa Rica, then Paris and Madrid. You move to Moscow for two years, to New York for four, to London for seven. From the ages of twenty to thirty, you visit thirty-seven different countries and live at eighteen different addresses. You live with roommates, flat mates, boyfriends, colleagues, strangers. In Moscow, in a two-bedroom flat with a single woman, her young daughter, and elderly mother. In Quepos, with an unmarried couple in a cement-block house with no hot water, no refrigerator, no stove. In Madrid, with a family in a lush, gated community surrounded by desert. Beyond its steep walls, a community of gitanos light fires at night and sing in strange, ghostly voices. Each new place makes your mind hum, your fingers tingle. None of them feel like home, of course, but this is irrelevant. No—this is for the best.

While you are abroad, your parents divorce. Your childhood house is sold. Your mother moves to a nearby town, your father closer to Boston. You avoid going back to visit them. When you do go, you feel itchy, restless. Everything seems small and dull. Every view looks stunted. Sometimes you drive past your childhood house and slow to look at it but you never stop. You drive the route you once walked to school and remember the dip in the sidewalk, the falling-down house with the dog, the yellow fire hydrant, the chestnut tree. You slow but you never stop.

Your grandfather says to you, shortly before he dies: I never felt at home. You wonder if perhaps your dislocation is genetic. Your grandfather was the son of immigrants, orphaned when he was eight years old, shuttled between friends and relatives for months, perhaps years, it is never fully clear to you. He tells you a story: one Christmas, he and his brother are staying at a family friend's house. The other children receive their presents, gaily wrapped packages, sweets and toys. Your grandfather receives a pencil. Another story: after he fought in Europe, he returned to New York and could not find a job. He begged, he said. He applied for anything, it didn't matter, and finally he found work selling shoes. Later, he owned a construction company on Long Island that made long, flat, unremarkable buildings for commercial use. Your grandfather is your favorite person in the world. After he dies, you wish in a selfish, childish way that he had not told you his feelings about home. It makes you indescribably sad to think of him with that burden. It also seems a prophecy. A fate.

You return to the U.S. and settle in Seattle with your English husband and children. You buy a house big enough for your family. There is a backyard with a swing set, flower beds in the front, neighbors with children, a library branch and coffee shop down the street. Seattle does not have old houses, not in the way of your hometown. In this house, there are no hidden ink stains. The toilets work fine, the cable TV, the wireless. Seattle does not get very cold in the winter nor excessively hot in the summer. You try very hard not to fight with your husband about money or each other or your depression. But you wonder why it is that, after six years in the Seattle house, you still have boxes to unpack. The light fixtures you called ugly the moment you first saw them still remain on the wall. The kitchen is still painted the same dark, oppressive red. After six years, the house bears no mark of you.

But your children? They have claimed it. They never want to leave. They say it's too rainy or too sunny or too early or too late to go outside; they want only to play with their toys, to build forts, to color at the rickety kitchen table that is scarred and bumpy from marker stains, dried glue, stuck-on food. Dirt from their fingers and faces mark every wall and you try to wash it off but still the stains remain. One day your daughter, who is eight, asks if she must leave home for college. She says: *I want to live here forever.* Your three-year-old asks: *Is planet Earth inside our house?* It is his whole world.

You think about your grandfather. You think about your old childhood home and wonder if the ink stain was accidental or a mark made with intent? You consider the ghost, the possibility that it did not choose to remain but instead found itself trapped. You remember the Moscow metro, the beach in Quepos, the place in Paris with hot chocolate so thick you had to eat it with a spoon. Soon you begin to itch. It is not the same itch as before. You are different now. You are a mother, you are a wife, you cannot shake off the life you have built, the city where you live in the same way you once did. But the longing fills you. You think maybe your marriage is over. You think maybe you need a new place to live, a place that is yours alone but not yours. A blank. A starting over. You realize that this is the exhilaration of a move. The idea that in a new place anything might happen. The idea that nothing has yet been ruled out. A true home requires choices, the taking of this over that, a loss of possibility. Once you paint the kitchen white, it will no longer be red. Once you claim a home, you are no longer an explorer.

Your mother sends you a link to a blog maintained by the newest owner of your childhood house. These people, a wealthy retired couple from New York City, have decided to undertake a complete renovation. They are very excited about the project, which represents to them a change of life, a dramatic fresh start after their frenetic jobs in the city. They post their architect's plans. They post photos of the gutted living room, of a large orange back hoe sitting in the front yard, of a board found in a closet upon which your name is written in a curving childish script. You visit the blog irregularly, usually at night, but you read every word and study every photo. On the day they post a picture of a crane lifting out the large window from the wall of your old bedroom—a window where you sat and looked out to the magnolia trees and apple trees, a window out of which you climbed to sit on the low pitched roof and imagine the places you might go—you begin to cry. You are as surprised by your reaction as you are by the image of the crane, which is a brilliant red and seems improperly built, the arm too long, the base too narrow, as though it will topple over at any moment. Do these people from New York know what they are doing? Do they understand the antiquity of the house, its delicate floorboards, its intricate molding, the fretwork of tiny holes in the mantel?

You remove the blog from your favorites tab. You vow never to visit it again. You want these new owners to have a fresh start in your old home. More than anything, you want to believe that you can too. You walk down the stairs of your house in Seattle. From the kitchen come the sounds of your children playing a board game, their voices impassioned and fierce. An orange late-afternoon sun cuts through the front window and illuminates the swirling, busy dust that fills—you see it suddenly, so clearly, so much—the hall. You wonder if an explorer must by definition remain adrift. You consider that home is nothing more than a choice you make to stay and place your mark. Lift a window. Paint a kitchen. Write your name upon a wall. Perhaps in the staying you find not the widest world but the best. *Want to play?* your son calls and you tell him yes.

———

Tara Conklin's first novel, *The House Girl*, was a *New York Times* best-seller, #1 IndieNext pick and Target Club pick, and has been translated into eight languages. Her second novel, *The Last Romantics*, is forthcoming. Her short fiction has appeared in the *Bristol Short Story Prize Anthology* and *Pangea: An Anthology of Stories from Around the Globe*. She is the recipient of a 2015 Artist Trust GAP grant. Before turning to fiction, Tara worked for an international human rights organization and as a litigator at a corporate law firm in London and New York. Tara was born in St. Croix, US Virgin Islands, and grew up in western Massachusetts. She holds a BA in history from Yale University, a JD from New York University School of Law, and a Master of Law and Diplomacy from the Fletcher School (Tufts University).

Annotating the First Page
of the First Navajo-
English Dictionary

Danielle Geller

Annotating the First Page of the First
Navajo-English Dictionary[1]

'ąą', well (anticipation, as when a person approaches one as
though to speak, but says nothing).[2]

---

1 The first, incomplete *Navajo-English Dictionary* was compiled
in 1958 by Leon Wall, a BIA official in charge of a literacy program on the Navajo reservation, and William Morgan, a Navajo
translator. The dictionary was published by the United States
Department of the Interior, Bureau of Indian Affairs.
2 I could begin and end here. My mother was a full-blooded Navajo woman, raised on the reservation, but she was never taught

'aa'adiniih, venereal disease.

'ąą 'ádoolnííł, it will be opened.

'aa 'áhályánii, body guard.[3]

'aa 'ą'ii, magpie.[4]

'ąą 'ályaa, it was opened.[5]

'ąą 'ályaa, bich'į', it was opened to them; they were invited.[6]

---

to speak her mother's language. There was a time when most words were better left unspoken. Still, I am drawn to the nasal vowels and slushy consonants, though I feel no hope of ever learning the language. It is one thing to play dress-up, to imitate pronunciations and understanding; it is another thing to think or dream or live in a language not your own.

3   Aug. 15. '15. I move to Tucson from Boston to join an MFA program in creative writing. I applied to schools surrounding the Navajo reservation because I wanted to be closer to my mother's family. My plan: to take rug-weaving and Navajo language (Diné Bizaad) classes; to visit my family as often as I can. It will be opened: the door to the path we have lost.

4   Magpies are the one bird I have not seen on the reservation. Birds I *have* seen in my grandmother's backyard: Cliff Swallows, Inca Doves, Sharp-shinned Hawk, Western Bluebirds, Western Scrub Jay, Phainopepla, Northern Flickers, Ravens, and other carrion birds.

5   It was opened: a PDF version of the Navajo-English dictionary. Curious which librarian from the University of Northern Colorado decided to digitize the dictionary. Most government documents, after they are shipped to federal depositories around the country, languish on out-of-the-way shelves and collect decades of dust before being deaccessioned and destroyed. I have worked in these libraries—I know.

6   One of the reasons Navajo soldiers were recruited as code talkers during World War II was because there were no published dictionaries of their language at that time—and because the

'a 'áán, hole in the ground; tunnel; cave; burrow.

'ąą 'át'é, it is open.[7]

'ąą 'át'éego, since it was open.[8]

'á'ádaat'éhígíí, the fundamentals, elements.

'áádahojoost'įįd, they quit, backed out, desisted, surrendered.[9]

'aa 'dahoost'įįd, t'óó, they gave up, surrendered.[10]

'aa dahwiinít'įįʼ, into court (a place where justice is judicially administered).[11]

---

grammatical structure of the language was so different from English, German, and Japanese. They were invited to: a world beyond the borders of the reservation. My mother always told me: the only way to get off the Rez is to join the military or marry off.

7 One of the first typewriters that could adequately record the Navajo language was built for Robert Young, a linguist who also worked with William Morgan and published a more comprehensive dictionary and grammar guide (*The Navaho Language*) in 1972. In the 1970s, a Navajo font was released for the IBM Selectric, an electric typewriter, which would serve as the basis for a digital font on early computers.

8 Navajo fonts are now available for download in multiple typefaces: Times New Roman, Verdana, and Lucida Sans. It is easier to write when 1:á, 2:ą, 3:ą́, and so on.

9 Spring. 1864. The "Long Walk" begins. The US Army forcibly relocates the Navajo from their homeland to Bosque Redondo in eastern New Mexico. Those who do not resist learn to walk, but death follows both paths.

10 There are many reasons parents do not teach their children the Navajo language: US monolingual policies, violence experienced in boarding schools, and perceived status. Those who speak English well will have a better chance for escape.

11 Sept. 13. '15. My cousin-sister is scheduled to testify in court in one week; she isn't sure if she wants to go. I pick her up anyway. Bring her back to Tucson with me.

'áádęę́', from there (a remote place).

'aadęę́', from there.

'aa deet'á, transfer (of property, or ownership).[12]

'áádeisįįd, they discontinued, stopped, or ended it.[13]

'aadi, there.

'áadi, there, over there (a remote place).[14]

'áádįįł, it is progressively dwindling away; disappearing.[15]

---

12 My aunt tells me we have land on the reservation, just off I-40. We've inherited it from our great-grandmother, Pauline Tom, one of four heirs to Hostan Tsi'najinii. Only, Pauline Tom had many children, and their children had many children, and after she died in 2008, all those children started fighting. It's a common problem, and it isn't unique to the Navajo Nation. Federal land allotment policies have resulted in too many heirs for too few acres.

13 "In the early 1970's, there were school-based efforts at reversing language shift, approved by the Tribal Government and supported in large part by the Federal Bilingual Education funds. A number of schools were active, but the movement did not take hold. . . . No more than 10% of Navajo children receive any Navajo courses" (Bernard Spolsky, "Language Management for Endangered Languages: The Case of Navajo," *Language Documentation and Description* 6, 117–131).

14 Sept. 13. '15. On the drive to Tucson along I-40, my cousin-sister points out the black-tar roofs of our family's houses. She tells me our relatives in Sanders called her Dibé Yázhí, Little Sheep, after the animals our great-grandmother raised. Dibé Yázhí points out the cemetery—a small, square piece of land—where our great-grandmother is buried. The cemetery is barely distinguishable from the rest of the landscape, and when I follow her gaze, look away from the highway, I see only the stark, white faces of the headstones and the silver glint of a ribbon in the wind.

15 In 1968, a decade after the first dictionary was published, 90 percent of the children on the reservation who entered school spoke

'áadiísh, there? thereat?[16]

'ąą dinéest'ą, they increased, multiplied (**'ąą** has the meaning of extension or spread).

'aadóó, from there.

'áádóó, from there on; and then; and; from that point on; from there. **Shash yiyiisxį 'áádóó shí nísel'ah.** He killed the bear and I skinned it.

'áádóó bik'ijį', after that.

'áádoolzįįł, I shall discontinue it.

'aahasti', care, respect; care or respect toward a fragile object; fragility.

'ąąh 'azlá, pawn.

'ąąh 'dahaz'ą, illness, sickness, an ailment.[17]

'ąąh dahoyool'aałii, disease.

'ąąh dah sitání, license plate.

'ąąh háá'á, debt.

'ąąh ha'ajeeh tó da'diisooligíí, chicken pox.

'ąąh háát'i, fringes (saddle).

Navajo; in 2009, only 30 percent knew the language (Spolsky, "Language Management for Endangered Languages," 117).

16 Sept. 22. '15. The second time I pass our allotment on I-40, I try to find the spot Dibé Yázhí showed me. I look for the headstones; I think of stopping and trying to find my grandmother's grave. My cousin-sister told me that if you don't do the proper blessing, the spirit will follow you home. ("What is the difference between a spirit and a ghost?") I don't know the blessing, but it doesn't matter; I can't recognize the cemetery or my family's land.

17 Sept. 19. I catch a cold from my students. Might be the flu. I tell Dibé Yázhí to stay away, but she says she won't get sick. We spend all day curled up on the couch watching *Shameless*. She rests her head on my shoulder, on my hip.

'ąąh naaznilę́ę, the pawns.

'ąąh nahóókadd, disappointment.

'ąąh ni'ít'aah, cast (plaster).

'aa hojoobá'í, poor.

'aahoolzhíísh, to be one's turn.

'ąąh sita', cervical.

'á'áhwiinít'į, kindness.

'aa hwiinít'į, trial (at law), molestation.[18]

'aa hwiinít'į bá hooghan, courthouse.

'aahwiinít'į̨igo, during the court session.

'aa hwiinít'į̨ihígíí, the court session that is to come.[19]

'ą́ą́hyiłk'as, body chill.[20]

---

18 How are these words (kindness/molestation) that sound so similar, so different? My second dictionary is no help: it omits the second incident. My aunt tells Dibé Yázhí that our maternal grandmother molested her sons. My mother tells me that my paternal grandmother molested her sons. ("Why would they tell us that?") It's hard to believe, but it isn't. There will never be a trial. These are words better left unspoken, forgotten, erased.

19 Sept. 16. '15. Dibé Yázhí is told that if she doesn't appear for the court date, a warrant will be put out for her arrest. I agree to drive her back to Window Rock on Monday night, after I am done teaching for the day. It is a six-hour drive, but I am almost happy to make it. I will be in Window Rock, with my family, on the two-year anniversary of my mother's death, not by plan but by circumstance.

20 I am sick with fever, alive with fever dreams. I dream of a two-story, sandstone motel, its three square walls opening onto the desert. A sun sets between two mountains, and heavy drapes are drawn across all the windows. My mother and my aunt and all my sisters are running in and out of the rooms, slamming doors, shouting at each other from the landings. I understand that

'**áaji'**, up to that point; up to there; toward there; to that point and no farther.

'**ááji'**, in that direction; on that side.

'**aak'ee**, fall, autumn.[21]

'**aak'eedą́ą́'**, last fall, last autumn.

'**aak'eego**, in, or during the fall or autumn months.

'**aak'eejí'**, near or close to the fall season.

'**ą́ą kwááníił**, it is expanding; it is getting bigger.[22]

'**ááłdabidii'ní**, we (pl.) mean by that.

'**ááłdeiłní**, they mean by that.

'**aa'na' (ee'na')**, **yah**, he crawled in (an enclosure, as a hole, house, etc.).

---

each door is a choice, each room a potential future, and that my mother's and my aunt's and my sisters' doors are closed to me. Standing on the landing and looking into the sun, I notice a solitary woman's figure in the desert. She wears a loose blouse and a long skirt, cinched by an elaborate concho belt, and though I never met her, I know this woman is Pauline Tom, our gnomon, casting her long, indecipherable shadow on our lives.

21 I start teaching my first freshman composition class in the fall. I'm convinced, like most first-year teachers, that I have no idea what I am talking about; I spend the entire hour sweating in front of my class. But afterwards, two dark-haired, dark-skinned girls walk up to me and ask me: What are your clans? Where is your family from? We are Navajo, too. We are all three nervous and unsure where the conversation should go, but I want to grab hold of them and root them next to me; graduation rates of native students are abysmally low.

22 Sept. 22. '15. Dibé Yázhí disappears in the middle of the night and leaves us a note: Went to Gallup with Heather and Faith need to get pads and face wash. Should be back soon. She leaves us a number, the wrong number. ("She prolly went to see *that guy*.")

'aaníígóó, t'áá, the truth.[23]

'aaníinii, that which is true.

'aaníí, t'áá, it is true; truly; really; verily.[24]

'aaníí, t'áásh, is it so; is it true?[25]

'áániligíí, that which is occurring; the happening; the event.[26]

'a'át'e', sin; injustice; meanness.

'áát'įįdę́ę́, what he did; his aforementioned act.[27]

'aa yílyáii, donation.

'abąąh náát'i', border, strand (of the warp of a rug).[28]

'abaní, buckskin.

'abe', milk, teat, dug, pap.

23

24 Dibé Yázhí tells me she didn't see her boyfriend again. That she went over to Shorty's and helped him set mouse traps in the middle of the night. He couldn't do it himself, he kept catching his fingers. But she would tell me if she saw him.

25 The answer is, in many ways, unknowable; for our mothers, the surest protection from the past was to spin truths and falsehoods into one story, one thread, impossible to distinguish in the weave.

26 I have been walking around the thing that happened, stepping around the truth, trying to protect Dibé Yázhí from myself.

27 Sept. 8. '15. My cousin-sister calls me at 4:30 in the morning, and I answer; her voice is thick with tears. She tells me her boyfriend got drunk and beat her up. She found out he was cheating, and she started a fight. He hit her, threw her down. I know this story. I know it. These are words better left unspoken; a story better lost to time. Still, I have no words to help her. I will come get you, I tell her. I will bring you home with me.

28 A Navajo blanket is woven on a loom and will never outgrow its frame. Do we finish the story our mothers began, or do we rip out the weaving and begin anew? It is not so easy to erase or forget the things that have come before us.

'abe' 'astse', udder, mammary gland.

'abe'é, ch'il, milkweed.

'abéézh, there is boiling.

'abįda'diisdzil, they were forced to . . . . [29]

'abid dijoolí, duodenum.

'ábi'diilyaa, he was made to be . . . . [30]

'ábidííniid, I said to him.

'ábidiní, you say thus to him.

'ábidiní, ha'át'íí shạ', what do you mean?[31]

'abi'doogį́, he was hauled away.[32]

'abi'dool'a', he was sent; he was commanded to go.

'ábi'dool'įįdii, t'áá 'aaníí bee, that with which he was really
     harmed.[33]

---

29 See footnote 53.

30 the kind of man who hits women. He crawled inside his father's
     shadow and filled it out.

31 One of my Navajo students interviews her aunt, who teaches
     Navajo language classes, and she writes a paper about revitaliz-
     ing Diné Bizaad. I ask her if she would put me in contact with
     her aunt to answer some of my own questions. Her aunt agrees
     to email me her responses, but I am so lost, I don't know the
     right questions to ask. I write a rambling email about adjectives
     and verbs and the state of being, and she never responds.

32 When I was little, my mother called the cops on my father,
     often. Usually after they had both been drinking. I remember
     standing on the street with our neighbors, watching the cops
     chase my father down the road, shove him into a police car, and
     haul him away.

33 What are the roots of domestic violence on the reservation? In-
     escapable poverty. Powerlessness. Untreated mental illnesses.
     Self-medication through alcohol. Cycles of abuse: fathers beating
     mothers beating sons beating their lovers and future mothers.

'abi'doolt'e'ígíí, yah, the fact that he was imprisoned.

'abi'doolt'e, yah, he was jailed, confined (as within an enclosure), imprisoned.[34]

'ábidoołdįįł, it will annihilate them.[35] **'ábidoołdįįłgo,** since it will annihilate.

'ábidoo'niidę́ę, what he was told; what he had been told.

'ábiilaa, it made him.

'ábíłní, he says to him.

'abíní, morning.[36]

34　Sept. 8. '15. Dibé Yázhí's boyfriend is arrested and thrown into the Window Rock jail. It isn't his first time there, but he isn't held long. He goes home to his mother. My cousin-sister is told not to contact him before the trial.

35　Rates of domestic violence and sexual assault are higher among Native Americans than any other ethnicity in the United States. A report by the Department of Justice estimates assault rates to be 50 percent higher than the next-highest demographic. A CDC study from 2008 reported that almost 40 percent of Native American women identified as victims of domestic violence during their lifetime. These are conservative figures; many assaults go unreported.

36　Sept. 13. '15. My first trip to the Rez. I wake before everyone and slip out of bed and out the door with my aunt's binoculars. My aunt's dog, Toro, follows me down the twisting dirt road and into the flowering sagebrush hills. Toro follows his nose off the path, under bushes, over piles of gravel and rock. He misses a pair of cotton-tails, who bolt out from under my feet as I cross the same ground minutes later; they reach the safety of a hidden burrow before he turns around. The cedar trees on higher ground are full of birds. As the sun climbs higher, I decide to head home; I call Toro's name, and he circles back to my heel. I pat his rib cage, scratch under his collar, talk cheerfully to him and the birds and the morning as we walk back to my aunt's house.

'abínídóó, from the morning on . . . .

'abnígo, in the morning.[37]

'ábi'niidįįd, it started to dwindle; it began to run out.

'ábísdįįdii, that which caused them to disappear, or become extinct.[38]

'ábizhdííniid, he said to him.

'abízhí, paternal uncle or aunt.

'ábizh'niilaa, he started to make it.

'ach'á, hunger for meat.

'ách'ááh, in front of.[39]

'ach'ááh na'adá, protection.[40]

---

37 Sept. 22. '15. I wake up to the sound of water lapping stone. I sit up in Dibé Yázhí's bed, peek through the blinds, am disappointed Tropical Depression Sixteen-E has followed us to Window Rock. If I were better rested, I would walk into the hills, look for water-logged birds, but my cough has kept me up all night.

38 The Navajo-Churro is a breed of sheep descended from the domestic Churra, brought to the Americas in the sixteenth century by the Spanish. The sheep were quickly integrated into Navajo life because of their low maintenance, resistance to disease, and ability to survive extreme climates. But the US government sanctioned programs to eliminate the Navajo-Churro: Before the Long Walk, Kit Carson slaughtered thousands; beginning in the 1930's, the government culled hundreds of thousands; and by the 1970's, there were fewer than 450 remaining.

39 Sept. 22. '15. My aunt and her neighbors clear the summer weeds out of the front yard and sweep them into piles. Toro has made a small rabbit's nest of them; he lies in a tight little ball. I call Toro's name, and he lifts his head, fixes me with red, watery eyes, but he does not move.

40 In 1977, Robert McNeal, a veterinary scientist at Utah State University, founded the Navajo Sheep Project, which rounded up

'ách'ą́ą́h neilyéii, that which he protects himself by.

'achą́ hwíídéeni, addiction.

'ach'é'é, daughter, niece (daughter of one's sister) (female speaking).[41]

'ach'é'édą́ą́', one's yard, or dooryard.[42]

'acheii (achaii), maternal grandfather.[43]

'achí, the act of giving birth.

'ách'į', toward oneself.

'áchį́į́h, nose, snout.[44]

Churro sheep from the hidden mesas and canyons they had scattered to as early as Kit Carson's campaign against them. They created a core genetic flock, and today the Navajo-Churro are threatened but not extinct.

41 After my mother dies, my aunt tells me that I am her daughter now—that she is my "little mother." This is how she introduces me to everyone: This is my niece! She's a teacher at the University of Arizona! This is how everyone responds: Hello, niece.

42 My maternal great-grandmother froze to death, and my aunt is shocked that I did not know. I don't understand because freezing to death in the desert, in the sun, surrounded by yellow sagebrush flowers doesn't make sense to me. My aunt tells me Pauline Tom fell while checking on a noise outside, and she broke her hip in the fall. My aunt curls her hands on her skinny little wrists, mimes our grandmother, crawling in the dirt, but she could not crawl far enough. My grandmother froze to death in the winter, in the deep dark of the night, in her own backyard.

43 I met my maternal grandfather once when I was very young. He was a Navajo police officer. When he got sick, my mother and my aunt started fighting over who would take care of him. My aunt talked too soon about pulling the plug, and they stopped speaking for years.

44 Sept. 22. '15. I call Toro's name again, and he stands on quivering

'áchįįshtah, nostril, sinus.

'áchį́įshtah dóó 'adáyi hashch'íí', catarrh.

'ach'į nahwii'ná, to have trouble; to have difficulty; to suffer.[45]

'ach'į na'ílyé, payment; to receive pension.

'ach'į niná'ílyá, repayment.

'acho', genitalia (male).

'achó, maternal great-grandfather.[46]

'acho' biyę́ę́zhii, testicle.

'acho' bizis, prepuce.

'ach'ooní, comrade, partner.

'ada', nephew (son of one's sister) (male speaking).

'ádá, for self (myself, yourself, etc.).

'ádaa, to, about-self, concerning, to one-self. **'ádaa 'áhojilyą́,** he takes care of himself; he is on the alert.[47]

'adaa', lip.

---

legs. He hobbles over to me and leans his entire weight against me. "Toro," I whisper, and I trace the black line between his eyes, smooth my hands over his head, down his sides. I rub his soft ears, over and over. "It's so hard, I know. It's so hard." I think of the stories Dibé Yázhí told me. All the times Toro has been hit, flipped over the hoods of cars. Gotten up, shaken it off. Has he been hit again? My aunt won't take him to the vet. He's a Rez dog, now.

45 My mother was homeless the six months leading up to her death, and she never called to ask me for help.

46 Young and Morgan's dictionary tells me **'achó** means maternal great grand-*mother*, that **'acho'** is not gendered. I am too embarrassed to ask, too scared my voice will betray me on the rising O.

47 My father would never admit his own violence, though I remember it like a mirage in the desert—the images came back to me in shimmers, a disturbing gloss over the horizon.

'adą́ą́dą́ą́, yesterday.

'ádaadahalni'go, when they tell about themselves.[48]

'ádaadįįh, they are disappearing, about to disappear.

'ádaadin, they are none of them; they are non-existent, they are absent.[49]

'ádaadinídíí, the ones that are gone; absentees; decedents.[50]

'ádaadzaa, they did.[51] **'ádaadzaa yę́ę́gi 'át'éego,** like they did.[52]

  'ádaadzaaígi 'át'éego, like they did.[53]

---

48 When my mother dies, I am the one who must go through her things: her diaries, her letters, her photographs. She says things in writing she would never say to me herself, and I feel some validation. I let my cousin-sister read some of her entries: there is truth in their stories, truth in our memories, if only we could let ourselves believe them.

49 Dr. William Morgan, Sr., the linguist and translator for both Navajo dictionaries, passed away in 2001. He was eighty-five years old, more than twice the age of my mother when she died. He received an honorary doctorate from the University of New Mexico and taught at Cornell, the University of New Mexico, and the Navajo Community College. According to his obituary, he left behind nineteen grandchildren and nineteen great-grandchildren. And though he is gone, he left a cultural legacy that will survive him and his children's children's children, perhaps.

50 I am unsure how many grandchildren and great-grandchildren survived Pauline Tom; there are too many blank spaces on the family tree my mother left behind. Many of my questions have no answers; the ones who could answer them are gone.

51 The court date is cancelled. I find out after I leave that Dibé Yázhí is back with her boyfriend.

52 My mother would leave the men who hit her, but she would always take them back.

53 I should know better, but I don't. I hook up with men from the Internet and drive long distances to meet them in hotel

'ádąąh, upon oneself. **'ádąąh áahast'ą,** he committed a crime; made a serious mistake. **'ádąąh dahosíst'ą,** I committed a crime.[54]

---

rooms. I let them tie me up, bruise my skin with ropes and clamps and leather, tear me up, and make me bleed. I tell myself that it's okay because I let them—that I am the one with the power. I cannot tell if it is a lie, or if there is truth there, too.

54 I should not have taken her home. I should have spoken the words I meant to say. That we are worthy. That there is another path. That we can weave a rug of our own design. I started to look for those words but did not find them; I found only the same ghosts haunting the page.

Danielle Geller is an essayist and MFA candidate in creative writing at the University of Arizona. She is also a grateful recipient of the 2016 Rona Jaffe Foundation Writers' Awards, and her work has appeared in *Silk Road Review* and *Brevity*. When she is not writing, she is birding in cemeteries or playing video games.

The Stars Remain

Claudia Castro Luna

Before

1970. Everything I know about the church, God, the devil and the spirit world comes from my Abuelita. She gives me instructions to insure that my alma, my soul, finds its way back into my body after its nightly excursions, teaches me what blessing goes with each occasion, shows me an altar's essential components: water, a candle, incense, and whenever possible, a clump of rue. All of this knowledge she passes down to me hand over hand, word over word, the way she learned from her own Abuela.

As soon as I'm old enough she teaches me how to cross myself. "Por la señal de la Santa Cruz . . ." she says and I quickly stumble after her. The words are matched step by step by a repeated pattern of hand gestures making the sign of the cross. She places my thumb over my index finger and guides me, pausing first over my forehead, then over my cheeks, then to navel and shoulders finishing on my lips. At each pause we draw the sign of the cross. "Kiss the cross," she says when we get to my lips. And I do. I kiss it and say a reverent "Amen."

Abuelita takes her time with me even though patience is not her virtue. By necessity she is a woman of swift action. Widowed in her early twenties, determination, grit, and an irascible temper exemplify the breadth of her emotional repertoire. In a fraction of a second she can go from laughing heartily to reaching perilous levels of anger. One of her searing and creatively strung list of insults can shake down all the leaves of a mango tree leaving bare branches with birds cowering at her words.

Lucky for me my Abuelita loves me, her oldest grandchild, and so she works hard to share with me the array of amulets, prayers, and rituals known to her so that I may live a long and fruitful life under the winning patronage of all the saints and angels in Heaven.

1971. Again and again Papá declares that things of the church are "Puras babosadas." Religion is the opium of the masses, Papá says, and says it without any hint at pretention or cynicism. Mami is not as strident in her opposition to church and spiritual things, but her silence lends a tacit agreement to Papa's more active opinions. In a 99 percent Catholic country, I belong to the 1 percent of families that reject any type of organized religion and deplore penchants of the spiritual kind. Everyone I know has one, two, or more of the following religious artifacts proudly displayed in their homes: the Holy Cross, a depiction of the Last Supper, the Sacred Heart of Jesus, a depiction of the Virgin Mary. By contrast, religious iconography is strictly forbidden in my house. Prayers, if any should cross one's mind, are to remain unuttered, trapped in the accordion-like bellows of the soul. And traditional spiritual ways, labeled superstitions, are swept away like crumbs from the rice cookies we call salpores that often accompany the afternoon coffee.

My parents are young teachers, raising two young daughters and working in the small town of Atiquizaya near the border with Guatemala. As members of the country's teachers' union they focus their energy on fighting for better salaries and improving the squalid living conditions of the students they teach. To them, understanding the social and political conditions under which we live, and doing something to change them, is all the religion we need.

1975. In fifth grade I wish nothing more than to make my Holy Communion. I want to have the experience everyone I know has had, including my parents. I long to have a picture of myself in a long white dress, a diadem of sparkling glass beads on my head, gloved hands and a white candle made elegant by a white bow. But I know that my wish is many rallies and marches away from becoming a reality.

When the heat of the day lies languid in the crowns of the tallest trees, Abuelita takes me down the length of our long cobblestone street to the town's square to hear late evening Mass. We return in darkness and find Papá pacing back and forth enrobed in the dim light cast by the lamppost in front of our house.

"Dónde estaban?" he demands in a rough voice. "Las busqué por todos lados!"

"En la iglesia" answers Abuelita, unconcerned.

"Què, què?!!!" Papá can't hide his annoyance.

"Que fuimos a la iglesia, hombre, solo por un ratito . . ." Man, Abuela says, we were at church just for a little bit.

"Pues, no quiero que la este llevando a la iglesia. Entiende?" Papá snaps and his eyebrows meet smack in the middle of his forehead.

If he were an animal he would have growled and snarled, but given that Abuelita is his mother, he offers a warning instead: don't take her to church again!

Abuelita looks back at him with heraldic bearing, the long striped shawl around her shoulders dignifying her stance. Without saying a word, she lets him know that if she wants to she will take me to Mass any day of the week she damn well pleases.

1976. One day while sitting on my bed reading a book, my Papá appears in the doorway, just out of the shower, a towel draped around his waist, water trickling from his wet hair.

"Qué esta haciendo esa mierda allí?" He demands.

I look up at the "shit" he's pointing to. A small bust of the Virgin Mary hangs from the wall, her face tilted downward. An identical figure rests over my sister's bed. The Virgins have been hanging for weeks, but Papá, who rarely comes into our room, has failed to notice them. I grow cold. When my sister and I decided to put them up, we knew we risked a confrontation that could end up settled with a belt, welts, and tears. But the little busts were too beautiful to keep in their newspaper wrapping under our beds and they matched perfectly and Tia Vicky said they would prevent evil spirits lurking at night from snatching our souls and Camila and I don't want our souls snatched.

I stare at Papá staring at me. I have been on the receiving end of his searing belt enough times to know that tears don't make welts go away. I glance at my sister, playing with her dolls on the floor between our beds, but she pretends not to hear anything.

I dredge up courage, "Nos las dió Tía Vicky la última vez que visitamos. Abuelita las compró en el Mercado."

He flicks water off his forehead and I wonder if the fact that his mother bought them for us will soften his response, but his face remains intractable.

"Son para velar los sueños," I inject by way of an explanation before he offers a response. From the floor Camila chimes in agreement, "Para los sueños" she repeats.

Safe dreams or not, Papá stands under the door's frame; his jaw locked, his mouth considering something. A grunt escapes him. The doll's hair winds around and around Camila's fingers. I wish that whatever is running through his mind, please, be not about hitting me. I feel like I'm always the one getting hit. My sister is pretty and cute, everyone says so, and three years younger. I'm convinced that rules in her favor.

"Quiere que las quitemos?" I ask ready to spring up and take them down.

"Solo son babosadas ustedes!" he says, spins around, disappears down the hall.

Nonsense he calls it, our gesture to hang the Virgins.

"Nos salvamos!" says Camila and the suggestion of a smile registers on her face. We are saved. Though I cannot see it, I know, a smile also registers on mine.

1977. Presidential elections. General Carlos Humberto Romero from the PCN (Partido de Conciliacion Nacional) is declared the winner. There are widespread accusations of voter intimidation and mismanagement of ballots. The outgoing President, Coronel Arturo Armando Molina, himself from the PCN and declared winner in 1972 through egregious electoral fraud, denies any wrongdoing. Eight days after the election a group gathers in San Salvador to protest the results and national security forces open fire killing hundreds—between two hundred and fifteen hundred—no official figures are ever released. The massacre galvanizes into action all sectors of society: from labor to rural workers, from students to professionals. Many political organizations, some with military arms, are formed at this time.

The ruthlessness perpetrated at this event marks the country for the next fifteen years.

1978. Señor C, another of my parents' friends and a fellow teacher, is killed while reading the afternoon newspaper. The killers leave a hand imprint on the wall outside his front door. I hear that teachers are killed because they plant seeds of insurrection in the young people they teach. Despite the intimidation, Papá and Mami continue teaching and Papá continues to occupy a leadership position in the National Teacher's Union. The level of violence and terror erodes Papá's objections against my religious inclinations. One day Mami tells him that I attended an Evangelical service with a neighbor. He stares at me and laughs.

1979. Since our move to San Salvador the sound of gunfire is as familiar as the sound of roosters breaking dawn was in Atiquizaya. Tanks crush asphalt and helicopter blades burst through clouds. My legs twitch every time a convoy, teeming with heavily armed soldiers, crawls along as I wait after school for my bus to arrive and take me home. I dread getting hit by a bullet. But what scares me even more is that Papá could disappear and never return home. We all know that to disappear equals the cruelest fate. Some of the disappeared are left on the side of roads dismembered and tortured. Others are tortured but kept alive as political prisoners and others are never found.

1980 is a terrible year. Terror and silence are the baseline of our everyday. These are the words that bind our existence: armed encounters, assassinated, bullet riddled, clandestine jails, communiqué, curfews, death squads, demonstrations, disappearances, kidnappings, massacres, military, MS-16, national police, political prisoners, ransoms, revolution, state of siege, strikes, tanks, torture.

I pick up and paste together scraps of information: what I hear on the radio, slogans I read on walls, books I find in the house. I scavenge for drifts of overheard conversation in buses or when adults visit our house and talk. No one ever considers sitting with us children to tell us what is going on. Like a blind person whose information gathering is deprived of eyesight, I feel my way through the viral terror that has spread over our lives. Few dare talk about it. Silence becomes an acknowledgement of fear. Fear an indication that death roams hungry day and night. One day running errands with Mami we pass by a church and in a move completely out of the ordinary she goes inside. Votives flicker in semi-darkness. I relish Mami's kneeling body next to mine, her bowed head and her lips moving in prayer. To kneel and pray with one of my parents has always resided solely in the province of my desires. Now, "La situación," the situation, as we call the unofficial war we live in, makes my dear wish come true.

"En nombre de Dios, en nombre de este sufrido pueblo . . .
les suplico, les ruego, les ordeno, que cesen la represión."

—Monseñor Romero, Bishop of San Salvador

The war makes people do the unthinkable. Papá has taken to tuning his transistor radio each Sunday to hear Mass. Mami, Papá, Uncle Ivan, Camila and I, and even the dog, Monina, huddle on the stairs leading up to the second floor to hear Monseñor Romero deliver Sunday's homily from the National Cathedral.

Monseñor Romero's voice rises and falls, filling the air with urgency and hope, and we cling to his every word. At thirteen I understand that to call out the injustice and repression, to speak against the military, is to risk your life and it is clear Monseñor risks his a lot. I believe Monseñor has to do with Papá's new attitude toward the church, but also something larger is at play, something I cannot grasp, and won't understand until decades later.

On March 26th, Monseñor Romero is murdered while officiating Mass.

On December 2nd three American nuns and a lay missionary are killed on their way from the national airport in the outskirts of San Salvador.

No one is spared. Everyone is suspect: the old for being old, the young for their youth, students and teachers for their knowledge, women for accomplices, and children because they get in the way.

The silver lining in this otherwise terrifying year is that the petition for US Resident Status that Mami submitted two years earlier is finally approved. To leave means survival. Since the news of our departure, hope crawls back into our lives. I skip more than walk. Only Papá drags his feet. I've heard him talking with aunts and uncles about leaving: how to survive in an unfriendly place without speaking English, how hard it will be to leave everything. "Everything" is code for the political movement he believes in and risks his life for.

At night the stars dispense their astral brilliance the way they always have and Papá stands in the back door's threshold looking up as if waiting for them to spell out a message just for him. I know the look. I myself have chased long-tailed stars in the hope of discerning a personal dispatch from them to me. Their flickering lights appear for us night after night. I know they would still be there if Papá disappeared. They would remain whether we left or stayed. I take in Papá's narrow shoulders, his hands clasped behind his back, and glimpse into the choice he needs to make: to abandon his comrades and convictions or to protect his family; to take a step off a ledge or to walk straight into darkness.

After

1982. Life in the U.S. is safe, yes, but also small. We are each other's only reference points in the absence of our large extended family and my parent's network of friends and work colleagues. Our world dulls in stark contrast to the tropical sun that suffuses everything in El Salvador. Concerns are of a different kind: finding jobs and schools, learning English. My parents struggle to make ends meet. Mami cleans houses and works an assembly line checking transistor parts. Papá washes dishes, mops floors, and mows lawns. They struggle with their marriage. They struggle to give us as much comfort as their pockets can afford and as much warmth as they can find in their wounded hearts.

Little by little Camila and I swap Spanish for English. At first, we practice single words with each other.

"Battery," I say in my thick accent.

"Battery," she repeats in her nascent American one.

School, *The Brady Bunch*, *Happy Days*, and other TV shows propel us into fluency. We go from words to phrases to sentences, and soon the day arrives when Spanish is no longer necessary, or wanted, between us.

With a university degree in English from El Salvador, Mami reaches fluency. Papá struggles. Washing dishes, doing janitorial work, and gardening require minimal English skills. He spirals downward: the less he is able to communicate in English the worse he feels about himself, the bigger the gap between him and Mami. English fills our world the way a cotton ball inside a narrow glass absorbs water. There is less and less space for him.

1985. With time the Spanish words that contain our experience and that might help us make sense of our exile get covered with thick dust, idling messages inside glass bottles bobbing at sea. We drift apart. Language differences, work exhaustion, the pain of remembering, all get in the way of communicating with each other. We retreat into ourselves and let sorrow, loss, fears, guilt navigate unresolved and unchecked in the tunnels of our subconscious. Silence layers upon silence. The silence of fear on top of the silence of forgetting. Layer upon layer until the communication between each other hardens, becomes impenetrable like rock.

1990. One morning, after twenty-four years of marriage, Mami leaves for work and never comes back. My sister is away at college. The two of us, Papá and I, and our shared sadness, are left in the apartment. I go to bed and leave Papá, sitting on the floor, his back against his bed frame, knees to chest. I wake up to find him in the same position, frozen in place.

1991. As a university student I travel abroad to study in Europe. Years later, back in the United States, I reconnect with a young German doctor I met while visiting exiled relatives in Holland. On a visit and somewhere along the coast between LA and San Francisco he proposes. Eager to move on, to have a home again, a family, I say yes.

1993. My marriage lasts almost three years. When I decide to leave my husband, I call Papá from Germany and ask if I can move in with him. Mami is remarried and living in Costa Rica. Papa lives with Tía Sonia, her two sons, and Abuelita, who came to the U.S. to support Tía Sonia while Tía works long days to establish her fledging Salvadoran restaurant. Papá and I share a room and the single bed in it, and since we have similar habits quickly fall into a routine: we read in bed and when each is satisfied with the night's reading we turn the light off, give our backs to each other, and fall asleep.

The best part about my return is reconnecting with my Abuelita. She is older and weaker but has lost none of her luster. She still laughs her full belly laugh and uses the same irreverent language. "Chimado! Venga para aca!" "Hijoeputa!" "Que mierdas son estas?" She sprinkles her days, and ours, with shits, whores, asses, and worse. After all the years she has not lost her spiritual compass. She still wears a scapular doused in holy water around her neck, still leaves a glass of water by her bed to insure that her soul never thirsts during the night. On Sundays I take her to Our Lady of Guadalupe Church in El Monte to hear Spanish Mass. For an hour we enter a borderless space. The brown faces and the Spanish spoken all around us exude a beloved familiarity. For that hour, next to Abuelita, I'm home. The rest of the time I'm dislocated: my body in California, my mind in Germany, and my heart, torn, somewhere in between.

My birthday arrives. Tucked in bed, Papá recounts, with as much detail as he can recall, the day I was born. After all the violence, the material lack, the loss of country, the weight of silence, the failure of his marriage, the failure of mine, the demise of family members, friends, and colleagues, after all this, he finds the memory folded tenderly, like a perfumed handkerchief at the back of a linen drawer. Papá is not a warm man. Warmth is Mami's territory. As a young child I yearned for his physical affection but the belt got in the way. That night, his words bloom in the devastated terrain we share. I am loved, his words say, always have been.

At dawn I open my eyes to find Papá standing in front of his dresser. Shadows grip the room, clothes pile high on a chair, and in a corner my two suitcases gather dust. A shoddy home-made bookshelf sags under the weight of too many books. The cramming all around makes the darkness more encroaching. Through the chaos I feel Papá's calmness. He contemplates a framed image of Saint Jude, patron saint of lost causes and si-lencer of demons, a gift from Abuelita he told me when I com-mented on it upon first entering the room. In shock I realize he is praying.

I pretend to sleep, but my heart gallops. That morning I learn that Papá is my Abuelita's son after all. And I learn that he is small, small like I am. We are both finding our way in the world, starting over again and again. Through him I recognize that to reach the fullness of light after deep darkness requires both bravery and humility. Like the thawing after winter, the softening that allows tiny crocuses to cut through soil, some-thing melts inside me.

2004. I am married again and the mother of two little girls. Twenty-nine years have passed since my sister and I took down the Virgins above our beds. Now, a framed icon of Monseñor Romero with the inscription, "Mi amor es el pueblo," hangs in my small office. Next to it, images of Our Lady of Guadalupe fill all available wall space. Roses, sequins, cherubs weave in and out of her robes, her head is slightly tilted to the right. Gently she holds her hands together at her chest in a gesture of prayer.

One December afternoon while on vacation from El Salva-dor, Papá visits me in my office. I sit at my desk; he stands in the doorway and points with a bony hand to a framed photograph of the Virgin. Where did I get that one? he wants to know, his stance gentle and inquisitive. A gift that my husband bought for me in Albuquerque, the photo is of Guadalupe painted on a gar-den courtyard wall.

Etched on Papa's face is the topography of time's passing: the shores of an arduous life visible in his hollow cheeks, the meadows of forgiveness around his softer eyes. He is no longer the man I feared.

"Esta bien bonita verdad!" I say, holding his eyes. I don't defend my actions; don't explain that I find solace in prayer, that in her image I find my compass, resilience and hope.

"Asi es," he says nodding softly. The suggestion of a smile registers on his face and though I cannot see it, I know, it also registers on mine.

———

Claudia Castro Luna is Seattle's first Civic Poet (2015–2017), a King County 4Culture grant recipient, a 2014 Jack Straw Fellow, and VONA alumna. Born in El Salvador, she came to the United States in 1981. Her poems appear in print and online in publications such as the *Taos Journal of International Poetry and Art, La Bloga, ARCADE,* and *Poetry Northwest,* among others. She is the author of *This City,* a chapbook of poems. She lives in Seattle where she gardens and keeps chickens with her husband and their three children.

The Leaving Season

——

Kelly McMasters

There is always something to hunt in northeast Pennsylvania. There is squirrel season and beaver season; grouse and bob-white quail season; mink and muskrat trapping season; bobcat and buck and bear season. There is both a fall and spring season for wild turkey. And you can shoot crow from July 4th through April 5th, but only Friday through Sunday. Starlings and English sparrows are fair game all year round, except during spring gobbler season, when these small birds can only be shot before noon. But, according to the state's 1843 Songbird Protection Law, you can never kill an Eastern bluebird, or you'll face a $2 fine.

Since moving here from Manhattan—first as a weekender for six years, then as a full-timer once I got pregnant with my second child—these are the rhythms to which I've grown attuned. Who is hunting what, who is harvesting what, and which chores need to be done. The old man down the road starts splitting logs for next winter on Memorial Day. St. Juliana's, the creaky wooden 150-year-old Catholic church around the corner, begins selling homemade pierogies mid-winter; the stooped and withered church ladies huddle together in the steamy warmth of the church kitchen a few evenings a week to make them. The camp traffic starts in June, shiny BMWs and Lexus SUVs speeding like dusty comets down the dirt roads, leaving an entire summer economy in their wake. During all of this, no matter the time of year, gunshot cracks break across the backs of the hills that surround our small farmhouse, echoing through the sky like an old-fashioned call and response.

They are the music to which I shake out autumn's last load of laundry to be hung on the line out back, and the beat I keep to as I thrust my thumb into the ground over and over and plug the holes with bulbs of garlic. Most of the men shoot bolt-action rifles, and the gunfire chirps in staccato pops throughout the day. My head spins in the direction of the shots automatically; left, right, left, right, over the hill beyond the summer camps, across the way near McGarry's swamp. The short bursts shake me out of naps and force my eyes to blink. Jerry, a neighbor who as a kid used to work the farm on which we now live, comes over and trudges deep into one of the old fields out back with M., my husband, to test out his .44 Magnum on our makeshift practice range of old tin cans. Jerry shows off his homemade bullets, melted and molded silvery nubs. M. is a good shot, and is thinking about buying a gun. I can barely lift the cold dark metal to my shoulder.

When we first moved from the city to the country full-time, it felt as though we were let in on a secret. Instead of cracked sidewalks or manicured lawn, my bare feet sunk into soft patches of clover and alfalfa. Instead of daily trips to the corner bodega for small bites in plastic packages and containers, I found food on my own land: sandy-webbed puffball mushrooms, strawberries the size of my fingernail, tart stalks of rhubarb, handfuls of delicately-haired raspberries that bled the same color as the scratches the thorns gave me on my arms. Instead of grocery store bouquets wrapped in clear plastic, the table bloomed with wild daisies whose stringy stems had fought to stay in the ground; tall curled clutches of garlic scapes, elegant and stinking; and, just once, bulbous heads of purple milkweed, teeming with black ants.

For a while, everything felt golden and magical. On top of turning our weekend dream into reality, we also had that hopeful first-home glow; although the farmhouse acted as a second home, it was really our first. Knowing we'd never be able to afford an apartment in Brooklyn or Manhattan, we'd set our sights on the country, pushing farther and farther out on the map until we were sufficiently far enough away from the city to make the property affordable. Three hours from the George Washington Bridge and just over the New York–Pennsylvania border, the 1860s farmhouse on the hill felt insulated, a small space on the planet that was untouched by time. Safe. Our water came out cold and clear from an underground spring. The property was tucked back off two dirt roads, so three cars passing our house was a busy day; I could open the door and not worry about letting my toddler run. In the city, I wouldn't have let him out into our building's hallway on his own. Late summer nights, instead of sirens and city sounds, the frogs were so loud we had to close the windows. In the morning, sharp bursting chirps from chipmunks or hysterical-sounding gobbles from roving packs of wild turkeys woke us. During walks, we collected bits of our new landscape and placed them on our bookshelves like evidence: soft spotted feathers, sweet wild roses, driftwood-like curves of spring-shed antlers. We learned a new lexicon of beauty, a new way of making home.

A vacation house is like an affair, I suppose. A weekend or summer house offers excitement, possibility, and contrast. Instead of being with a different person, you are with a different house. When you choose to be with a person other than your partner, and usually for small bits of time compared to the time spent with your main partner, part of the allure is the freedom to be a different person yourself. The same happens when you are with a different house. Sometimes that fantasy feels so real and so much better than what you've already got going on, you leave your partner for the affair. But ultimately, you still have to figure out how to pay bills and who is going to make sure the propane tank is full and who is going to change the toilet paper rolls. Suddenly, the person you imagined you could be is eclipsed by all the same small worries that took up your time before the switch.

Marriage is also a kind of fantasy; in my mind, in our farmhouse we would write and paint and raise our children with intention and integrity, surrounded by the beauty of the natural world. I'm embarrassed to admit this now, and it sounds so childish, but it is true. I imagined our new home would have a dollhouse quality, with our worlds taken up by moving from one room to another and another, a tiny galaxy of four planets held within our creaking walls.

But the longer we lived full-time in the farmhouse, the farther away from one another M. and I drifted. By our second summer there, neither of us were finding the work we'd hoped and the aging house required more funds to keep it running than we'd planned; our mortgage was an unspoken weight yoked between us. M. spent more and more time away from the house, taking the truck we shared and visiting the woodshop or barn where the local men spent their days, downing cans of watery beer and talking about spring fishing or ice fishing, their horseshoe league, their dilapidated cars, their pole barn project, hunting. He bought his first gun. Then another.

In a way, when we moved to the country, M. fit in so well that I stopped recognizing him. He has a feral quality that always made the city a bit difficult for him—he couldn't hold a normal job because he couldn't (or wouldn't) bear to show up at the same place day after day or be told what to do, so he spent his days painting pictures. He couldn't read menus, couldn't keep track of bills, and his phone was always getting disconnected. He slept on the floor of his painting studio, bathed in his sink, traded paintings when he was short on rent, boiled hotdogs for dinner in his percolator one night and went to a five-star restaurant with his art collectors the next. He allowed other people to buy him shoes and winter coats, stole toilet paper from public restrooms. There was a wildness to him, and this was one of the reasons I was so attracted to him when we first met; he was like a tiger prowling the city streets, beautiful, untamed, out of place, and different from anything I'd seen before.

But in the city, being a painter often became the excuse for some of his strange behavior ("He's an artist; what did you expect?"). In the country, the other men—mostly a band of similarly feral men living alone and scraping by in rented, rusted single-wide trailers tucked away in the hills—recognized him as their own, accepted him, brought him into their fold. Being an artist was something they tolerated (read: lots of gay jokes), whereas in the city it was the reason people put up with what were seen as his eccentricities. His wildness became compounded, and although he still painted, it didn't define him as much. His studio in our old dairy barn was as full of power tools and chop saws and 2x4s as it was paint and canvas. Not having a job or income, patching things on the house yourself, day-drinking, shooting guns, burning garbage, wearing the same outfit five days in a row—this was all status quo in the hills. After a while, he crossed over, was so in his element, that I stopped recognizing him. In a way it felt like I was Wendy Darling, watching a sleepwalking child from cobblestoned city streets find his band of lost boys in the forest.

Many of our friends who lived in the city and had weekend or summer houses in the country had warned us about making the move full-time. Living in the country was for storybooks; it was something out of *A Year in Provence*, and even Peter Mayle's move wasn't permanent. We imagine, somehow, when the place is still just our vacation house, how much better life will be there, how happy we would be if that could only be our every day, if only we didn't need to return to our real life. But the reality is, vacation homes feel magical because they truly are: going to a vacation home is like playing house, where we put on different clothes, cook different food, have sex in different places or positions, fall into different routines. There are elements of high imagination and low stakes that allow us to fool ourselves that we really are the make-believe characters we are playing for the weekend. But then we go home, to our real home, while that fantasy bubble remains intact and separate. Once you make your vacation home your permanent residence, in a way, you lose your real self. This can, it turns out, be very lonely and rootless. You don't recognize yourself. And everything that once gave you joy suddenly feels like a noose.

As I looked around, I realized there were many other couples who'd tried the same thing. Nina and Eric had moved up to their country house after the birth of their second child so she could write full-time. Eric planned to work as a carpenter, but quickly realized what felt like "experience" in the city just held him on par with everyone else since the locals here grow up fixing everything themselves. They stuck it out for a year and even started their son in public school, but left after Nina contacted the ACLU over a flier for Sunday school came home in her son's backpack and caused quite a stir. "Thank God we kept our lease in New York," Nina said. "Otherwise, I guarantee we'd be divorced right now."

There were our friends Paul and Bill, whose gorgeous house I'd written about for a magazine and whose home decor shop was one of the most successful stores in town. But they hadn't quite moved completely either; like Nina and Eric, they also still kept a small apartment in the city and they both returned to the city periodically for consulting jobs for weeks at a time. Micki and Graham had two kids and a rambling old Victorian, but Graham drove the daily three-hour commute to Manhattan to work as a lighting designer on Broadway most of the year.

Before we'd decided to move to the farmhouse full-time, M. and I had been to dinner at another couple's house a few towns away. I approached the evening as a science experiment, gathering data on yet another potential model. This couple, an artist and an advertising executive, also split their time between rural Pennsylvania and Manhattan, like us, though the wife had moved up to the house full-time and only the husband went back regularly to the city for work. She painted large canvases full of birds and lizards and, from what I knew of her, she chose the peace of isolation and the opportunity to live within the natural world over the city and constant presence of her husband. I was hoping to see how she was faring.

They are both tall and spindly and own a very small car, and they look folded up, like a sheet of ticket stubs, when they drive around town. They were standing outside of their small A-frame house tending to the barbeque when we pulled up in our truck. They left the chicken and steak and sausages on the grill and took us up the rickety front steps and into their home, which was like a little blue birdhouse perched on a cliff. Bits of ribbon and feathers were tucked into wooden slats that made up the kitchen ceiling. The four of us stood out on a small deck overlooking their pond and watched hummingbirds dart around some flowering bushes.

"Once, I came home and a hummingbird was stuck in the screen door," the wife said. She was from South Africa and her c's came out like g's, her r's non-existent. "His beak was like a little dart through the netting. I plucked him out and he just shoomed away." She fluttered her long fingers in the direction of the pond.

We sat on the deck picking apart a cluster of delicate, tart table grapes and grazing on a cheese plate while the meat smoked on the grill. The wife identified different flowers in her garden for us, and when we turned one way we noticed a doe close by, munching on a bush. Her tawny down looked soft and shiny in the light, and she stared up at us for a moment with her dark black eyes.

"Uch. I hate them! They are teak boxes!" The wife cursed at the deer, with a vehemence that surprised me.

"Teak boxes?" M. asked.

"Tick boxes," her husband translated.

"They're the one animal I could imagine shooting," she said.

There is a brutality to the country, and to part-time country houses turned full-time residences. There is so much that you miss when you click on your alarm and drive down the road back to your real life elsewhere. You can choose to miss the piles of snow, the icy roads, the constant black-outs from electric lines down from wind or trees, the smells when something dies in your wall, the scorching summer days where the heat makes little waves dance on the metal roof. You have somewhere else to go. But when the place where you hide from the real world *becomes* your real world, you suddenly realize you have nowhere else to go.

Then there is the way the paint blisters on the house in the sun, the sudden stink of a septic system revolting under the strain of regular use, the unrelenting smell of dank earth emanating from the dirt basement. There are the swarms of ladybugs coating the walls in masses too thick to be sucked up by the vacuum; the heavy orbs of carpenter bees at work on the front porch; fleets of angry sleek-bodied wasps hiding in the folds of the unopened patio umbrella, the soffits of the poorly executed metal roof, buzzing behind the thin drywall inside the house. Pat, a dairy farmer and retired corrections officer from down the road, stands in our three-bay English barn and pokes at the piles of sawdust created by the powder post beetles boring structur-ally compromising holes into the beams and says, "Everything's gotta have a place to live, I guess." Yes, but if this place belongs to them, what belongs to me?

Then, of course, there are the myriad varmints that are tol-erable on the outside, but demand to come inside the house: the mice and the rats, the snakes and the bats, the blind felt-soft opossum babies stuck to the glue traps in the kitchen with their small searching snouts quivering. And there is the jewel-blue Eastern bluebird I scoop out of the cinders in the belly of the wood-burning stove one summer morning, who got trapped in the stovepipe trying to start a nest and couldn't make it back out. Not everyone can make it out here in the wild, not even those who are wild to begin with.

And there is the hunting. In northeast Pennsylvania, school-children get the first day of hunting season off instead of Mar-tin Luther King Jr.'s birthday. The opening of the season truly is treated like a holiday, and weekenders and summer folks gen-erally aren't included. For the first few years, the closest I came to a hunting party was an open bed of a pickup truck full of ten or twelve men decked out in full camouflage, large black guns slung against their shoulders. They usually head out in the early morning, when even lovely days are still cold and wet, and many wear black or orange ski masks pulled down on their faces. Only their voices or a familiar wave will reveal them as neighbors. Once we moved here full-time, it wasn't long before the men knocked on the door and asked M. to join the push.

A deer push is exactly what it sounds like; at the end of the season, the men fan out in a line across a swath of forest and, with whoops and claps and the clear tang of their own musk, they drive the remaining deer toward another group of men waiting with guns. There are no houses visible from our porch. There are only a handful of homes, including two single-wide trailers, two ranch homes, and one other farmhouse like ours dating back to the 1860s, within the surrounding six hundred or so acres. The property looks out onto craggy shelves of blue stone, dark and dense hemlock forests, and stands of tall, skinny poplar trees whose round golden leaves shimmer in the wind. Our hill is a thruway for animals heading toward the swamp for a drink. Which means our house is also a great place to shoot animals heading toward the swamp for a drink, a perfect place for a push.

Although we posted No Hunting signs when we bought the house, the locals continued to stroll up our long dirt driveway during deer season, carrying wooden sawhorse-like contraptions, small seats that they pound into trees, front rows from which they scan the forest. For years, when the house sat abandoned in the 1970s and 1980s, men would sit in rocking chairs and lawn chairs on the porch, or prop themselves up on the wooden banister, one leg on the beer cooler, and pick off the deer as they crashed through the tangle of rosehips and thorny crabapple trees that mark the edge of our property.

One morning, as I mashed banana for the baby's breakfast, our friend James showed up on the porch before the coffee finished brewing. His Day-Glo orange hat and vest were visible through the blinds and when M. opened the door I could see his camouflage jumpsuit and the strap of his rifle slung over his shoulder like a purse. It was the last Saturday of deer season, and they always ran the push on this morning—anyone who'd already bagged an animal would form a line and spread out, slowly creeping through the woods for miles to flush any deer left out of the swamp and over to a line of men who hadn't shot their catch yet that season.

M. pulled his orange hat and gloves on and grabbed his rifle, following James to the line of trees just beyond the garden. I watched them fade into the forest.

Not long after, I stood in the kitchen as sounds from a horror movie track echoed across the landscape: sharp whoops and high-pitched shrieks, catcalls and curses. The men were invisible in the forest and swamp, but their sound surrounded us. Every so often I would spy a flash of orange or yellow. Every time I passed a window, I looked out into the emptiness. The children piled blocks, we read and we slept. We stayed inside. Then a gun would crack close by, and the whoops would grow louder, like coyotes after a kill.

Hours passed. I kept looking out into the woods, searching for human forms. I felt blind and on show at the same time, like being onstage for a concert and knowing the audience is there but not being able to see past the glare of the houselights. After a while I drew the blinds, sealing the kids and myself inside. Alone, just the three of us, closed off from the men and the landscape outside, we could have been anywhere.

One of our favorite annual events was Venison Night at the local bar and grill, The Red Schoolhouse. Held at the end of deer season, hunters dropped off extra meat to contribute to the $9.99, all-you-can-eat feast of venison. I also liked making my own venison at home; when people hunted our property—a right that many viewed was inalienable, no matter who owned the property now—often they'd leave a bag of frozen meat hanging from the doorknob a few days or weeks later. I knew most of the neighbors brought their deer to our friend Ned for processing, and I was intrigued to see what this "process" entailed.

Much of the meat we received was mixed with pork, a way to get some fat into the very lean venison. Most of the men recommended the venison kielbasa and burgers Ned prepared, but they were too greasy for my taste, the pig-to-deer ratio not quite right. I preferred the loin, but since I wasn't hunting my own I had little choice in the matter. I mentioned this once to Ned, who suggested we come over at the end of the season—lots of people drop the deer off, but then don't have the money to pay for the processing and so the meat just sits in Ned's freezer. If he had any leftover loin, I was welcome to it.

I told Davey, one of the men who'd helped us on some building projects around the house, about Ned's offer. Davey has a metal plate in his head, as well as a rod in his back and another in his leg from a car crash he had as a teenager. He lived on the hill opposite ours in a rented singlewide trailer and was considered the best cook in the neighborhood. Davey is a woodworker, and he'd recently unearthed old grey barn boards and planed them until they turned honey color, buffing them soft and smooth and joining them into a countertop for us. At the end of the kitchen project, M. shuffled a two-bay industrial stainless steel sink into the room. He'd used it in his painting studio in the city; when he lived in his studio, it was where he took his baths.

He and Davey pushed the sink into position then stood back.

"How do you think it looks?" M. asked.

"I love it," Davey said emphatically. M. and I exchanged a look, surprised that this man who'd lived in these hills his whole life appreciated the way the modern sink mixed with the built-in farmhouse cabinets and reclaimed barnwood counter.

"Thanks, Davey," we said.

"Sure. That's the best sink I've ever seen. I mean, you could dress a whole deer in there!" Davey's face broke open in his strange smile, his lips pulled taut against the open spaces where he was missing teeth.

Davey's favorite way to eat deer is canned. He likes to spread it on soft sandwich bread. He said Ned's canned venison is a little salty, so we were to tell him that Davey said go easy on the spices.

⌒

Driving up to Ned's house we were greeted by two giant English Labradors, a yellow and a brown one. More solid and square than American Labs, these two were stout and close to the ground with big jaws, better for hunting fowl. Ned walked down his laneway, calling the dogs that were pawing at us and slobbering into our cupped palms.

"Want to see the workroom first?" he asked, nodding to the outbuilding next to which we had parked. M. followed him in, but I was pinned by the chocolate lab that was trying to give me a stick from her mouth, mistaking my son's leg poking out from the baby carrier on my chest for my hand. I closed the door over quietly, leaving my other son asleep in his car seat.

"Come here, girl," I said, motioning to my side. I tousled the soft hair on her head and then looked more closely at the stick in her mouth. It was sprouting hair from a knob. The dog brushed my leg with the deer bone—probably part of a knee from the looks of it—as I made my way to the workroom.

Passing through the doorway into the dark, I was engulfed in a thick cloud of gristle. I was suddenly coated and slick with the stuff, halfway between the smell of a hamburger frying in its own fat and the foamy muck I skim off my turkey broth. My eyes adjusted and I was in a large room, a small mountain of heads to my left. One deer had a cut like a staircase in its head, as if it had been a brain surgery patient. Only later did I realize it had been pillaged for its antlers. I looked away from the pile of heads to see the body of a deer stretched as if in flight from a hook dangling down from the ceiling. It was stripped of its skin, and its brown muscles were threaded with white. The hook was fished into the deer's neck, its head lolled to the side, legs slack along its body.

I had somehow imagined Ned's to be more of an industrial kitchen than a place of such death and disassembleage. I had heard about caping, looked it up on the Internet because I loved the sound of the word, some kind of superhero deer coming to mind. Instead, the photos I saw online were ghastly and graphic, stripping the faces off of the animals and reforming their empty stares to adorn a wall. With a carefully orchestrated dance of surgical cuts starting at the back of the neck and continuing down the spine, a deer's entire skin could be lifted from its flesh in one piece. I imagined holding my arms out in front of me open as if for an embrace, shouldering my body into the caped hide like a hospital gown, pressing my eyes into the holes like a Halloween mask, a skin mask.

In the photos, the single deer made caping seem almost artistic, if brutal. But in Ned's shop, the sheer quantity of death was too much. My son's head sweated into my chest from his sleeping perch and my heart fluttered beneath his brow in alarm. The men were blurry movements beyond the carcasses, walking around in the next room, as if we were in a bakery, or a flower shop, or a gym. I tried to move my legs, but found them stuck. My throat tightened and my pulse began to race. Finally, after a few moments, I uprooted my feet and left the thick darkness of the workroom, finding my way from the piles of death and bones and back out into the light, into the air, into life.

The dog still sat in the dirt driveway, licking at the puffs of dust his paws kicked up as he gnawed at his prize, turning the white knobbed bone over and over and over in front of our red truck.

∽

When I lived in the city, I'd never imagined myself as the kind of woman who, with a baby on her hip and a toddler by her side, would collect bouquets of pineapple weed, pressing out the plant's juice with the pads of my calloused fingertips to dot behind my ears and under my children's noses. There was a fierce pride when I thought of my life on our little hill, what we could withstand.

When we'd straddled both worlds, I would exhale as we hurtled up our long driveway, ending the three-hour trip. Our city exterior would be punctured and my brain and body came alive, senses alert to the smells and rough feel of wild ramps and rhubarb, cupping a baby to my breast. I felt alive to the tips of my fingers and toes.

But then, once that world became our only one, a familiar numbness set in, similar to the days before the farmhouse when I would stare out my city apartment window, dreaming of coconuts or crisp hotel sheets or the sea. Where do you escape to when you've escaped full-time to your escape?

That's the trick of the dollhouse—you can never really live there. You store all of your ideas and dreams of the perfect home inside it, make the figures go about their business with their tiny plastic dishes and lace curtains. But if you could actually live there, if you could shrink down and fit inside, you'd still be inhabiting someone else's house, cracked open for all the world to see. You could never feel home. I could lace my arms into the deer's caped skin, but I could never inhabit its body.

Standing there in Ned's dirt driveway, I realized that over the course of the years coming up here and living in this falling-down farmhouse in the middle of the woods, surrounded by thousands of empty acres and bobcats and bear and soft-tipped fern and untamed men I didn't understand, I'd finally had my fill of the fantasy. I could no longer stand the relentless pounding of gunshots, the winters, the wild. That day at Ned's, my baby tethered to me by a sling, my toddler asleep in the pickup truck, I stared at that dog and understood that I needed to leave.

I thought we would bloom in the country; M. took root, but I withered. I tried growing things, to offset the blood and brutality that seemed to accompany the country life, but I couldn't— I am no farmer. All I could do was pull tangles of berries that were already growing wild, yank yet another damn zucchini from the garden when we were tight on grocery money. The house belonged to the wasps, the powder post beetles, the mice and snakes and voles. The property belonged to the hunters. Both belonged to the bank. I thought I was gaining space with all those acres, but I had no room to breathe.

I had tried to inhabit the skin of another person, of another house, to shrug into a cape of chicken feathers and garlic scapes and wood stove cinders, of the staccato of soft-nosed homemade bullets and the angry silence of broken men in the hills, of separating meat from skin with a knife and nimble fingers, gently loosening jawbones and limbs and antlers, until all that was left was a jumble of parts on the floor. In the process of trying to become someone else, a part of me floated off over the hills, just another bit of loose late-summer hay on the wind. I wasn't sure how to get it back, but I cupped my baby's soft-socked foot in my palm like a talisman and steered us away from that loamy-smelling hut and the carcasses and stack of heads. I looked back, saw my husband's orange-capped head through the foggy window and waved desperately, but he couldn't see me.

So I got into the pickup truck with my children and closed the door tight.

———

Kelly McMasters is a former bookshop owner and the author of *Welcome to Shirley: A Memoir from an Atomic Town*, the basis for the documentary film *The Atomic States of America*. She is the recipient of a Pushcart Prize nomination and an Orion Book Award nomination. Her essays and reviews have appeared in the *New York Times*, the *Washington Post* Magazine, *Paris Review* Daily, *American Scholar*, *River Teeth: A Journal of Narrative Nonfiction*, and *Newsday*, among others. She holds a BA from Vassar College and an MFA in nonfiction writing from Columbia's School of the Arts and is an Assistant Professor of English and Director of Publishing Studies at Hofstra University in New York.

In the Kitchen

Margot Kahn

A t 7 p.m. on a recent evening, I'm standing in my kitchen scrubbing the broiler pan in our double-basin stainless-steel sink. It was a mistake, this sink, neither basin really big enough to wash the big things. Out the window, tree-leaf shadows shift on the neighbor's stucco house and the new auralias I planted for a backyard party reach their variegated, palm-shaped leaves out over my son's toy dump trucks. The trucks are scattered in a patch of dirt that's too shady to grow vegetables or even grass and that for years now has been left empty as a simple place to play. Each of these choices has been made deliberately, carefully: the kitchen, the sink, the plants, the child. And yet, come 7 p.m., when I've been standing in the kitchen for at least two hours, I am chafing at the nagging reality with which I have not yet come to terms. I am the one who is home, in the supporting role, in the same way my mother and my grandmother and all the women before her were. And I always thought I'd be the one to break the chain.

My grandmother spent the majority of her life in the kitchen, seen only from the waist up behind the counter that separated the kitchen table from the sink and stove. The cupboards and counter of her kitchen were pale yellow and cream, the color of eggs and butter beaten together, and I saw her against the backdrop of them as I sat at the kitchen table eating broiled lamb chops and carrot pennies cooked with syrup and butter. While my mother was divorced and I was an only child, I spent a good deal of time at my grandmother's table. But I never inquired after my grandmother's work and she never narrated it. The meals appeared before me as if by sleight of hand. If I spent the night, there would be fresh orange juice and a bowl of Cream of Wheat for breakfast, or a plate of French toast with sugar, syrup, and jam. On occasion, my grandfather would sit across from me at the table, eating a bagel with cream cheese and fork-smashed sardines.

My grandmother had her specialties and she made them in rotation. Out of her kitchen came a consistent string of briskets and kugels, matzo balls and chicken noodle soups, rum balls, banana cakes, macaroons, rugelach, and chocolate chip cookies. When her children were young, they came home from school for lunch, so my grandmother, like most other immigrant women of her generation, was making a hot meal three times a day, and my mother swears that she and her siblings never ate anything canned, processed, or store-prepared. The family joke was that the one time they ate a TV dinner, my grandmother finally having relented after the children begged for it (it was what every other family ate, the American way!), they all got sick. But as adults, all my grandmother's children will say they resented their mother for spending so much time in the kitchen. They wished she had done something other than feed them. When my son was still a baby and distracted at the table, my mother admonished me for all the things I did to entice him to eat—counting peas, making the spoon swoop like an airplane. "Your grandma used to chase my brother around the house with a fork!" she said, as if warning me against a future fate.

My grandmother's hands were arthritic and talon-bent, large knuckles giving way to fingers tipped with long, lacquered nails. With the curl of her finger she would scrape batter from the edge of a bowl and add it to the pan; she would open any jar no matter how tight. She did each task with a consistent sense of purpose: that her children should be nourished, flourish, and grow. It never occurred to me to ask my grandmother, who fled persecution in one country and landed in another to make a home for herself from scratch, if the simple routine of the meals, day in and day out, was enough. Did it save her, sustain her? Did she long for something more? Never, in the years I knew her, did she express any regret.

She did, however, tell me a story once, and only once, when I visited her in Florida after my grandfather died, in the ground-floor condominium that smelled like a Wallace Stevens poem, all green and orange and pink. The living room there looked out onto a screened porch where, as a girl, I kept lizards caught in a shoebox; outside, in the man-made lake, the little shower of a sad fountain seemed to hang in the humid air. The compact kitchen had a view of the parking lot, boxy Buicks and Cadillacs glinting in the sun. We were sitting at the kitchen table with bowls of tuna salad, egg salad, and cottage cheese between us, when she told me that she'd wanted a divorce. She'd wanted it so much that she'd asked for it several times, and each time my grandfather's anger rose. "The last time I asked for a divorce," she said, "he told me that if I ever mentioned it again, he would take out his gun from the closet and he would shoot me. And then he would shoot the children, and then he would shoot himself." So she stayed married. Brisket, kugel, banana cake. Brisket, kugel, banana cake.

One other clue: my grandmother never taught her children to cook. Women grooming their daughters to be good housewives teach them how to cook, no? A woman grooming her daughter to be something else in the world would keep her out of the kitchen.

In the house I grew up in, the kitchen was renovated in the 1980s with a Modernist white-gray-black palate—gray floor, white cabinets, white counter, white fridge, white stove. In this kitchen, my mother cooked regularly, but never with pleasure. There was no joy for my mother in this kind of ephemeral creation, a thing you labored over only to find it consumed quickly and often without appreciation. Her flank steak was always the same, marinated in soy sauce; her chicken breasts usually came to the table raw inside, returning to the oven only to end up overcooked, tough and dry. Dinner was a necessity and it was her job to put it on the table, my mother told me time and again, because my stepfather worked and made the money to keep us housed and clothed and fed. She held to this belief even after she got her own job and made good money herself. My mother worked as a consultant, part-time, while the house and the children were still her primary responsibility. Her outside-the-house work gave her an identity other than homemaker, an outlet I think she needed as a way to be sure she would not become her mother. But her consulting career, so long as she had children in the house, was always secondary.

Meanwhile, in my best friend's basement, our favorite game to play was restaurant. From a bin in the play kitchen we took plastic drumsticks and sunny-side-up eggs, piled them on plates, ferried the plates and cups back and forth to the invisible customers, back and forth, back and forth. We dreamed of one day being waitresses. We dreamed that we owned the restaurant. But I never imagined being the primary breadwinner for a family. Professions for women, so far as I understood, were best when they were flexible and ended early enough in the day to pick children up from school, to have summers off. Whereas a friend whose single mother was a doctor received the implied message that she could grow up to be a working mother and the primary breadwinner for her family (and she has), men around me said things like, "Do something you want to do. Someone will take care of you." This was a strange middle-step of an idea, the approval of a woman's freedom while keeping her imprisoned, tethered, powerless.

Even as late as my high school and college years people said, "You can be anything you want to be," but didn't outline the reality of working as meaning you'd see your children for one or two harried and exhausted hours most days. "That's a hard career to choose if you want to have a family," I was told more than once, planting an idea long before I chose a career that, for women, regardless of what you chose to do or the degree of difficulty it would require, homemaking still ranked before profession in order of priority. Others say, now, "You can come back to your work later." "You have plenty of time." Depending on the profession, returning to work after a long absence in which wages and professional contacts are lost may be possible, but not quite the same as never having left.

My husband has said he would be happy to stay home if I could make enough money to support us, and I think I believe him. After all, when the husband stays home he is given a big pat on the back. Women look at him with starry eyes. He is so liberated, so supportive. He is enlightened, a word we use for a crucial age of innovation in the history of Western civilization, a period of rational thinking triumphing over all, when traditional authority was questioned and science determined the truest and best ways of being.

Most of the women I know who out-earn their husbands—and there are many—have at some point longed for their husbands to stay home and take care of the house and children, letting them really focus on their career. But the husbands, for the most part, won't consider it. Meaningful work outside the home provides not only a paycheck but a sense of purpose and sometimes power; a project, clearly defined goals and rewards; a review, a bonus or recognition; the possibility to complete something. Housekeeping and child-rearing can be too cyclical, solitary and amorphous to provide the same satisfaction on a regular basis.

"If you got a bi-weekly paycheck and an annual review and a promotion every now and again for the work you do at home, and you had time to pursue your other interests and hobbies 'after work' so that you had something else to talk about besides potty training and menu-planning, would you be happy?" I posed this question to a friend on the brink of reentering the workforce after a seven-year gap. She thought about it for a minute and said unequivocally, "Yes."

Last year a friend said, "If I have to choose between my work and my marriage, I will choose my work."

"Remind me," I said, "why this has to be a choice?"

Her career was going great. Her husband was not supportive of it. She got a divorce.

∽

When my husband and I first married, and for the first five years of our marriage before we had a child, we both worked full-time. We shopped and cleaned and cooked together, sharing the household duties equally. This was a modern marriage, an equal partnership we'd both grown to understand as the way things should be. We made decisions about our home—where we would live, how we would decorate, and the kinds of things we'd surround ourselves with—together, and we shared a similar aesthetic, which made things easy. The fact that he out-earned me was the cause of many conversations, but eventually we sorted that out, too; we had made different career choices that would dictate our earning potential, and we were supportive of each other's choices, in technology and the arts, respectively. When we talked about having children, we talked about sharing that task equally, as we had everything else. After the birthing part, we imagined.

When our son was born, I took a six-month maternity leave from the nonprofit arts center where I worked. I thought that after that amount of time, I'd have things figured out and I'd be ready to go back to work. Only there was no precedent of an employee having had a baby in the organization's twelve-year history and I didn't have the energy, not having slept more than three consecutive hours in half a year, to advocate for what I needed. For example, I worked in a cubicle and couldn't imagine where in the building, besides the already-occupied offices, I could pump breast milk. This assumed, of course, that the baby would take a bottle, which he never did. I was also experiencing vision-blurring migraines, and it inexplicably still hurt for me to sit or stand for long periods of time. The questions sound simple now, but I was unable to answer them. Who would take care of my baby? What would he eat? Where could I lie down? The prospect of going back to work at that time felt entirely overwhelming. Furthermore, because the arts, like homemaking, are wildly undervalued, I would have to spend most of my income paying someone else to take care of my child. While my career, in the long run, might benefit from this arrangement, I figured it might also be a wash. So I quit.

Two and a half years later, Sheryl Sandberg's book *Lean In* came out and I read it in hardcover before giving it to my husband. I was inspired and outraged and for a few minutes I wanted to put our son in full-time daycare so I could go back to work. But the kind of arts administrator job I had given up wasn't an easy one to find. And our son was not an easy-going child. At every preschool pick-up there was a report of hitting or screaming or pushing. He wouldn't go to the bathroom. He wouldn't nap. He wouldn't eat the snack. There were children who would sit doe-eyed on the carpet and play all day until someone picked them up; our son screamed and screamed. He wanted to be home where it was quiet, and I couldn't blame him, so I worked part-time and came home every afternoon to take care of him. It was a privileged position to be in, to even have had this choice to make; this I understand completely. And yet this was never the choice I thought I would make.

Now here we are nearly seven years after our son was born. I drop off at school and I pick up; I drive to swim lessons and monitor play dates; I shop and I cook and I clean up; I do bath time and bedtime most of the time. I arrange the doctor's appointments, the flu shots, and the refills of allergy medicine. I bring in the class snack, the library books, the pinecones for the school project. When we bring home the class hamster, I help feed it. Because I am the one taking primary care at home, I need to check my husband's schedule and make arrangements for childcare if I need or want to travel alone; if my husband needs to travel, he simply tells me when he must go. This is what's been called the role of the "primary parent," a sort of theory that explained why, no matter how equally you think you divide things with someone, one person in the household necessarily is the project manager of the home—the homemaker. And even when both parents work, this person is more often than not the woman.

When we talked about having a child, we didn't talk about the reality of this because we didn't know what it would really be like. Our mothers had stayed home with us, and our mothers (and fathers) had told us how important it was to be home with young children, and we believed them—and we still do. But they all made it sound like this was a very temporary situation. Children grow up, we were told—they go to school, soon they do not need you very much at all. Only now that we're in it, surrounded by contemporary parents with their own stories to tell, I would argue that this isn't exactly true. Or, it's true but the timeframe might be expanded. Parents of older children no longer need to help with teeth brushing or bath time, but they need to be present to deal with gender and sexual identity issues, learning disabilities, medical and mental health needs, social situations, and the generally tumultuous teenage years of emotional growth. More than one parent has told me that they need to do as much personal work as their children to navigate this growth with true understanding.

After a family celebration in my hometown, a family friend, Judy, drives me and my son to the airport. Her children are grown now and her car is impeccably clean in a way we couldn't keep ours even if we tried. While my son looks out the window at the other cars speeding by on the freeway, Judy and I talk. Her daughter is in her late twenties and engaged to be married, and Judy tells me she will go wherever her daughter needs her. Judy is a tall, assertive, smart woman. She went to Mount Holyoke. She was a lawyer before she had children. "And then I made my children my life," she tells me. Now, without her children or her career, she feels adrift. But the daughter is working her way up the corporate ladder, and she loves her job. Judy doesn't want her daughter to have to choose between a professional career with children in daycare and homemaking. I've seen this again and again—the mothers who had wanted to be something more, now helping their daughters and their daughters-in-law return to work by taking care of the children. My grandmother must be counted as one of them, taking care of me so my mother could support us without a husband.

When I moved and made a home far away from my mother, I wasn't thinking about children or the support system that an extended family can provide. In my family and my husband's family, for better or worse, the work of mothering is seen as a responsibility like any other work, and staying home with children is understood to be a privilege for both the parent and the child. But with each successive generation, there's more left on the table—more career choices, more opportunity, and more responsibility to lead and spur social change.

Another email arrives in my inbox from the local political action group advocating for paid family medical leave and affordable childcare legislation. One in four women go back to work within ten days of giving birth because they don't have access to paid leave. Half of all working mothers—41 million Americans—can't stay home with a sick child because they don't have paid sick days. In every state in the U.S., a month of childcare for two children costs more than the median rent. I sign the petition. I call my congresswomen. I'm insanely privileged to have had the ability to stay home without financial hardship, but this system is rigged.

The title "homemaker" is not something I will put on my resume. And yet, in the quotidian handiwork, handwork, hands-on work of making a home for my family, I find there is creativity and, sometimes, satisfaction. There is a necessary commitment to the space and time each task requires—sweeping the floor, changing the sheets, folding the towels, sorting silverware, watering plants, hanging a picture—each motion a ritual, an act of devotion. It feels good to be nurtured and it feels good to nurture, my child, my partner, the houseplants, even the physical structure of windows, decking, pipes, and wires.

So this is the paradox of modern homemaking that I cannot resolve, I can only frame: There is a beauty, a necessity, in the making of a space where we are safe and comforted, a place that reflects who we are and what we hold dear; and there is the mundane drudgery of the daily tasks this requires—folding laundry, cooking meals, rearing children. But while a woman with a corporate job and board positions who farms out her

household tasks to nannies, decorators, cleaners, and garden-
ers is regarded as powerful and successful, a woman who cares
for her home and raises her children is seen as . . . what? I have
trouble even finishing the sentence. There is a void here, as if
irrelevant, though irrelevant isn't the right word. But it is an
empty space, a space unseen. Or, as another friend who started
and owned a business for fifteen years and sold it to raise her
two boys put it, "A woman who cares for her home and raises
her children is seen as 'not working,' and without a job title she
isn't even considered when society is labeling her as successful
or not."

Most days, when I pick my son up from school he is exhausted and wants a hug. This day is no different. After the hug
he wants to sit down on the school steps and show me the pictures
he's made—several mazes for me to trace my finger through, an
autumn tree, a paper mosaic, an A-B-A-B pattern of red and yellow squares. It's a beautiful day, sunny and cool, and we go home
to relax on the porch, eat a snack, and tell a story. We walk to the
store, me clapping out a beat and my son singing on top of it, and
at the store the owner offers my son a job, when he turns sixteen,
"If you are very good at math," she says. "Study hard at math!"
So we walk home practicing: two plus two, four plus four. "But I
might want a different job," my son pauses to say. "I might want
to build freeways. Or I might want to be a vacuum cleaner."

Back in the kitchen, he pushes a dining room chair up to the
counter declaring his desire to help. I give him a cutting board, a
butter knife, the soft balls of mozzarella. A brown ceramic bowl
with a marine blue glaze on the inside to backdrop the glistening tomatoes, the creamy cheese, the bright basil leaves. Some
of the cheese falls on the floor. The basil is bruised between my

son's strong fingers. He will refuse to eat this salad, despite having helped make it, which all the parenting books will tell you is the way to get kids to eat things. The leaves on the tree outside are shifting, ready to fall.

Above us, on the wall, in a collage my mother made, photographs of my grandmother and great-grandmother stand side by side, both of them layered onto a recipe in my grandmother's handwriting for Mother's Apple Cake, a recipe I tried once with uninspired results, the cake too sweet and too dry. But the chicken I put under the broiler with a brush of barbeque sauce comes out tender and moist; the tomatoes from our community garden are meaty and sweet, the best we've ever grown. At the sound of the front gate opening, my son jumps down and runs to open the door, shouting, "Daddy! Daddy! Daddy!" There's good food on the table, the windows are open, and the sun is flooding the room with light. It's a nice way to be welcomed home.

With the meal comes the mess, and twenty minutes later I am at the sink again, sponge in hand, scrubbing the broiler pan. I hate the broiler pan with its sharp edges, the grease clinging to the small openings, lurking in the hardest places to reach. I try to be patient with it. In the periphery of my attention are the voices of my husband and son down the hall where there is a bubble bath and a happy boy and much splashing and singing. This is the moment, I remind myself, like a meditation, like a mantra. This is the moment, this and no other.

———

Margot Kahn is the author of *Horses That Buck*, winner of the High Plains Book Award. Her essays and reviews have appeared in *Tablet*,

River Teeth: A Journal of Narrative Nonfiction, the *Los Angeles Review*, and elsewhere. She lives in Washington State where, on July 7, 2017, after ten years of advocacy, the most progressive family leave policy in the nation was signed into law.

Of Pallu and Pottu

Hasanthika Sirisena

M y mother has never attended a church service before, but she does know she has to dress up. She outfits me in my favorite gingham dress trimmed with white lace. She picks a pair of neat black slacks for herself. She has recently given up wearing saris. They aren't practical for the wet, cold fall in Goldsboro, North Carolina, and she has also begun to like the way she looks in pants: lithe, elegant, and modern.

My mother isn't Christian. She's a practicing Buddhist. But when my parents first arrived in North Carolina in 1975 they enrolled me in Faith Christian Academy, a Free Will Baptist school. The choice was pragmatic. My parents shared one car, and my mother needed to find a school she could easily walk me too. My parents picked the closest private school, and in Sri Lanka it wasn't unusual to enroll your child in a religious school, even a Christian one; the country was predominantly Buddhist, after all, and Buddhist culture dominated. At Faith

Christian Academy, the principal had promised the school was open to and respectful of all faiths. When my kindergarten teacher invited my mother to attend church one Sunday my mother agreed, not out of any desire to learn about Christianity, but to be polite.

At the church, a parent of one of my classmates nods hello. Others offer handshakes. Still, others look at us politely but curiously. By the beginning of the service, the church is full. A clutch of women line the pew in front of us, their hair teased up into cotton-candy bouffants; my mother and I crane our necks so that we can see over their heads. I accidentally kick the back of their pew and one of them turns: a pale profile, heavily rouged, skin pulled taught over high cheekbones. I spy some of my classmates with their parents, but they don't look in our direction. Maybe they don't know we are here.

At the beginning of the service, everyone rises. The woman next to us shows my mother where in the program to find the hymns. My mother doesn't sing and, later, during the prayers, she doesn't pray. She stares ahead. At one point, she places a hand on my thighs to keep me from fidgeting and shushes me when I ask why I can't sing with everyone else. Everyone around us knows what to do—which hymn to sing, what line of the psalm to repeat in response—and as my mother watches she wonders why she has come.

The minister walks up to the pulpit. He is wearing a blue polyester suit with wide lapels and a tie with blue stripes that match his suit. He is massive and ruddy. The minister pauses, seems to consider his words; then he runs his hand through the sparse tufts of blonde hair. I can imagine his deep Southern drawl. My mother also remembers and can recount in detail all that is going on in the culture at the time that disturbs and frightens

the minister so much that he feels he must speak out passion-
ately. These events frighten my mother as well. Gerald Ford has
just survived an assassination attempt by Squeaky Fromme, a
member of the Manson cult. The police have apprehended Patty
Hearst, scion of an iconic American family, victim of a brutal
kidnapping, member of the Symbionese Liberation Army. The
trial of Jeffrey MacDonald, the charismatic and very possibly so-
ciopathic Green Beret who is accused of murdering his family, is
about to begin. A perfume branded with a boy's name, Charlie, is
being hawked in local drugstores and women proclaim, with no
hint of bashfulness, that they wear short shorts.

The minister feels a deep need to speak out, to bear witness,
to warn his congregation. He must lead them out of this wilderness or they too might end up like Patty Hearst—brainwashed
by the forces trying to hold them captive. He rails against
women who want to act like men and proclaims the word of
someone named Paul who warns of the importance of the sexes
knowing their place. He grips the side of the lectern and leans
forward, "Look out around you. You are surrounded by Legion,
living among you. Look at what they do. They cut their hair
short? Paul wrote in Corinthians 'if a woman has long hair, it
is her glory.' Your glory!" A round of no's rumbles through the
audience. "And these women, they disobey their husbands, they
disobey God and his desires for them. They choose to wear . . ."
he pauses a moment for effect, "They choose to wear pants."

Pants? My mother blinks, not sure at first if she has heard
the minister correctly. He repeats the last line as if for my con-
fused mother alone. My mother looks around the church and
notices that all the women sport dresses or skirts. She imagines
suddenly the woman next to her looking surreptitiously at her,
the women sitting in front sneaking glances at her. She looks

down at me. Had I noticed? But I was concentrating very hard on swinging my legs as close as possible to the pew in front of me without actually touching the wood.

In Sri Lanka, by 1975, women wore pants, even jeans. But here she sits believing one thing—America is where women live emancipated existences, go to college, work jobs—while being told by a man what she shouldn't do as a woman. She, who for so long did exactly what her father, and then later her husband, asked of her, is the most liberated person in this church full of Americans.

We imagine the move from a developing country like Sri Lanka to America as a move from oppression to progress, from backwardness to enlightenment, especially for women. The truth is much more nuanced. Many Sri Lankan women of my mother's generation attended medical school, became lawyers, accountants. The women in my family are strong and forceful. Some even practiced careers before marriage. None of them easily fit the stereotype of South Asian femininity: demure, submissive, ultimately oppressed by the patriarchal society.

Much of the progress Sinhalese women achieved in Sri Lanka was due to one man, Dharmapala, a Buddhist monk considered by many the father of the Buddhist revival in the late nineteenth century. Dharmapala had contact with American feminists during the time he studied in the West and was aware of the American and European feminist movements. He was also a keen and savvy politician who recognized the need to accommodate the growing political and social clout of Sinhalese women. But there was a dark side to Dharmapala's ideas. In Dharmapala's view, the woman as wife and mother was integral to a singular ethnic, national identity. His prescription for the burgeoning women's movement was particular to the point of counseling Sinhalese women how to drape—wrap and pleat—their saris.

As a teenager, I noted, with no real understanding of what I was seeing, the change in how my Sinhalese family dressed over several generations. The women of my family, in formal portraits dated during the late 1800s, adopted fashionable Western clothes—long skirts and high-collared bodices. The women in photographs dating from the early twentieth century, however, sported the Kandyan sari. The blouse—the fitted article of clothing that goes underneath a sari—covers the waist, and the pallu—the stretch of fabric that wraps around the body and over the shoulder—is carefully pleated. This contrasts to the far more well-known Indian sari, where the blouse ends at the bottom of the ribcage and the pallu is left flat and arranged so that it conceals the waist and stomach.

The real significance of the sari is cultural. Kandy is an area of Ceylon revered by the Sinhalese as the seat of successive Buddhist kingdoms and as the home of a powerful Buddhist monastic order. The Kandyan style of draping is unique to this area, so to don a Kandyan sari meant associating yourself with that region and that Buddhist tradition. Dharmapala, when he pushed Sinhalese women in the early twentieth century to wear the Kandyan sari over the Indian, understood this significance. The Sinhalese woman was not simply declaring a national and Buddhist identity, but positioning herself as the distinct opposite of the Tamil woman, who drapes her sari in the Indian style and applies a pottu to her forehead. Dharmapala's attitudes became embedded firmly in Sinhalese culture. I remember my mother chiding me, when I was a teenager, for expressing an interest in getting a nose ring. She suggested it would make me appear to be Hindu and I imagine, though she didn't express this explicitly, to be Tamil.

Dharmapala's claims of the purity and the primacy of Buddhism had serious political and social consequences for Sri Lanka. Scholars argue about the extent to which Dharmapala's ideas have been misused and misconstrued. It cannot be denied, though, that they underpin the virulent Buddhist chauvinism that led, in part, to the nearly two-decade civil war between the Sinhalese dominated government and the Liberation Tigers of Tamil Eelam. This nationalist movement also managed to cripple Sri Lanka's vocal and active women's rights movement by appearing to be progressive—for example, supporting women's suffrage—but by promoting what was, in truth, an image of woman tethered firmly to household and home. Yes, women had power; but their agency came from their nurturing roles as exemplary mothers and wives, the inculcators of Buddhist values and traditions. Sinhalese women accepted and internalized this and donned Kandyan saris for their wedding portraits.

My mother's course tracks that of her nation. When my mother was twenty-five, she agreed to an arranged marriage—partly to escape her family—and was introduced to my father. She was told she had a choice. She did not have to marry my father. I also know all the social pressure she faced. Both families would have charted my parents' horoscopes to assess their compatibility. My father was of the same caste and was already a successful doctor, his family successful farmers. My mother is a strong woman capable of considerable resourcefulness when necessary, but she's also the sort of person who wouldn't say no when she couldn't imagine a reason not to, especially back then.

I admit I spent my teenage years and my early adulthood looking down on my mother. I thought her weak for having acquiesced so easily to an arranged marriage, for being a good mother to us. And I have scorned the idea of home, connecting it to homemaker—a role my mother adopted, in my opinion, too readily. What I didn't understand then, what I see now, is that home is a political act. How can it not be when so many ideological, religious, and nationalist movements use home as the fundamental building block of social and cultural identity? And while she never verbally expressed any desire to oppose Dharmapala's vision, I do see her act of moving her family—her three daughters—as an act of rebellion. She did, after all, steal three of the country's native daughters and allow each to thrive independent of any single image of who she must be and who my mother, herself, was forced to be. My memory of my mother's home is a place where I was allowed to dress as I wanted—my own hybrid envisioning of British and American punk—choose the career I wanted, and willfully and purposefully declare without approbation that I myself wouldn't marry and have children. (I've done neither.) Her openness seems to me its own type of bravery.

The word *home* is, for me, tied to the word *land*—home, homeland. Like many immigrants, I hold simultaneously two images of home: one feels transient and impermanent even though my family has resided here for forty years, and the other is, by now, almost entirely an imagined construct. And yet that imagined construct has remained potent and formative. From the Baptist preacher's reactionary strictures, to Dharmapala's nationalist identity, to the independent state that Sri Lanka's Liberation Tigers of Tamil Eelam fought for, homeland, and home, has always felt, to me, a battleground. I cannot deny my ambivalence to the concept of it.

I've read a number of accounts of a poster—a piece of propaganda—distributed in the 1980s during the Sri Lankan Civil War. It depicted the image of a Sinhalese woman breastfeeding an infant. The caption read: "Give Your Life Blood to Nourish Our Future Soldiers." Propaganda depicting the mother as homeland, as the source and succor for war, is ancient. But this image is particularly troubling to me. I have spent two decades haunted by the Sri Lankan Civil War, and I know what this image of mother and home has cost a country.

I try to envision what the counter to this image is. All that comes to me is my mother dressed in her brand new pair of black pants, perched on the edge of her church pew, staring past the minister, into the chancel, at the bare, glowing rectangle of light in which floats a single white cross. She pulls me closer.

———

Hasanthika Sirisena is the author of *The Other One*, a collection of short stories. Her essays and stories have appeared in the *Globe and Mail*, *WSQ*, *Narrative*, *Kenyon Review*, *Glimmer Train*, *Epoch*, *StoryQuarterly*, *Narrative*, and other magazines. Her work has been anthologized in *Best New American Voices* and named a distinguished story by *Best American Short Stories* in 2011 and 2012. In 2008 she received a Rona Jaffe Foundation Writers' Award. She is currently an associate fiction editor at *West Branch* magazine. She is the winner of the 2015 Juniper Prize for Fiction.

Nuclear Family

———

Amanda Petrusich

I grew up in Buchanan, New York—a tiny, mostly working-class village in northern Westchester County, tucked into a crook where the Hudson River bends, narrows, juts east. My parents were public school teachers, and we lived in a split-level wood house they built themselves on Lake Meahagh, a man-made pond dug by the Knickerbocker Ice Company in the late nineteenth century. It was, by any measure, a sweet place to be a kid. In the summertime, my sister and I fished for carp on the lake's soft, reedy shores and chased hissing swans through the black mud ringing its perimeter; in the winter, we laced up our figure skates and carved broad figure eights into its big, imperfect surface. There was a dusty corner store up the street—Teresa's—where we pedaled our rickety, ten-speed bicycles and bought Hostess cupcakes and cans of fruit punch. The village had, somewhat improbably, a sizable public pool with an extra-pliant diving board. I could walk home, downhill, from my elementary school. Its pleasures were small, but precious. Buchanan is a community of just around 2,200 people (the village itself comprises less than 2 square miles); when people ask where I'm from, I usually say Peekskill or Croton, the two closest mid-size towns. For the most part, Buchanan is known only to itself.

But on occasion—after the attacks on the World Trade Center; after the 2011 earthquake and tsunami in Japan, and the subsequent failure of the Fukushima Daiichi nuclear power plant, which led to the meltdown of three nuclear reactors and the discharge of untold amounts of radioactive material—Buchanan becomes a regional fixation. The village is home to the Indian Point Energy Center, a three-reactor nuclear power plant that generates enough electricity to satisfy 10 percent of New York State's total energy needs. Because the plant sits just thirty-odd miles north of Midtown Manhattan, newspaper and magazine articles bullhorn its precariousness during tense times, detailing the many reasons it should be shuttered, and soon: its vulnerability to terrorism, the 1,500 tons of radioactive waste stored on-site, the implausibility of its established evacuation plans, and so on.

But to residents—I live in Brooklyn now, but my parents, aunt, and uncle all reside within a mile or so of the plant—Indian Point's noiseless menace is old news. After all, it's been there since 1962.

When I was a child, the plant loomed strangely in my mind. Its reactors—housed in massive containment domes, built with four-to-six foot-thick walls of steel-reinforced concrete—signified something peculiar and unsettling, something I didn't entirely understand, although I'd heard, as children do, that it had something to do with glowing in the dark or, if you were particularly lucky, with manifesting a third eyeball. At some point, my sister and I decided Indian Point was funny. Periodically, the plant would test its emergency siren system—a high, violent wail suddenly pierced the calm air—and we would scream "Meltdown!" at my parents before collapsing into giggly heaps on the cold kitchen floor. Fishing with our father on Lake Meahagh—he would stab balls of stale bread or kernels of canned corn onto the craggy points of our hooks when we were too squeamish to pierce a night crawler ourselves—we would gleefully throw back any catch we ultimately deemed a "nuclear fish." (The qualifications were arbitrary.) Every now and then, with a certain relish, we would attribute each other's various imperfections ("your face") to massive and irreversible radiation poisoning.

The plant became considerably less funny after my sister found an old paperback copy of *Hiroshima*, John Hersey's staggering, devastating book on the aftermath of the atomic bomb, and spent the next several nights shaking in her bed in the room next to mine, dreaming of endless flashes of light. Hersey describes the moment of impact as "a sheet of sun." The aftermath, he suggests, was dimmer: "Such clouds of dust had risen that there was a sort of twilight around." It only got darker.

Certainly, there were quirks to a childhood in Buchanan: power lines extended in every which way, a complex web of black rubber. The medicine cabinet always contained a plastic bottle of potassium iodide pills, a salt that helps block the absorption of radioactive iodine by the thyroid gland. When my father took us out on the river in his aluminum canoe, a sickly warmth spread over the floor of the boat as we paddled closer to the plant. Still, signs declaring the plant's safety ("Safe, Secure, Vital," they swore) were tacked to telephone poles all over town. The village seal included the atomic symbol with two hands next to it, holding tools. Buchanan was proud of its industry—Indian

Point employed around one thousand people locally, and subsidized my excellent public school education, and, by extension, my parents' jobs—and of the citizens who made it run.

My father grew up in neighboring Verplanck, an even smaller Revolutionary War town that has since lost some of its historical luster (about 22 percent of its residents now live below the poverty line). In 1779, Stony Point—a port directly across the Hudson from Verplanck; the two points were twin termini for the Kings Ferry, a crucial river crossing—was reclaimed from the British by the Brigadier General Anthony Wayne and his Corps of Light Infantry following "a brief bayonet assault." Gunners from the Continental Artillery re-aimed their captured weapons across the river, attempting to take back Verplanck, too (they ultimately failed, though the British army moved south by the following fall). Verplanck continued to be a crucial outpost in the war (per the *Journal of the American Revolution*, "Stony and Verplanck Points saw one major battle, a number of amphibious landings, various forts, one treason, almost daily crossings, one Grand Encampment, a mutiny, and even a visit by a future Marshal of France"); in 1781, Washington's army used Kings Ferry to cross the Hudson en route to Yorktown. Though it has since become something of a pejorative, native Verplanckers still proudly refer to themselves as "Pointers."

By the 1830s, Verplanck was being figured as the new "capital of Westchester"—which helps explain its too-broad and grand-seeming boulevards—but it was ultimately bypassed by the railroad, and became something of a blue-collar immigrant enclave. My paternal grandparents arrived there from Croatia in the 1930s. My father's childhood home was less than two miles from the site where the plant was eventually built, then an idyllic spot called Indian Point Park. In the 1930s and '40s, stately

Hudson River Day Liners chugged north from New York City and deposited smartly dressed tourists at the park, which had a dance pavilion, a public swimming pool, ball fields, picnic areas and amusement rides. My father remembers curling into the branches of the park's copious cherry trees as a child, and filling his mouth with ripe fruit.

Francis B. Stein, my elementary school principal and Buchanan's late, beloved historian, collected and saved postcards of the park. Muted but enthralling, the cards show beaming visitors wading into the river, bounding toward the dance hall and lining up for 75-cent rides on a boat called *Miss Indian Point V.*

Approached from the east, Indian Point is set back from the road so that its reactors are visible only from a distance. When I was young, and my family drove together down Broadway toward my aunt's house, where my sister and I caught the school bus most mornings, I would twist my neck from the back seat of our Ford to glimpse the tops of its domes—dull and squat, turning pinkish-gray as the morning sun climbed higher. You could spot them from the riverfront in Peekskill, too, but the best view was from the other side of Annsville Creek, near the kayak launch. There, the domes ("Domes of doom," my aunt joked) rose clumsily from the horizon, odd and oafish, cold. Even now, that juxtaposition—organic versus synthetic, ancient versus new—feels ominous.

One day, when I was still in elementary school, my mother discovered a man with a sack of unwieldy equipment roaming our backyard, uninvited. My mother, who is unusually fearless, marched us outside and confronted him. Apologetic and bumbling, he said he had been sent to survey our land—and all areas surrounding Indian Point. Why? He mumbled something about fault lines.

I had already learned a bit about earthquakes in school. As far as I could tell, they involved giant, lightning-bolt-shaped gashes in the earth. As the man nervously packed up his instruments and left, I began wondering what it would feel like if our house slipped into a gaping crack in the ground. That worry changed shape when we were told that Indian Point was built on the Ramapo Fault Plane, a 185-mile system of fractures in the earth's crust that snakes from Pennsylvania into the Hudson Valley. The plant claims it was designed to absorb an earthquake of up to a 6.1 magnitude (the earthquake that felled Fukushima Daiichi was a 9.0), but as of 2010, Indian Point still ranked number one on a cautionary list compiled by the US Nuclear Regulatory Commission—meaning it has the highest risk of suffering core damage from an earthquake of any nuclear plant in the nation. Twenty million Americans live within fifty miles of it.

Eventually, I went away to college in Virginia and didn't think much about Indian Point until the fall of 2001, when I moved back to New York and enrolled in a graduate writing program at Columbia University. In the days following the 9/11 attacks, I would pull fliers—for chemical suits and build-your-own nuclear bunker kits—from underneath my windshield wipers every time I went home and parked my Honda on the street. Camouflage-clad armed guards stood at the entrance to the plant, and the whole area was cordoned off like a prison, with stretches of razor wire. Those fences remain.

That fall, the National Guard started camping out in the forest behind our home, near the cemetery where my grandmother is buried. On the evening news, we watched anxious anchors speculate about Indian Point's vulnerability as a terror target. We ourselves had whispered conversations with neighbors about whether rolled-up blueprints for the plant had really been found in a cave in Afghanistan. When I stood at our living-room window during those days, gazing out over the lake and drinking coffee with my father, I half-expected a tank to slowly roll by. There was a sense, then, that danger of some sort was imminent, though we couldn't specify its origins or potential. This is the most odious and creeping kind of fear.

A few years later, my aunt was diagnosed with thyroid cancer. She recovered, but I still wonder if Indian Point contributed in some way to either the genesis or progress of her disease. (There has yet to be a definitive study of thyroid cancer rates in Westchester and Rockland Counties and local nuclear radiation, though plenty have and continue to speculate about potential correlations.) Not long after, our veterinarian found a lump growing on our old cat's thyroid gland; he was treated, successfully, with an injection of radioactive iodine. Now, when I go to the dentist for a checkup and all the attending X-rays, my mother still cautions me to request a thyroid guard, an extra bit of lead-lined apron that can extend up and over the neck. Secretly, I want to ball up under the bib like a hermit crab, shielding my entire body from any more radiation. It is a curious, shapeless, and omnipresent enemy: electromagnetic waves, shooting from somewhere to somewhere else.

I don't live in Buchanan anymore, but I still spend plenty of summer weekends there, grilling steaks and ears of corn in my parents' backyard, helping my father plant potatoes, idly picking ticks off the cat. In the last few years, the county has been developing the waterfront more, building bike paths and picnic areas, converting old factories into lofts or hotels or craft breweries. The plant remains, unmovable, nearly stoic. We look at those domes and shudder, or shrug, as we have all our lives.

Amanda Petrusich is the author of three books about music, including *Do Not Sell at Any Price: The Wild, Obsessive Hunt for the World's Rarest 78rpm Records*, which was named one of the best books of the year by NPR, Slate, and BuzzFeed. Petrusich is the recipient of a 2016 Guggenheim Fellowship in nonfiction, and is a contributing writer for the *New Yorker*. Her work has also appeared in the *New York Times*, the *New York Times Magazine*, the *Oxford American*, *Pitchfork*, *GQ*, *Esquire*, *Playboy*, *The Nation*, *The Atlantic*, and elsewhere. She is a commissioning editor for Bloomsbury's 33 1/3 series, a 2015 MacDowell fellow, a 2014 New York State Foundation for the Arts nonfiction fellow, and an assistant professor of writing at New York University. In 2015, she was named one of the most influential people in Brooklyn culture by *Brooklyn* magazine. She lives in New York City.

Keeping My Fossil Fuel in the Ground

Terry Tempest Williams

———

My husband, Brooke Williams, and I recently bought leasing rights to 1,120 acres of federal public lands near our home in Utah. The lease gives us the right to drill for oil or natural gas. We paid $1,680 for it, plus an $820 processing fee.

We put it on our credit card.

I hadn't planned on leasing these lands when I attended an auction run by the federal Bureau of Land Management, a government agency that manages hundreds of millions of acres of public land across the West. I was there to protest the leasing of these lands to oil and gas companies planning to drill for fossil fuels.

But I ended up in the shorter line to get into the auction, the one for people registering as bidders. So I signed a registration form and was given the number 19. I followed the other bidders inside and found a seat in the front row.

My husband entered with the protesters, who were assigned to a separate space set aside for them.

As people filed in, a BLM agent approached me and asked, "Are you aware that if you have misrepresented yourself as a legitimate bidder with an energy company you will be prosecuted and you could go to prison?"

His tone moved from inquiry to intimidation to harassment. "I am asking you, are you aware . . ."

I said I was aware of what happened to Tim DeChristopher, who attended a similar auction in 2008, where he bid up prices and ended up with 22,000 acres, worth nearly $1.8 million that he had no intention of paying for. He was doing it to protest the auction. He was sentenced to two years in federal prison on felony counts of interfering with the auction and making false representations.

"As an American citizen," I told the agent, "I have a right to be here and witness this auction and decide if I am going to bid or not on these leases on our public lands, correct?"

"I am saying, if you choose to misrepresent yourself . . ."

"But I have this right . . ."

"What energy do you plan to develop?"

"You can't define energy for us. Our energy development is fueling a movement to keep it in the ground."

"You will be prosecuted if . . ."

We were interrupted as the auction began. Parcel after parcel was sold to the rhythmic bantering of the auctioneer until voices in the back of the room began singing, "People got to rise like water . . ."

The singing became louder and louder until the bidders could no longer hear the auctioneer. The auction stopped. The protesters were told to be quiet. They kept singing. They were asked again. They sat down. The auction continued.

"Two dollars, two dollars, do I hear 2.25, I hear 2.25, 2.50, 3, 4, 5, are you in, are you out, do I hear 5, I hear 5, do I hear 6, 6 dollars, do I hear 7, 7. Sold! Bidder No. 14."

And so it went.

Then the protesters began to sing again. This time, they were escorted out by the police. They offered up words of protest as they departed, ending with "Keep it in the ground!"

The doors were closed. The auction continued as the singing of protesters echoed from the stairwell.

"Come on, men, are you in, are you out, or are you stayin' home—this is a lot of scenery going to waste," the auctioneer joked when no one bid on a parcel.

As the auction closed, we were told that if we wished to lease parcels that had not been sold, we could go to the BLM office and purchase them "over the counter" at a discounted price. Call it a fire sale.

Which is exactly what my husband and I did. We were interested in buying leases within the county where we live specifically, on land where oil and gas exploration might threaten sage grouse, prairie dogs and other wildlife. We met the qualification: we're adult citizens of the United States.

With maps stretched out before us, we found what we were looking for. The $2-per-acre base price had been reduced to $1.50. We took out our credit card, and sealed the deal. The land sits adjacent to a proposed wilderness area. When we visited, we were struck by its hard-edge beauty and castle-like topography.

We have every intention of complying with the law, even as we challenge it. To establish ourselves as a legitimate energy company, we have formed Tempest Exploration Company, LLC. We will pay the annual rent for the duration of the ten-year lease and keep whatever oil and gas lies beneath these lands in the ground.

Those resources will remain there until science finds a way to use those fossil fuels in sustainable, nonpolluting ways. After ten years, we will lose our lease if we haven't drilled.

We're not suggesting that everyone who feels as we do about the exploitation of our public lands should do what we did. We aren't going to be able to buy our way out of this problem. Our purchase was more or less spontaneous, done with a coyote's grin, to shine a light on the auctioning away of America's public lands to extract the very fossil fuels that are warming our planet and pushing us toward climate disaster.

Out here in the Utah desert, we are hoping to tap into the energy that is powering the movement to keep fossil fuels in the ground. Some 32 million acres of lands managed by BLM have already been leased to energy companies to drill for oil and gas, even as some climate scientists tell us the world needs to keep most fossil fuels in the ground to avert a catastrophic future of runaway global warming.

The energy we hope to produce through Tempest Exploration is not the kind that will destroy our planet, but the kind that will fuel moral imagination. We need to harness this spiritual and political energy to sustain the planet we call home.

———

Terry Tempest Williams is the author of *Refuge: An Unnatural History of Family and Place; An Unspoken Hunger: Stories from the Field; Desert Quartet; Leap; Red: Patience and Passion in the Desert; The Open Space of Democracy*, and *Finding Beauty in a Broken World*. Her most recent book, *The Hour of Land: A Personal Topography of America's National Parks*, was released in 2017. She is currently writer-in-residence at the Harvard Divinity School. Her writing has appeared in the *New Yorker*, the *New York Times*, *Orion Magazine*, and numerous anthologies worldwide.

Sea Home

KaiLea Wallin

Today we are anchored in a wide bay, the swell has dropped for a few days and the boat is pleasantly becalmed. When I climb out of bed and poke my head above deck, this is what I see: a dozen other sailboats anchored a comfortable distance around us. Low clouds waiting to burn off the humid mountains on the opposite side of the bay. Flocks of Heermann's gulls and pelicans pestering fishermen as they drift by us, cleaning their catch from the night before. A lone paddle boarder, racing no one out to sea.

Back aboard our floating universe I see surf wax and dinghy fuel and our tiller draped in rash guards. There are small drool rags of various colors tucked in handy nooks, like under the dodger and from hanging lines off the mizzen mast. A long row of rinsed cloth diapers are clipped to our lifelines and wave like surrender flags in the breeze. A faint odor rises up from forgotten damp flip-flops.

I tuck my head below and survey the interior. The port or left side berth cradles instruments: guitar, ukulele, drum, baby rattles. The starboard or right side berth holds dry goods and fruit: rice and cereal, limes getting squished by grapefruits, bright bananas hanging above ripening mangos. As I climb down the ladder back into the main cabin, I see my husband with Etolin in his arms, headed for the changing table. While they debate, using mostly body language, the merits of wearing clothes versus spending the day in the nude, I put on water for oatmeal. Eventually Etolin concedes to Rob's persuasive arguments and removes his foot from his mouth, allowing the proper placement of his diaper followed by a cotton onesie. Rob takes over breakfast preparations and I carry Etolin up to the cockpit to look for whales.

Six months a year, this boat is our home. She's a good boat and we love her. She is ample and stately, no-nonsense, with sexy curves and a confident air. We are proud of her classic lines, workhorse nature, and simple, modest systems. We don't mind that she's lacking a few luxuries, like hot water or a shower.

Before we met and married, Rob and I separately satisfied our travel itch and distaste for office jobs by working seasonal, often maritime-related, jobs in Alaska, Hawaii, New Zealand, and beyond. Independently we lived on schooners and barges, fish boats and yawls. We accrued hundreds of hours of sea time, learned how to fix engines and outboards and studied both high tech and ancient forms of navigation. We were pretty salty before we met and after we joined forces, our time on the water doubled. Eventually I moved aboard his 38-foot sailboat and we merged our varying visions of the future into one: quit our nonprofit jobs and sail the boat south.

Two thousand and seven hundred miles later, here we are in Mexico. What was supposed to be a quick stop on our sailing journey has turned into a lifestyle. The longer we stay in this deep bay circled by lush green mountains, this balmy climate, the more our ties to the community grow and the anchor lodges deeper. I will concede that Mexico will never be home to the same degree as the nostalgia-rich Pacific Northwest that we sailed away from. But bringing your house with you really helps bridge that divide.

We first lived on our ship in the rainy harbors of Puget Sound and the Salish Sea that connects Seattle to Canada. Then we lived on her offshore in giant seas and epic gales. Then we lived on her in the foggy coastal towns of California and the dusty desert pueblos of Baja. Now, in tropical mainland Mexico, she fits us like an old pair of boots. She's worn in where we have tread the most (the galley, the head) and she's scuffed and cozy in comforting ways. We can dinghy to shore, explore new towns, eat foreign food, and speak Spanish all day then return to the same bed we've slept in for nine years.

But for all the joys of this maritime life, after a long winter on a rocking home, I'm feeling a little green. Plus, we have bills to pay. So every spring we leave the boat and head back to America. Six months a year, our home is on land. This is our working home. While families around us prepare for summer vacations, we start working 10–14 hours a day, sometimes every day, for months at a time. Some summers we slay salmon in Alaska, others we lead wildlife tours. If we work hard enough and save our pennies we can turn them into pesos and go back to our boat for another season of aquatic adventures. Compartmentalizing our lives into one home where we play and one where we work is a bit extreme in terms of work-life balance but it averages out to nearly normal hours and income if taken over the course of a whole year. We like to think of it as trading stock options for a reoccurring, annual, six-month retirement.

April is the month we leave our water home for our terra firma home. To prepare our boat for Mexico's summer hurricane season, we have pages of "To Do" lists that dictate our days. We painstakingly remove every stitch of fabric and every single line and clean, dry, and stow them below. That includes all the sails, sail covers, cockpit cover, dodger, weather cloths, and safety netting. We wash, dry, and fold all our clothes and put them in trash bags with dryer sheets to prevent mold and mildew. We bag every single book for the same reason. We give away perishables and dry goods that bugs would enjoy and bag up cans and sealed food with bay leaves and rodent traps. The engine, the batteries, the dinghy, the outboard; every single thing onboard gets some kind of special check up, tune up, and treatment for stowage until the entire boat is almost bare above deck and below deck looks like a bursting storage unit. We even take the booms off and put them below to preserve their Sitka spruce cores from baking in the summer heat. Surfboards and solar panels get stuffed below. Meanwhile the temperatures soar into the nineties, we often miss meals because we can no longer cook in our torn apart galley, and our heads and backs ache from hauling heavy objects up and down the ladder. Patience runs thin.

Once we've finally crossed everything off the list and raced to make our flight north, it's unpacking time again. We cross our fingers that our renter has left our little apartment in good condition and we don't have any major repairs that need attention. We try to remember what we shoved where in the frantic rush of leaving the previous fall (the shed? the storage unit? the laundry room cupboards?) and we hope our car is not too disgusting from spending another winter under a tarp. Eventually we find our sweaters and shake out the moths and put them back on and start our summer jobs in earnest. We restart our cell phone plans, our insurance plans, and our friendships. During all this, we try to ignore the nagging thought that in six months, it will be time to do it all over again.

I'm not angling for sympathy here. We had a dream and we made it a reality. I know it is an extreme privilege to have the opportunity to live this wacky life. But I do have some concerns. Because I'm not a carefree vagabond in my twenties anymore, skipping from lucrative boat jobs to unpaid internships all willy-nilly. I have a family to think of and a child to raise. For now, he goes between our dry and wet homes with ease. But for how long? What will he make of all this as he gets older? Will he glow with the special feeling of having love, community, and friendships in not just two homes but two countries? Will he be pleased to be bilingual and savvy with a soccer ball? Or will he come to tire of the constant motion? Will he resent this family tradition of uprooting? I worry one home can never be enough for me and that I am passing this trait on to my son. I worry our family will never fit in, full-time, in either home and we will be doomed to be outsiders wherever we go. Having too many homes can diminish the power of the original concept: home as the place where you feel you most belong.

Sometimes I fantasize about a home that embraces both our worlds. Four walls and a roof, concrete foundation anchoring it to land but inside paintings of whales and sailboats and a cozy galley-like kitchen with teak and brass. Mexican oilcloth on the table in bright, primary colors and loads of maritime books, telling stories of the high seas. A land boat, a boat house. And no chance of seasickness. But even the mere fantasy triggers a wave of sea-homesickness. I would miss the turquoise sparkle of the sun glinting off the water! I would miss the digital detox of living without smart phones and Internet. I would miss the sense of possibility, like we could up-anchor and go anywhere in the whole world, at a moment's notice. Clearly, I'm in pretty deep.

When my thoughts get all twisted in knots like this, I come back to what I know. I love the sea but I can't live on it year-round. We want and have to work and it's easier to do so in our home country. Dividing our world in half makes sense for now and someday I will look back and wish I had just enjoyed the ride. Embraced the good and the bad, the stressful transitions and the lessons they teach us. I think moving between two homes can foster agility, adaptability, curiosity, and a Zen-like detachment from material things. Combine that with a healthy dose of respect, kindness, and empathy and I can't think of better values to pass along to my son.

Back out on deck, Etolin gurgles and points at the horizon. I catch a glimpse of a lingering column of mist hanging in the air. A humpback whale exhales again, then dives under the surface with her newborn calf close behind. Seasonal migrants like us, this whale swam north thousands of miles while pregnant to feed in the nutrient-rich waters of the Pacific Northwest. Now that she is back in tropical waters she has given birth and will teach her calf the same route and lifestyle. Hard to say, but from here they look pretty happy.

Maybe we aren't crazy after all.

———

KaiLea Wallin was born on an island in Alaska, spent her childhood on boats, and gets habitually seasick. Nevertheless, she has worked, lived and taught on boats for most of her life. She writes personal essays, feminist fiction, and travel stories between boat projects and chasing her offspring.

Size Matters

——

Sonya Chung

Your average portable vacuum cleaner features a retractable cord that is 12 feet in length. Square 12, multiply by π, and you get 452—roughly the square footage of the area that can be cleaned without having to move the plug to another outlet. This is also the ideal size of any dwelling that I might call home; it is in fact the size of the studio apartment in New York City that I do call home.

❧

It's taken me a long time—forty-four years—to feel at home somewhere. But I do, finally.

It's unexpected, and lucky. We acted out of necessity—limits and constraints. We might have chosen otherwise, with more resources. We imagined we would trade up sooner than later.

Now, I sit at my six-foot desk, built in under the kitchen window and within reach of espresso-maker and air-pop popper (doggie-dining and recycling underneath), and I think, *perfecto*.

Now, I think: how can we hold onto it. I could grow old and die here.

Now, when I browse real estate for one-bedrooms in the Bronx or Queens, I think, That's too big.

Which came first, the claim that "size matters" or the assurance that it doesn't? It occurs to me, in any case, that the expression is guilty of *weak specification*. The unaddressed question isn't *whether* size matters but, rather, *which* size is preferable.

In the case of penises, "size" is assumed to mean *large* size, and that of course is the joke: "size matters" is much funnier than "only large penises satisfy sexually." These days the joke extends into nonsexual realms, while maintaining its innuendo: think Martha Stewart whipping up egg whites into formidably stiff peaks, coaching us through with banter—*Keep whipping, there are no shortcuts here: size matters.* A faint smile, shift of the eyes. Har har.

So let's be clear: when we say size matters, what we're saying, without saying it, is Bigger is Better. And when we say size *doesn't* matter, we offer comfort in the face of insecurity: don't worry, small is okay.

I'm saying: Small is more than okay. Small is home.

What is "big"? What is "small"?

In Manhattan, a 700-square-foot apartment is "spacious"; in Paris, *très grand.*

A 10x10 bedroom can fit a full-sized bed frame (with under-storage drawers), nightstands on either side, a chair, and at least 30 feet of wall-mounted shelving.

For my sister, who lives in the suburbs with her husband and two children, her 2,500-square-foot house is "too small."

In Grahamstown, South Africa, circa 1994, students at the elite University of Fort Hare—alma mater of soon-to-be-elected President Mandela—hosted a group of us from US colleges. The rooms were modern and clean, with modular furniture; 75 square feet if I had to guess. The students were distinctly proud to share their accommodations. Seeing each room's hard lino-leum floors and single twin bed, we all wondered if blow-up mattresses or mini futons were stowed away in the closets. Then the light of realization dawned on us: for three nights we slept snugly, head to toe, with strangers. Those of us who keep in touch still talk about it.

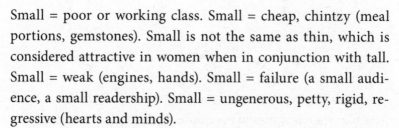

Small = poor or working class. Small = cheap, chintzy (meal portions, gemstones). Small is not the same as thin, which is considered attractive in women when in conjunction with tall. Small = weak (engines, hands). Small = failure (a small audi-ence, a small readership). Small = ungenerous, petty, rigid, re-gressive (hearts and minds).

A small business is an independent business, a sign of healthy entrepreneurialism and a thriving community. Small =

the underdog we root for (the runt, the little engine that could). Every parent wants a small classroom for their child. Small = luxury, specialty, elite (small-batch bourbon, beer, cigars, ice cream). Small = nimble, permissible, advanced (pets, luggage, electronics).

Small = limited, constrained. We forget—or perhaps, in the U.S., we underestimate—that while limitations and constraints can be damaging, they are just as often constructive. Better than okay.

Better than big.

✌

We've lived in our small apartment for seven years. One of us is 6' 1". We had a big dog until two years ago; now we live with two little dogs, four rubber trees, and several herb plants. We are not twenty-somethings, or even thirty-somethings, on an adventure. This is home.

Perhaps I mention it too often. *We live in a studio apartment. 450 square feet. And we both work from home.* Why do I do that? Like name-dropping, it's some kind of badge, a need to prove something.

We like it. It works. We've figured it out.

What is "it"?

✌

While it's far from commonplace for Americans to favor small over big when it comes to necessities, this may be changing.

Consider: *Tiny House Nation, Tiny House Hunting* (FYI Network); *Tiny House Big Living, Tiny House Builders, Tiny House Hunters, Tiny House Luxury* (HGTV). *Tiny, Small Is Beautiful,*

Living Small, We the Tiny House People (feature-length documen-
taries). Tiny House Listings, Tiny House Trailblazers, Misfits Tiny
Homestead, Tumbleweed Tiny Houses, Tiny House Living, Tiny
House Design, Tiny House Swoon, The Tiny Life, Tiny House
Talk, Tiny House Blog, tinyhousefor.us, ilovetinyhouses.com.

A quick Internet search for tiny house designers and builders yields easily twenty-five reputable specialists, evidently quite
busy.

Tiny House Hunting, Season 1 Episode 1: the first house that
Gus and Kyle look at is a whopping 650 square feet—a significant downsize from their 2,000 square-foot house in Boston, but
not small, and not nearly tiny. By episode's end, they've "learned
a lot about what tiny really means"—not just square footage, but
lifestyle and philosophy, e.g., economical use of indoor space
to encourage outdoor activity. They settle on a 400-square-foot
modern cabin. (Hoorah for tiny!)

In her 2016 BuzzFeed article, "Who Is the Tiny House Revolution For?," Doree Shafrir writes, "[A] few common themes
emerge . . . They want to rid themselves of unnecessary possessions; to not feel beholden to maintaining a too-large house, particularly cleaning it; they want to be out of debt; they want to live
more 'green' . . . they want to spend more time with each other
or with family (. . . are forced into a small space together); they
often want to live off the grid, or at least in a remote area . . ."

We don't exactly fit the profile.

Neither of us are pack rats or collectors. I do hate cleaning
and am serious about one-plug vacuuming. We do recycle and
compost and are mindful of lights and running the a/c, but

that's just what you do these days, isn't it (size doesn't matter)? We work at home, so definitely on-grid.

We moved here because at the time buying was cheaper than renting, and it was what we could afford. Now, seven years later, contending with career transitions and increasing maintenance fees, our housing cost is inching steadily beyond our means.

We do spend quite a lot of time together; that's been an adventure.

∽

Some things we've figured out:

- No radio, not even news, between the hours of 8 a.m. and 5:30 p.m.
- Same, obviously, for TV.
- Music with no lyrics is okay; music with non-English lyrics (opera, for example) is okay. A decent set of headphones is a good investment.
- No way this works if only one of you is a smoker.
- Schedule business phone calls during lunchtime or at 5 or while walking the dogs.
- Your chargers are not my chargers.
- Togetherness does not always involve verbal communication.
- Even so, after a full day of not-talking and not-listening, cocktail hour is a beautiful thing.
- A sleep mask is a good gift from the person who reads late into the night to the person who is highly light-sensitive.

- In 450 square feet, with thoughtful planning and arrangement, it is possible to have a living area with TV, a dining area, a sleeping area, a full-sized kitchen, sufficient closet and pantry space, bathroom with tub, and two home-offices.

- Books are not so different from clothes: if it's been on the shelf for a year and you haven't read it or referenced it, it's not earning its shelf-space: pass it on.

- An hour is as long as you can sit, fully clothed, in a bathtub after an argument. Better to walk around the block in your pajamas or find a bench—even late at night, even in the cold.

- Whatever "it" is, when you're living with another person in 450 square feet, you can't fake it or avoid it.

∽

Easy for you to say.

In high school, a friend was talking about missing his father, who'd died of cancer. They had a close relationship. *You're lucky you miss him,* I said. The words just came out. *You're lucky you had a good father.* My friend looked at me like I'd kicked him in the shins—pained, but also bemused. Then he laughed, almost pityingly.

Easy for you to say, he said. *Your father is still alive.*

My father was an angry, miserable man. (He is still alive.)

Was it easy for me to say?

450 square feet is more than enough living space for two adults.

Okay.

450 square feet is the ideal amount of living space for two adults.

Easy for you to say.

∽

Our family of five lived in a two-bedroom apartment when I was born, the third of three girls. We moved to a three-bedroom, two-bathroom ranch house when I was still an infant. My middle sister and I shared a room, while my oldest sister had her own, and we all shared the second bathroom. I have only scant memories of those years or that house. The photographs indicate that we three girls were together most of the time, not infrequently dressed identically.

Soon, we moved again. I don't know why; school districts, most likely. I was starting pre-K, my oldest sister third grade. My father's medical practice was growing; my mother was learning to manage, and spend, money. The new house was enormous: five bedrooms, five bathrooms, on three floors. A living room, a den, a family room, a dining room, a kitchen, a laundry room, a full basement. The dining room and living room were hardly used, since my parents rarely entertained: by this time they had few friends, because my father was increasingly not friendly.

Both my parents came from poor families, my father's much more so—country people, uneducated, twelve children, never enough food to eat or shoes to wear. He's the one who wanted, needed, a big house. Today, he lives alone, still unfriendly, in 3,000 square feet.

Memories from those years, in that house, are abundant and too-clear. The house was not big enough to shroud my father's chronic anger, self-loathing, and their effects; it was the perfect size, on the other hand, for isolation and loneliness. My oldest sister's room was at the end of a long hallway, with its own bathroom, and two large closets that she filled with clothes and shoes of which she became intensely possessive. Both sisters became teenagers before I did and often kept their doors closed. I spent a lot of my childhood in the backyard talking to myself, in the damp, dark basement watching TV by myself, in my room scribbling in a diary.

One night not long ago, my middle sister and I spoke honestly for the first time about those years: she knew and saw things I never knew or saw—ugly scenes and words exchanged—and vice versa. We drank wine and we cried, sad and regretful, and it helped; it was also too little too late. Our adult lives have been marked, and addled, by those years (failed relationships, lots of therapy). My oldest sister, I'm told, still hoards shoes and clothing; she lives far away, and I hardly know her.

In college I made friends with other women whose fathers were awful. They are all very close with their siblings. I'm convinced it's because they shared bedrooms.

That house was too big.

∽

Is that easy for me to say?

According to Shafrir, Tiny Housers comprise, "by definition, a middle-class movement, one that eschews identification with people who have lived in 'tiny' homes for decades—whether that 'tiny' home is a mobile home, an RV, or just a really small apartment . . . the tiny house movement has an inherent privilege built in: Going tiny is a *choice*."

Indeed. We are in the realm of choice. But when presented with choice, the inclination toward bigger too often, too easily, prevails. Size matters, but *how so*? My test case plays out like this: I imagine that a friend of mine—who grew up poor, one of four children in a two-bedroom apartment in the South—comes into some money: a major promotion, a smart investment, what have you. She asks me to go house hunting with her. She wants a BIG place—eat-in kitchen, dining, living, an office each for her and the boyfriend, a separate room for each of three children, a guest room, nine closets. Finally, space! She asks me what I think. I say, you're really asking me? She says yeah. We've been friends a long time.

I say, *It's too big.* I say, *Think about the children.* I say, *Size matters.*

～

How much space do you really need? What you need and what I need are different. In a small space, however, the question must be asked, over and again. The persistence of the question is the thing. In 450 square feet, there is no auto-pilot, no passive accumulations or retreating into your pod. You have to—I won't shy away from the word—*curate* your life; the result of which is more likely to be beautiful, truthful, healthy.

Whatever it is, you are always, every day, figuring it out. Together.

Does my hypothetically newly rich poor friend have to experience big space before she can choose small space? Maybe. But I'm still going to tell her what I believe to be true: curate is not a word reserved for the middle class; nor is healthy. I would want anyone in my friend's position to have access to both.

⌒

If we have to move, then yes, we have the privilege of options. I'm trolling tiny houses, learning about permits and trailer widths and metal roofing. I especially like the ones with rooftop balconies—a much better option than the bathtub.

I do not want to let go of the place I have finally called home. I have found home in small. But small in itself isn't the point. The point, ultimately, is what matters.

———

Sonya Chung is the author of the novels *The Loved Ones*—a Kirkus Best Fiction 2016, *Library Journal* Best Indie Fiction, Indie Next List, TNB Book Club, and BuzzFeed Books Recommends selection—and *Long for This World*. She is a staff writer for *The Millions* and founding editor of Bloom, a site that highlights the work of authors who debut after age forty, and is a recipient of a Pushcart Prize nomination, the Charles Johnson Fiction Award, the Bronx Council on the Arts Writers' Fellowship & Residency, a MacDowell Colony Fellowship, and a Key West Literary Seminars residency. Sonya's stories, reviews, and essays have appeared in the *Threepenny Review, Tin House, BuzzFeed, Huffington Post, The Late American Novel: Writers on the Future of Books*, and *Short: An International Anthology*, among others. Sonya has taught fiction writing at the Gotham Writers' Workshop, NYU, and Columbia University. Currently she lives in New York City and teaches at Skidmore College.

The Sound of Horse Teeth on Hay in the Snow

Pam Houston

This morning the wind woke me at first light, howling against the storm window and threatening to tear a loose piece of flashing off the kitchen gutter. I'd been awake writing till two, and hoped to sleep till eight, but William the wolf-hound was worried, emitting a micro-squeak the way he does every thirty seconds—just long enough for me to have nearly dropped back off to sleep, and now I was worried too, not about the house but the horses.

We have made it to February first, which means, hopefully, that there won't be too many more nights of thirty-plus below zero. We've had a lot of those nights this year, in December and January, too many for the comfort level of my elderly horses who just keep hanging in there year after year. A storm like this will elevate the temperature, possibly even above zero. Still, a forty mph wind can turn twenty above into twenty below, and I am starting to suspect that Isaac, the mini-donk, who has a bit of a Napoleon Complex, has begun bullying the horses, keeping them out of the giant stall I leave open for them. If he is successful, it means that two tiny donkeys are (relatively) warm and dry right now while the horses are doing their best to use the angles of the barn to stay out of the wind.

I roll out of bed and cautiously open the door to the wood porch. (I've lost doors to big wind plenty of times in the past) but this wind seems to be from the south, and though the snow is swirling around the porch like some kind of ghostly special effect, the door opens normally. I tump the snow off of a couple of logs and bring them inside, knock the coals around in the wood stove and add the new logs to the fire.

If there is any doubt about how cold this winter has been, my wood and hay supply attests to it. I am going to run out of both, probably by mid-March, and since the pasture doesn't come in until late May and since it can snow anytime until the Fourth of July, I am going to have to buy another two cords and another hundred bales.

It's not the buying that is punishing; hay and wood are reasonably priced around here. It's getting the hay from the plowed part of the driveway to the barn, and getting the wood from the same spot across the front yard and around the house to the covered porch—all of this with four feet of snow still on the ground. That will involve packing a trail with snowshoes, and then sledding the rounds of wood/bales of hay, one or two at a time to their destination. And then there is the stacking them once I get there.

Rick Davie, my hay man, will help me move and stack the hay—he's too much of a gentleman not to, but I tend to move the wood alone, a half cord a day if there is no snow in the forecast threatening to bury it, or all at once if there's a storm coming in.

It's easy to lose track of the days out here, but I know this is Sunday because the blizzard was supposed to arrive Thursday, but turned out to be flurries until yesterday (Saturday) morning, when it started to snow in earnest. The forecast kept edging the winter storm warning forward, increasing its duration by two or four hours at a time, like they didn't want us to notice, but now they have gone ahead and said we are in for it pretty much continuously until Tuesday night. There is so much wind it's hard to say from the kitchen window whether we have gotten two feet or four feet, but I know the drifts will have made the driveway out of the question, even in the old reliable Toyota truck with the manually locking hubs.

I'm mostly here by myself during the winter, or I guess you would say more correctly that I am the only human on the ranch, which feels the opposite of being alone to me. I am in the good company of two wolfhounds, two elderly geldings, a bonded pair of miniature donkey jacks, three Icelandic ewes and a ram, and one aging mouser named Mr. Kitty. I have well-stocked cabinets and there is always something in the freezer to make soup out of. Randy Woods, who plows my driveway, usually gets to me within twenty-four hours, unless it is a three-day storm and then he gets to me twenty-four hours after it stops. Being snowed in on the ranch with the wolfhounds, tending the barn animals, doing my work, makes me happier than just about anything else on earth.

I make some cinnamon tea—double warmth—and dress in layers of wool, fleece, down, and whatever it is that snow pants are made of these days, and step out onto the dog porch into the blow. I squint to the see the horses in the corral, their manes, backs and tails frosted with snow. No sign of the donkeys nor the sheep, who have wisely decided to stay inside their enclosure.

I have always preferred the company of animals to the company of people, and I know that when I say that you'll think I am emotionally stunted in some way, and maybe I am. But when I compare myself to the many people I have known who can't seem to handle being alone for five minutes, I think I might be less emotionally stunted than they are. My childhood home did not have any safe places—when my father was drinking, stomping through each room of the house looking for a target, I often hid in the basement, in the clothes dryer with the round Plexiglas door barely cracked. But life is long, and in the decades since then I have felt safe in the presence of enough human beings to offset, at least cognitively, all the ways I was conditioned to distrust them. Still, it has still been a rare human who has given me an animal's worth of love back.

My partner Greg is pretty good at giving love of the human variety, and my decade with him has made me better at giving love to a human too. But if it were not for the fact that both Greg and my fourteen-week-a-year teaching job are in California, I'd probably have thirty rescued donkeys and at least five dogs, if not ten. I'd become the crazy old dog lady who wears so much fur all her clothes tend to look the same color. (At the airport the other day the TSA guy gave my black fleece a once over and said, "So, you decided to bring the dog with you today . . . huh?") I'm not sure in that scenario I'd be any less happy, or any less loved.

The wind stills for a moment and the whole world is silent as a church. In the aftermath of a blizzard, the snow looks more like a painting of snow than snow itself. Everything sculpted and softened by all that force pushing it for hours in one direction. The hill that rises behind the homesteaders' old cabin looks less like landscape and more like contemporary art. White on white, a tiny row of fence poles the only distinguishing factor. And then the wind starts howling again.

I go back inside and call Randy Woods and get on his schedule for Wednesday morning. I slice two apples and break eight carrots into pieces while Livie hops around on the kitchen floor and William sits patiently beside me. I don the hat I bought right out of an Inuit lady's kitchen in Arctic Bay, Nunavut, Canada, last year (the warmest hat I have ever owned), my neck gaiter, my winter work gloves, and my Carhartt barn jacket. No need to call the dogs, who are competing for the pole position in the mud room. I open the door and off we go.

From what I can see, and I can't see all that much in this gale—even though it is full daylight now—we've gotten about two and a half feet of new snow since midday yesterday. But the drifts between me and the barn run anywhere from one to three feet higher than that. My beautifully engineered two-weeks-in-the-making snowshoe-packed trail to the barn is nothing but a distant memory, but it still behooves me to try to stay on top of its old footprint, because when I fall off of it, I sink yet another foot and a half down into the last storm's snow. I get about thirty steps into my trek when a wind blast stops me cold and I realize I have left the porch without the snow shovel, so back I go, using the boot-sized post holes I have just created to retrieve it.

The dogs don't really love snow this deep. It gets up in their paws and makes ice balls which eventually bleed, but they are nothing if not loyal and so they return to the porch with me. Thirty steps doesn't sound like much unless you are walking in snow that varies from eighteen inches to four feet deep and you are trying to use your memory to stay on a trail that is now at least a foot and a half under.

I don't need to shovel my way to the barn (though one year we got five feet in one storm and then I did need the shovel just to get there). In this wind, any progress I would make trying to use the shovel to remake my old trail would be erased, literally, in minutes. I'll need the shovel once I get there, to shovel out the orange gate, which lets me into the corral, and then to shovel out the barn door, which lets me get to the hay.

But first things first. The remaining hundred or so steps to the barn. It seems impossible, but it is snowing even harder than it was five minutes ago. A giant gust of wind lifts more snow into the air, and the barn, which is only about a hundred yards from the house, disappears entirely. This is the kind of day that makes a person believe in those stories where the farmer gets lost between the house and the barn and freezes to death in a snowdrift while his wife cooks his dinner. If I get lost in a snowdrift today, no one will know I'm there until the spring thaw.

One time, after a big storm, I fell off the side of the ghost of my old trail into a very deep drift. My legs were trapped under me in a strange position, and being more or less armpit deep in snow there was a moment when I wasn't sure I could get myself out. I gave it another try, and got one leg around to the front and then another, until I was more or less in a half-buried sitting position. I tried to use my arms to roll myself over, to get on my hands and knees, but everything beneath me still felt bottomless. I wasn't exactly scared, I hadn't yet had time to get scared, and though it was well below zero with a moderate wind, the sun was shining.

I decided to rest for a minute before the next try, and laid back in the little cave I had inadvertently fashioned for a minute to look at the sky. No sooner had I gotten into that prone position and let out a long slow exhale than William was right by my side—the windward side—the whole length of him tight against the whole length of me—body to body. His first instinct was to block the wind, to keep me warm until I got out or until help came.

Today we make it without falling to the corral where the horses are waiting and I distribute apples and carrots through the rails. The horses seem calm, in spite of the wind, which must be a function of the temperature. Fifteen above beats thirty-five below in their book no matter what the weather channel tells us the wind chill "feels like." When it is coming down like this it simply can't be thirty-five below—those conditions are mutually exclusive, and I believe the horses, at this stage in their lives, would choose the snow over the deep-freeze on every occasion.

When it is thirty-five below, the sky is clear, the wind is still and it is as quiet outside as the beginning of time. Ice crystals form on the aspen tree outside the kitchen window, on the lead ropes that hang from the barn door, on the horses' coats and eyelashes and whiskers. When the light is right, and you train your eyes just a few degrees off the direction of the sun, you can even see tiny crystals suspended in the frigid air. When it is thirty-five below, I take one step outside and the inside of my nose freezes, and the crunch of my boots on the packed powder path is the definition of the word *dry* on my tongue. On those mornings, the equines eat the apples and carrots out of my hands quickly, before they turn into carrot- and apple-flavored popsicles, and I must do everything with great care because one minute with exposed skin is enough to cause frostbite.

But today there is time to pet under a forelock, to reach down into the snow to pick up a dropped apple or carrot bit. The mini-donks, Simon and Isaac, crowd in for their share. Simon won't eat carrots, only apples. In between bites he occasionally likes to take a benign flat-toothed love nip out of my hip or thigh. Isaac thinks he's the boss around here even though he is shorter than the wolfhounds. He puts his little hooves up on Roany's neck sometimes just to push him around. Roany, a big Roman-nosed quarter horse, seventeen hands at the shoulder, has been on the planet for more than thirty years, getting along with pretty much everybody, and so lets him.

At one time, Roany was the most powerful beast on the ranch by far. He could have kicked Fenton the wolfhound over the fence with one back hoof if he wanted to stop his barking once and for all, stop all his showing off. But even when Fenton would chase Roany from the middle of the pasture all the way back to the barn, the big gelding would take care where he put his feet, would turn and pin his ears in warning, but never do anything more than that.

Roany was thin this September and thinner in December. He's staying closer to the barn than he ever has and I fear he might be losing his sight. I've been sneaking him a coffee can of senior sweet feed most afternoons when the others aren't looking. In December I feared he might not make the winter, but here we are in February, and he rubs his ice-crusted eyelashes against me and reaches his giant lips toward my pockets to get another carrot. Maybe the old Roan will get to see another summer on the ranch.

When I made the decision some years ago to slash my time at UC Davis in order to spend the coldest part of every winter here, I thought a four- or eight-week solo stint at the ranch might make me antsy or lonely, or just plain weird from only talking to animals. It mostly has not.

You might be thinking right now that I don't like people, but my writer's life puts me around them, 24/7 for weeks at a time, and I like that version too. This summer I taught eight back-to-back seven-day workshops with only two days off over the entire period and for the most part managed to keep both my humor and my good will. I have friends spread from coast to coast and elsewhere whom I visit, or who come to visit me, and so I always have someone to go travelling with (if I want), someone to spend the holidays with (if I want), someone to call in some long, troubled middle of the night. And for the last ten years I have had an honest-to-goodness—if long distance a lot of the time—family in the form of Greg and his daughter Kaeleigh.

I am deeply grateful for all of those things and would not trade any of them, but I've also recently realized that what I have never had enough of since I was a kid is alone time. That kid who hid in the clothes dryer had almost unlimited alone time and she came to realize that alone time meant both safety and the possibility of unrestricted adventure. At eight, on a vacation to London with my parents, I memorized the entire map of the Underground, got myself to the Tower of London, and took the terrifying beheadings tour at sunset before my parents—who were quite happy in our hotel bar—ever realized I was gone. At five, in the Bahamas, I befriended a giant dappled grey horse and his Bahamian rider, who scooped me into the saddle, galloped me all the way down the beach and chest high into the waves before my mother looked up from her beach towel. (From that moment on, I was horse crazy.) From the time I was ten until I turned sixteen, I rode my bike through the cornfields of Bethlehem, Pennsylvania, to the truck stop on Schoenersville Road, where I racked up ten games on each of the pinball machines and sold them at half price to the truckers. My solo adventures this winter have mostly involved snowshoes, cross-country skis, and an occasional run down to Pagosa Hot Springs.

Last month, after three solid weeks alone here, I went outside after the last blizzard with my good camera, took a bunch of photos and sent them to Channel Four CBS news in Denver where, during the weather report, they flash the best photos from viewers and sure enough that night they chose mine. Several people in Creede called the house to tell me I was "famous," and a good friend in Denver who had seen my photos called to ask if I was sure I didn't want to come down to the city for a day or two.

The concern in her tone was not lost on me, and so I tried to explain how much I delight in the simple—some would call it selfish—pleasure of living alone in an isolated place. I can ski as far as I want for as long as I want. I can sleep with the dogs in my bed, or out on the couch near the fire, or even with them in their dog beds if I want to. I can take a bath in the middle of the day and I can stay in there until I shrivel. I can (and did) take the bathroom door off of its hinges so I could bring a four-foot silver water trough in there and raise six Plymouth Barred Rock chicks. I can clean the pantry at three in the morning, or do a thousand-piece jigsaw puzzle on the kitchen table or eat a whole bag of frozen peas for dinner with one pat of butter and thirty six shakes from a bottle of Crystal hot sauce.

Every time an alone spell comes to an end and I am about to welcome a guest, or a friend, or Greg and Kaeleigh, or I have to go back out into the world to teach or speak or be public, along with the excitement there is always a shred of regret as I watch the hours wind down. On the last day alone I invariably find myself wishing for just one day more.

Today, though, all potential visitors will have to be dropped in by helicopter. On a Sunday, mid-storm and this late in the season, I doubt I'll even see the plow out on Middle Creek Road. My octogenarian neighbor to the west, Margot Lamb, descendant of one of the original homesteaders of the Soward Ranch, moves into town every winter. So usually, for these months, I am the last occupied house on this side of the river. My closest neighbors back towards town are the Albrights, and they're about two and half miles walking, when it is walkable, which today it is not.

The big orange gate swings out from the corral. It is the main access to the barn as well as to the large pasture. In the fall, Rick Davie backs his flatbed loaded with 120 bales of hay through it, backs it up to the barn door, and we buck the hay off it and stack it along every available wall and every available corner, six bales high.

In winter, the gate does not need to open big enough for a truck, but it's important to shovel it out wide enough that if a horse had to be taken out in an emergency, the horse would not be afraid to walk through. The gate is about twenty feet wide so, with a couple feet of snow drifted against it, it takes about twenty minutes of bust-ass shoveling to get it to open double-horse-width wide. Then there is the barn door, which is smaller, but has the added challenge of the frozen-solid horse briquettes that seem to collect there, and must be pried up along with the snow. By the time I finish both tasks I can feel a new set of blisters rising on top of my calluses.

In this much wind, I would normally put the hay in the three-sided windbreak on the barn's south side. But this is an unusual wind, from the south, which accounts for its unseasonably warm bearing, so I drop the bale in the corner of the corral, on the north side of the barn, hoping the sheep pen will block most of the wind when it starts to clock around to the west, as it is predicted to do in a few hours.

I cut the orange twine with the hay hooks, making sure to pick it up and zip it in my pocket (hay twine wreaks havoc with a horse's digestive system), and close up the barn. If it were grain day, I would give the horses their mix of beet pulp and senior mix for horses with metabolic conditions, joint formula, multivitamins, Gut-Sure, and a scoop of Horseshoer's Friend. (We are all big believers in supplements in this house.) Deseo does have a metabolic condition—something a little like diabetes, or Cushings, that means he can't handle grain too often, so we stick tight to our every-fourth-day plan. Today is day two, which is going to work out great, because Tuesday, when the storm moves out and it really gets cold, they will be happier for the grain to warm them up, even than they would be this morning.

The wind has calmed for a moment and I stand and listen for a few minutes to the altogether satisfying sound of four equines chomping good grass hay on a snowy morning, and think about all the mornings, over the last twenty-five years, I have spent just like this, standing out in the snow.

2009 was the coldest January. We went through four whole cords of wood even with propane back-up. For the first time ever the dogs had to be encouraged to go on walks, and Mr. Kitty wouldn't even go out to the barn to hunt. He stayed in the basement for days at a time, cozied up to the big gas heater.

There were five feet of snow standing and no warm days to melt any of it. The white ground reflected back all the sun's rays and couldn't soak up enough heat during the short days to raise the temperature even to ten below. The three-foot split rail fence that surrounds the house went completely under in early

December and we walked daily on a white moonscape between the house and the barn. The roof slid so many times eventually there was nowhere down for it to go and it formed an igloo around the house that actually kept the wind off and raised the temperature in the back bedroom by several degrees compared to a lighter winter. The house threw off enough heat to cauterize the insides of the igloo—like what a candle does on the inside of a jack-o-lantern. It was beautiful, for the month it lasted, living inside a big jack-o-lantern of snow.

But today it is edging toward twenty above, and the horses are feeling it. The wind picks up again and Isaac lets out a big donkey bray that means he is either mad at the wind or happy about the hay or about to climb up on somebody's neck, so I exit the orange gate and start the hundred-yard trek to the water trough.

On a normal day, even on a normal winter day, this is easy, but today I have the challenge of memory again, trying to stay above my old trail. Sometimes if I hold my head just right, I can see the faintest ghost of the path on top of all the brand new snow. It's kind of like one of those magic-eye drawings, the way I have to look not directly at it and soften my eyes to see. Only then can I sense the slightest change in the snow surface that, princess-and-pea-like, indicates a change in the surface several feet down.

I know the trough will barely need topping off—snow has been falling into it for twenty-four hours and this kind of weather does not engender big thirst in the horses. But I have learned, over the years, that the best way to care for animals, especially barnyard animals, is to repeat the exact same tasks, in the exact same order, every day, forever and ever, amen. A change in the barnyard often means trouble, and if I do the same things the same way each day, I am more likely to notice a change. Also, any local will tell you that Murphy lives on a high-altitude ranch in a snowstorm. Were I to decide the trough did not need topping off today, this would be the day the trough heater failed, or the bottom seal wore out, or the pump froze, or a rat with Hanta virus drowned himself in there and Isaac would be just churlish enough to eat it.

I am not a good farmer. I am not even a real farmer. Rick Davie is a real farmer and I am only pretend. But the hypervigilance I learned in childhood does serve me well on the ranch in general and in big weather in particular. My mind runs a series of potential calamities, and my actions, in so much as they can, guard against them.

The trough is less than an inch down, but I top it off anyway. All systems go. Then it is back along the trail, easier the second time through, to the sheep pen, and another door that needs to be dug out.

I decide to feed the sheep inside their enclosure, something I don't do often because I try to keep the amount of inside poop down. But even with five pounds each of the warmest wool money can buy on their backs, the sheep don't want to be outside today. I give them their four flakes of hay, and drag my feet around in the snow in the outside portion of their pen until I find the three black rubber feeders which went under hours ago. I dig them out and split a coffee can of grain among all three so they don't ram each other fighting for it.

Outside the fence, the dogs are watching Sheep TV. The whole time I am in the pen they sit perfectly still in the same exact place they sit every day, staring hard, waiting for one of those sheep to make a wrong move so they can tear the chicken wire open with their teeth and rush in to rescue me from them. Their faces are so intent, so utterly concentrated, so perfect in their tandem motions every time either I or a sheep takes a step; it is a daily sight gag, a relied-upon and appreciated moment of hilarity.

I leave the sheep pen and head back on my water trail to the frost-free pump and fill a bucket to carry back to the pen. Last winter, because my back was ailing, I discovered that if I carefully plucked all the icicles that hung on the back of the barn—there were hundreds hanging at half inch intervals in accordance with the corrugated tin of the roof—and added those to the sheep's water, I could save myself a good many bucket carries. The icicles are beautiful; they renew themselves every day until it warms up enough for the roof to slide, and they feel delicious when you hold them in your hand.

Every time I walk one of these little connector trails I improve the conditions. The dogs walk with me, so it's three of us packing down the trail each time. But when we turn back toward the house the trail we made an hour ago has been utterly obliterated. I decide to wait at least until it stops howling to shovel the walkway to the house, or—a much bigger job—remake the path to the propane tank.

Last month, in a long spate of thirty-below-zero nights, the propane company called to say their man couldn't deliver propane because I did not have an "appropriate path dug from the driveway to my tank." In twenty-five years here I had never been asked to dig a path to my propane tank—appropriate or otherwise. I'd always figured that any propane man worth his salt owned a pair of snow pants. But perhaps the propane company had hired a new delivery guy who had recently moved here from Florida.

The day I got the call I channeled my outrage into action, went outside immediately and spent three hours digging a walkway to the propane tank so beautiful you could have rolled a red carpet out on it and used it for the Oscars. When I got to the tank and checked the gauge it turned out the lady on the phone had been wrong, that the guy had crawled through the deep snow and filled it after all, which made me feel better about him generally, and happy to have spent my afternoon making him such a nice path.

Today has eliminated that path, along with the driveway, which is just a suggestion of itself between the ridges Randy Woods made the last time through with his plow. Back inside, all three of us shake off snowballs in the mudroom. I put some oatmeal on for breakfast, the steel cut kind that takes forty-five minutes because why not? It's as good a day for writing as there has even been so I join Livie on the couch, open my laptop, and get to it.

Monday and Tuesday are much of the same, but Wednesday morning dawns clear, as predicted, and thirty degrees colder. I open the back door to utter stillness and ice crystals in the air. Every living being in the county, it seems, is either resting this morning or frozen in place. When I start across the path toward the corral with my apples and carrots I can hear a car crossing the cattle guard three miles and two deep bends of river canyon away.

In a few hours, Randy Woods will be here with his giant blade to reconnect me with the rest of the world, and after I finish shoveling the walkway and the path to the propane tank, the dogs and I will drive to town, pick up the mail, drop off the recycling, get a few fresh vegetables and a pint of Talenti sea salt caramel ice cream.

It will be nice, after all these days, to speak to a member of my own species, someone who can speak back in the same language. But there is another part of me, some eight-year-old part, who wants Randy's plow never to come. It's not only that the eight-year-old feels safer at the snowed-in ranch than anywhere,

it's that the snowed-in ranch was a story she used to tell herself—she is certain of it—when she needed a place for her mind
to go, when she needed a reason to make it to nine, and then ten
and eventually seventeen, and freedom.

———

Pam Houston is the author of *Contents May Have Shifted*; two collections of linked short stories, *Cowboys Are My Weakness* and *Waltz-
ing the Cat*; the novel *Sight Hound*; and a collection of essays, *A Little
More About Me*. Her stories have been selected for volumes of *Best
American Short Stories*, *The O. Henry Awards*, *The 2013 Pushcart Prize*,
and *Best American Short Stories of the Century*. She is the winner of
the Western States Book Award, the WILLA award for contemporary
fiction, The Evil Companions Literary Award and multiple teaching awards. She directs the literary nonprofit Writing By Writers, is
professor of English at UC Davis, teaches in The Institute of American Indian Art's Low-Res MFA program, and at writer's conferences
around the country and the world. She lives on a ranch at 9,000 feet in
Colorado near the headwaters of the Rio Grande.

Undergraduate Admissions Essay Draft

Elissa Washuta

———

First-Year Applicants:

Robert Frost once wrote, "Home is the place where, when you have to go there, they have to take you in." Thomas Wolfe once wrote, "You can't go home again." In an essay of 500–1000 words, explain which author you agree with and why.

I did not apply for admission to the University of North Carolina at Chapel Hill in 2003 because I couldn't, at that time, respond to their prompt.[1]

INTRODUCTION

The introduction should include the thesis statement, tell the reader what the essay is about, and contain a "hook."

———

1 This is not the exact wording of the prompt; it's my best recollection of it.

The summer I visited colleges, my younger brother and I watched *The Skulls* every day. I needed to choose the college that was most likely to have a secret society like the one Luke McNamara joined: a secret society with robes and tombs and power. My brother and I only spoke to each other in movie quotes:

"You've been digging, Luke, and if you keep digging, you'll be digging your own grave."

"Our membership has its pleasure, its hardship, and sometimes its pain."

"Our rules supersede those of the outside world."

"We have been watching. We will be watching."

"We live by the rules, we die by the rules."

I didn't know, then, that there were places without crickets, without mothers. I didn't know that the rubbing of tiny legs was happening outside my body because it had always been in my ears. I wanted a dead place, anyway, having dreamed about the city. When fall came, I applied to colleges with brick buildings choked by ivy. In the spring, I chose a college built in a place where I had made only two memories: campus tour and scholarship interview. In the summer, I bought bed sheets out of a catalog and, with every bright plastic item I acquired that matched the sheets, I felt my grip clenching upon my tidy new world. I lived on the seventh floor, which is a height so extreme that nothing can grow there, like on Saturn. This is not the room where my body died, but it's the room that taught me what it would be like to live without my old body and grow a new one.

You might want to write the introduction last.

First Body Paragraph

The first body paragraph should contain the strongest argument

- *or the most significant example*
- *or the most illuminative illustration*
- *or a good starting place*

and it should include a topic sentence relating to the thesis.

In the freshman dorm, unlike at home, the residents are nasty. Some people learn to use the microwave for the first time. Some people learn to vomit. I learned to sleep in a room with another body in it. I didn't learn to be naked in front of another person; I didn't know I was supposed to. My roommate and I changed in the bathroom behind closed stall doors. Some people learn to fuck each other in the freshman dorm, but I didn't. I learned that nobody was like me. For example, every night, I sat in the dark and watched *Fight Club* or *American Beauty* while my roommate hung out with her friends, an activity I could not imagine, describe, or replicate. When I returned to my parents' house for Thanksgiving, I recognized the smell of the forest soaked into the walls—I had thought that was the smell of the universe, or of the skin inside my nose. When hardwood creaked under my feet, my legs shot taproots into the floor. I hadn't known that the whole world wasn't made from smoke and ferns. When I was a child, I asked my dad why the world smelled different in springtime. "It's the bacteria released from the thaw," he said. Later, I would learn that I was full of more bacterial cells than human cells. I was made of thaw. The dorm was made of grime on the undersides of things. I could not live there.

Second Body Paragraph

Each body paragraph will have the same basic structure. Body paragraphs are the middle paragraphs that lie between the introduction and conclusion. A strong body paragraph supports your thesis statement or central argument using claims, evidence, and

*analysis. It is in the body of the essay that your preparation comes
to fruition: your topic must now be investigated through argument.*

I learned that college had nothing to do with ivy. Some of
the buildings must have been throttled by the vines' tiny fingers,
but I don't remember which. What I do remember from that
first year must be what college was about: eating as many eggs
per day as I wanted without concern for cholesterol; avoiding
the protestors outside the biology building who displayed photos of mangled flesh labeled "MURDERED BABY, 16 WEEKS,"
or something like that, alongside photos of people in Nazi con-
centration camps; weeping in two professors' offices in a single
hour; handing my completed calculus quizzes to my TA, watching him look them over, feeling his warm whisper in my ear,
returning to my desk to write down the solutions he gave me,
and receiving a perfect score in the class; eating two slices of
chocolate cake on my birthday, alone in my dorm in the dark
with styrofoam balanced on my knees; passing the football
stadium but never entering because I was afraid of young men
who raised their voices; knowing about Route 1, the road bor-
dering the campus, a boundary between our brick and the frat
row brick, but never going there because I was afraid of people
who gathered after basketball games to burn couches and throw
rocks through windows and rip off their shirts; consuming the
contents of my parents' care packages in a single sitting; knowing about the cow outfitted with a hole in its side through which
people could reach, for research or spectacle, without harm-
ing the cow; encountering black squirrels, whose large population on campus resulted from the introduction of eighteen
black squirrels at the National Zoo during Teddy Roosevelt's
presidency for reasons unknown. All of this differs from what
my house was about: fingering moss; sitting on the porch and

listening to Ace of Base for hours every summer night; speaking with cats; swimming in the lake while never forgetting for a moment that I believed it to be packed with water snakes; being quiet with the three people who knew me deeply because we were made of the same bacteria; never, for a second, thinking about taxonomy when I picked berries and salted slugs and sat under trees and yelled at black bears who strolled through the yard, and never identifying any insect sound because it never occurred to me that those sounds were made by individual creatures rather than a vast field of living energy. Home was a place unlike campus: at home, I was one of the animals; on campus, there were no animals, only installations.

Third Body Paragraph: Try an Accordion Paragraph!

Accordion paragraphs are written according to a specific structure:
Topic sentence: position, "power statement," claim
   Reason/fact/detail
     Analyze/explain
   [Repeat several times; the paragraph can expand like an
     accordion!]
Conclusion: summarize, convince, challenge
Remember to use transitional words and expressions to unify
your paragraph.

During freshman year, my boyfriend Arthur—leftover from high school, two years older, and a college dropout—moved to College Park, despite my protests, because he had nothing better to do and thought he might become useful by bearing down upon my newly unfettered life.

He thought that without him there, the way I walked on campus alone after dark, I might be raped.

That there were streetlights meant, to him, that there were treacheries needing illumination; every person was a potential threat, and even in crowds, I wasn't safe, because in this concrete place, nobody would look out for me.

Also, he thought that without him there, I might never figure out how to comport myself among the dangers.

For example, every dorm-residing student was either required to get the meningitis vaccine or get their primary doctor to sign an exemption form. Arthur told me the vaccine would eat my flesh, starting with my brain, and I could never go back to the person I was before. I didn't believe this—I believed meningitis was everywhere, and would surely work its way into my brainstem and make my spine swell until it burst through my vertebrae, sending their splinters like shrapnel into my organs, but two years into this relationship, I had run out of the energy needed to challenge him. When I presented the doctor with my form, my mom, a nurse, looked on in horror. Usually, she and Dad let me make mistakes and learn from the pain, but this one required intervention. "Do you remember what I told you about infections? What they are?" Dad asked. Of course I remembered. "There's a war going on," I said. "Exactly," he said. Sometimes, the body has everything it needs to fight the war; other times, the body will wage the war but die when facing an unknown enemy for which it never could have prepared. Inside the campus clinic whose mental health floor would, years later, become more familiar to me than the dining hall, I received my meningitis vaccine. I tore off the little round Band-Aid and never told Arthur what I'd done.

Additionally, he thought that without him there, I might forget about him.

He knew I logged off instant messenger for hours most nights, and he didn't believe that I was doing what I said I was doing: walking around campus. And anyway, I shouldn't be doing that, he said, because I might be raped. And anyway, where was I walking and why? To clear my head, I said, but actually, I was walking around looking for the history TA I believed I loved, though we'd never spoken. Somehow, Arthur knew. He got an apartment not far from campus and took two buses and a train so he could accompany me to my history lectures. The next year, when I first tried to break up with Arthur, I told him that—*still*—I loved a man to whom I had never spoken. "I think you should go for it," Arthur said. "I think you should walk into his office wearing no shirt and a bra." I told him I wasn't going to do that and I didn't want to talk about it anymore. "Just go in wearing a sports bra, like you've just been running," he said. "I think you wouldn't like that," I said, "I think you'd be jealous." And he said, "Not at all. I want to know that someone is doing the things to you that you never let me do." He meant sex.

I believe he put a hex on me.

Fourth Body Paragraph

Sometimes, during the writing process, we realize that we have omitted key information that will provide background to the reader. Fear not—the work of reorganization is a key component of the revision process! While drafting, get down as much relevant information as you can, knowing that you can move it, cut it, or

*expand upon it later. Sometimes, we only come to know our posi-
tion fully through engaging in a written support of an argument.*

I realize now that I'm supposed to talk about my *background*, which is a code word for my status as an enrolled member in the Cowlitz Indian Tribe, and the struggles I have faced as
a Native American. But my *background*, as I understood it at age
eighteen—which was a limited understanding because it didn't
extend back into the generations that came before me—did not
include struggle. I grew up in Mountain Lake, New Jersey—not
a town, not even a township, but a community within a mostly
forest township. At the center of this community was a lake. At
the periphery were streets, including mine, set above the road
circling the lake. I grew up in the woods, in a sense—there were
neighbors, but there were also acres of forest. I found paths
where none had been cut. Every time I stepped into the woods, I
met new wonders: the dozen foot-long night crawlers that raced
across dead leaves when I lifted a broad stone; the heap of stones
where I believed snakes were living. The cicadas sent unified
shivers through the air between the trees. I set my pulse by their
rhythm. Growing up in the woods, I became so accustomed
to magic that I watched Disney's *Alice in Wonderland* on loop,
wishing our backyard moss would turn, in the dark, into Alice's
mome raths, a cluster of small, helpful, multicolored creatures
with bug-eyes. At night, I locked the doors and gathered the cats
when no one else thought we needed to; I was afraid of the sinis-
ter unknown. I couldn't explain why I thought the woods would
rush in through the unlocked door to consume me. Really, the
only unsafe time was hunting season, when we were reminded
what, to other people, the forest was meant for. None of this,
though, is relevant to a college admissions essay; I must demonstrate that I have overcome obstacles.

You can always develop this key information in your second draft.

Fifth Body Paragraph

While in high school, you may have only had experience with the five-paragraph essay, in college, you may find that you are expected to write considerably longer essays. You might treat the entire essay as an "accordion essay," expanding as needed to explore your topic and support your argument.

When mom would ask to have a bite of my ice cream cone, I would protest: at health camp, I had learned that communicable disease could be spread through saliva. "We have the same germs," she would say, and I didn't think that was right. However, it was. According to Lax et al. in an study of families and the microbial communities in their homes, "Humans sharing a home were more microbially similar than those not sharing a home," and when an individual leaves the home even for three days, that individual's contribution to the microbiome is measurably diminished, suggesting that the human microbiome signature on surfaces quickly disappears.[2] In "Sources of Airborne Microorganisms in the Built Environment," Prussin and Marr write that microbial communities in different indoor environments—schools, houses—are markedly different, in part because of different sources of airborne microorganisms in the built environment: "humans; pets; plants; plumbing systems;

---

2 S. Lax, D. P. Smith, J. Hampton-Marcell, S. M. Owens, K. M. Handley, N. M. Scott, S. M. Gibbons, P. Larsen, B. D. Shogan, S. Weiss, J. L. Metcalf, L. K. Ursell, Y. Vazquez-Baeza, W. Van Treuren, N. A. Hasan, M. K. Gibson, R. Colwell, G. Dantas, R. Knight, and J. A. Gilbert. "Longitudinal Analysis of Microbial Interaction Between Humans and the Indoor Environment." *Science* 345, no. 6200 (2014): 1048–1052. doi:10.1126/science.1254529.

heating, ventilation, and air-conditioning systems; mold; dust resuspension; and the outdoor environment." However, the greatest impact upon the microbiome in a space did not result from human occupancy; "Rather, microbial communities observed in indoor air were closely related with those in outdoor air, and changes in microbial communities in outdoor air were mirrored by changes in indoor air."[3] Therefore, when I left my home, I changed it completely; when I was away, I was altered; when I returned, it was to a place I'd never been to.

Sixth Body Paragraph

Have you adequately provided support for your thesis statement? Read it over again and use your final body paragraph to present any additional findings.

Throughout this essay, in exploring the question of whether or not one can go home again and whether or not they have to take you in if you do, I have avoided directly addressing my most persuasive and consequential fact: that, halfway through my sophomore year, the night I broke up with my longtime boyfriend, I was raped by a boy I knew only a little; that I didn't tell my parents for a year because I believed it was my fault and wasn't even sure it was rape; and that I would never fully inhabit my home again, in some ways, because it was a sanctuary and some part of me believed my presence might defile it. But I was the only one who ever wondered whether home should take me in when I came back altered. The moss was there, and the blue jays were there, and the night crawlers were there, and the ferns were there, and the cedars were there, and the cats were there,

---

3 Aaron J. Prussin and Linsey C. Marr. "Sources of Airborne Microorganisms in the Built Environment." *Microbiome* 3, no. 1 (2015): 3, 7. doi:10.1186/ s40168-015-0144-z.

and the people were there, all thriving in a place where the only constant was change.

Conclusion

This final section brings the essay to a satisfying end, summarizing the connections made in the body paragraphs to the thesis statement. The reader should experience a feeling of finality and a thorough understanding of your point. The conclusion should contain the strongest and clearest statement of your message because it is what the reader is left with. Do not bring up new information or the other side of the argument; less is more.

In conclusion, in college, I learned about the change that happens when someone gets deep inside a body and puts his bacteria there. I learned that my wound was infested with microbes I'd never known. I learned that my home is a body: it lives by regeneration, turning over its every cell until it is both completely new and completely recognizable. A creature in flux, I belonged there.

And Now, Rewrite Your Introduction

After completing your first draft, you may want to revisit your introductory paragraph, rewriting it now that you know the ground you will cover in the essay. The introduction should serve as a "map" for the journey you will take the reader on over the course of the essay.

Cicadas' dead bodies littered every campus sidewalk during the spring of my freshman year of college. Growing up in the woods as a child, I heard cicadas, and I saw their translucent brown skins sloughed off and clinging to peeling cedar trunks. But I had never seen anything like the mass appearance and death of cicadas on campus. This phenomenon was known as

Brood X, a huge group of cicadas that, every seventeen years, tunnels to the surface of the ground to lay eggs and then die. When I returned home and saw their husks clinging to trees, I could imagine the corpses, knowing now that these skins were shed by animals with wings, animals that had hidden dormant underground for most of my lifetime, safe from predators. They emerged in a massive group so they would be too plentiful for predators to consume them all, increasing the cicadas' likelihood of surviving long enough to reproduce. They live in trees. They feed on sap. They are *cryptic*, avoiding predator detection by concealment. And so, when I returned home after my first year of college and saw the delicate exoskeletons I used to collect in jars, I realized I had never paid attention to what I was meant to learn: that I could never truly go home again, because the woods had been telling me all along that some places provide protection, and others provide none, but we need to tunnel out from under the ground. Because we are humans, and humans believe we are not part of nature, maybe we'll find parts of ourselves consumed by others' violent actions that defy the universe's instructions for living in it. Maybe we will do the work we will exist to do. Certainly, we will die. The forest is made of death and change, and as I will demonstrate in this essay, I am made of the forest, made of change, made of the sound of hundreds of millions of the body's cells dying every minute.

———

Elissa Washuta is a member of the Cowlitz Indian Tribe and the author of two books, *Starvation Mode* and *My Body Is a Book of Rules*, named a finalist for the Washington State Book Award. She is an assistant professor of English at the Ohio State University.

Inheritance

———

Elisabeth Eaves

A t twenty-five, I was looking for a way out—of town, of my relationship, of the life I had created—when my mother invited me on a trip to Baja, Mexico. A trip with my mother, however temporary a solution, was at least an opportunity for respite. That winter I was working part-time jobs while applying to graduate school, a bright goal that kept me going when I felt mired in quicksand, which was most of the time. From the point of view of my parents, or indeed anyone over the age of forty, it might have looked like I had my whole life ahead of me, but I wanted to start over. I felt old, and disconcerted that I had come dangerously close to messing everything up before even really getting started.

My parents, meanwhile, had recently gone in on property in Baja with a windsurfing-obsessed Oregonian, and intended to build a house. I was floored by this out-of-character behavior. They had always travelled, frugally and independently, sometimes returning with books, pottery, or yards of fabric. As a family of four we had lived abroad, and taken vacations during which we piled into Turkish minivans and Mexican buses. My mother is a psychologist who taught me to shop for clothes in thrift stores, and my father was a math professor who, among his off-hour activities, enjoyed poring over stock market reports and family balance sheets. We never wanted for anything, but we were not the kind of people who bought luxuries or owned a second home. Vacation houses were for families with more money and a different definition of leisure, one that involved cocktails and golf. Or so I thought. As I boarded the plane, I tried to reconcile what my parents had taught me about travel in Mexico—you take the chicken bus—with the new reality that we would have a place of our own.

It would become much more than just a vacation house. As my parents were reborn there, so it grounded me through many transitions. And perhaps because I moved so often in my outside life, saying unceremonious goodbyes to one urban apartment after another, over the seventeen years that we owned the place in Baja, it came to feel like my true home.

On that first trip, we flew into the languid seaside city of La Paz and rented a convertible Volkswagen Bug, a model still ubiquitous around the region in the late nineties. A two-lane, mostly shoulder-less highway circled the cape, and we drove it, top down, taking turns at the wheel over several days, eating lunch on beaches where pelicans flocked to incoming fishermen. We spent a night in the mission town of Todos Santos, another amid sun-burnt sailors and margarita slingers in Cabo San Lucas. We drove north along the east side of the cape and stayed in a whitewashed, hillside inn in Los Barriles with a view of the Sea of Cortez, the sparkling, 700-mile-long expanse separating mainland Mexico from the Baja Peninsula, imbuing the latter with its sense of isolation. Cut off from the rest of the continent by water on three sides and an endless two-lane highway running north, southern Baja was a world apart, vast and sleepy, where natural forces never seemed far away. Bright colors delighted me at every turn: a turquoise pottery duck for sale in a market, a garishly striped woven rug on a hotel wall, a colonial-era building painted two tones of vivid pink. I resuscitated my lapsed habit of journal writing, and took pictures of the homemade roadside shrines erected to commemorate the victims of car accidents. The sky was sharp blue by day, teeming with stars by night. Cardón cactuses, among the world's largest, assembled in abundant forests like many-limbed Wild West outlaws.

One morning we drove a couple of hours north from Los Barriles. The road, rutted by hurricanes, was, in places, washed over with sand. Cows crossed unhurriedly. We had to put up the Bug's top and roll up our windows to avoid choking on dust along stretches of unpaved road. Finally, a spur led us to a wide bay called La Ventana, or "the window," named for the way the wind rolls straight in through a frame created by the southern tip of Cerralvo Island and the northern tip of Punta Arena de La Ventana.

On this bay sat the village of El Sargento, a handful of one-story homes, some made of raw cinderblock and others candy-bright. There the road turned to dirt again. Ten minutes further on, we parked at a spot marked by a few iron stakes. A plateau of desert plants sloped down gently to a low bluff, which dropped to a sandy beach and the aquamarine sea. This was where the house would stand one day. A few small, vivid sails cut across the bay as an invisible hand whipped up the morning's first white caps. I felt a sense of desire that was simultaneously

fulfilled, the scene stoking a wish and granting it all at once. I
began to believe I could untangle the knot I had created. Look,
my parents seemed to be saying, you can start a new life. If they
could change course in their sixties, surely I could do it in my
twenties. I knew then that I would return from this vacation
with a greater sense of detachment from what I wanted to leave
behind—the boyfriend, the house, the city—and more hope for
the future.

It was almost two years before I went back to La Ventana, on
a winter break from graduate school in New York, and by then
my parents had built their new house. It was a one-story home,
the color of warm sand, with terra cotta tiles and interior walls
that were white, yellow, and red. The master bedroom, office,
living room, dining room, and kitchen all faced the sea; standing at the kitchen sink was like standing on the bridge of a great
ship, looking out over the water. I watched the steely, disciplined
pelicans flying in tight formation while I washed dishes, waiting
for a bird to break off and dive-bomb the surface. Sometimes,
from the patio or roof deck, we would see a whale breach far
out towards Cerralvo Island, mighty blues or humpbacks on the
annual migration to their breeding grounds.

I was still unused to the idea that my parents had built a
second home, and not in some brooding landscape of dark ever-
greens and opaque waters like Vancouver, where my younger
brother and I were raised, but under Baja's expansive sky, where
the sun lit up even the underwater world. My newly retired father sank his teeth into the project of operating a home in a
barely-on-the-grid corner of Mexico, somehow completely in
his element. No public utilities ran to the house when it was first
built. He relished the opportunity to put his Spanish to practical
use as he dealt with builders and banks; now he could stay on

top of accounts in two languages, which was his idea of a good time. Over the course of his retirement, he would also take up Italian and Chinese.

Together my parents bought ornately painted ceramic sinks and rustic wooden furniture. They had balky solar panels installed. My mother planted cactuses, aloe vera, and bougainvillea. They hired a gardener and caretaker, Manuel, for the months when they weren't there. He was exactly my father's age—born in 1933—and a former fisherman with a large clan and a fenced compound near the church. The two of them had long, winding conversations about water supplies, insects, and plants, my dad struggling with Manuel's dropped consonants. My mother found an old cowbell on one of her walks and affixed it to the wrought-iron gate to our courtyard. It became our de facto doorbell, alerting us with its hollow music whenever someone arrived.

My parents made Baja friends—windsurfers and gringo retirees—and even consumed the occasional margarita. These new friends, who I would meet on my visits, all seemed to know a slightly different pair of people than I did. To them, David and Linda enjoyed leisure. They had people over for drinks. They owned kayaks. These things resonated with nothing I had ever observed during the eighteen years I had lived with my parents.

I snorkeled in the Sea of Cortez for the first time, descending the newly built concrete stairs to the beach and swimming out in front of the house. Floating above the rocks, I tailed yellow and black angelfish, sergeant majors with their vertical stripes, clusters of tiny puffer fish, and long, silvery cornetfish. Schools of blue-and-gold snappers swam in towards shore, then darted back out to sea. Reef fish are highly territorial, and every day I swam out I saw the same individual boxfish loitering around the same rock formation. I would float on the surface until I spotted it, about six inches long, deep indigo-black and covered with white polka dots.

At dawn, six days a week, a droning, rhythmic buzz rose from the water. It was fishermen leaving the village in the simple, sturdy outboards called pangas, bows slapping the water like metronomes. They paralleled the shore, heading north every morning, and returned before the afternoon winds picked up. If you timed it right, you could intercept a fisherman on the beach upon his return, and buy a huachinango—a Pacific red snapper—before he sold his haul to the trucks that came from Los Cabos and La Paz. In the afternoons, windsurfers steered their taut, triangular sails on miles-long reaches towards open sea before tacking back to shore. We watched them like we watched the birds, admiring color, grace, and the way they knew how to use an air current to their advantage.

In those early days there were fewer houses around, and the wildlife still had a tendency to encroach. One morning I opened the door to the bathroom and there, coiled into a spiral on the tiled shower floor, was a disturbingly long, thick snake. I caught my breath, stepped back, and slammed the door shut. Then I slowly cracked it open and peeked back in: I hadn't imagined it. It was pale and scaly, with distinctive black and brown blotches in a symmetrical row along its full length, the marks of a rattlesnake. It was larger than the ones I'd seen, alive and dead, on nearby roads, or maybe it just looked bigger because it was curled in my shower. I closed the door and heard my heart pound.

Immediately regressing, I did what any child would do in the situation: I called my dad—the professor, the suburbanite, the late-night mathematician. And he, after taking a look at the creature and closing the door with great care, scratched his head and stroked his beard as he pondered options. It wasn't as though there was some snake removal service you could call, even if we had had a telephone. Still, I was surprised when he returned from the garage with a machete. "We have a machete?" I asked my mom.

I did not see the ensuing operation. I heard clanging and grunting; forever after there would be gash marks on the tile. "Don't go in there," he said when he emerged, sweat beads visible on his forehead. "It's a mess."

Most of the specific, fully articulated advice I remember my dad ever giving me had to do with cars and money: Check your oil. Carry tire chains in the trunk. Buy real estate and index funds, and don't try to game the stock market. On a long, late-afternoon walk through the cactus-covered hillside, earth rosy in the waning light, he urged me to open a Roth IRA. He rarely weighed in on anyone I was dating, but when he did, he tended to be right. I called home in tears once from a sublet in New York's Soho; the man I was seeing had broken it off. My chattier, more outwardly emotional mother was absent, so I laid it all on my father. After listening for a while, he said simply, "it sounds like he's bad news for you." And somehow that made the truth suddenly obvious and actionable.

When I got pulled over for speeding in my Ford Escort at the age of nineteen, my father, who I feared would be mad, sat down beside me and with no rancor, compared me to a loaf of bread that just wasn't quite baked. Even two decades later, during what would turn out to be his later years, I wasn't entirely sure that I was. In the years after my parents built the Baja house, I moved to New York, then to Washington, DC, then to Paris. Then New York again. My parents visited me in every city where I lived. In Brooklyn my father, by then well into his seventies, hoisted a heavy armoire onto his back, where it dwarfed him, and carried it up the steps into my apartment building.

Living back in North America, I discovered a five-hour direct flight from Newark to Los Cabos. The southern cape was developing, and the state had paved one of the dirt roads between Los Cabos and La Ventana, cutting the three-hour drive from the airport in half. I could leave Brooklyn in the early morning and be at the house by mid-afternoon.

We kept a stick-shift Nissan pickup truck with a broken air conditioner at the house. During absences, mice sometimes took up residence in the engine and we had to make sure they didn't chew through anything essential. I drove around in flip flops, Mexican folk music blaring from the radio, now happily reminded of my own primordial muck, before Baja and writing for pay, a time of crummy cars, poor decisions, sunshine, and bare feet. All the locals who had sold lots to foreigners had purring, big-tired, shiny trucks, amid which our Nissan was an eyesore. Friends who came to visit asked if we couldn't please use their rental cars instead. I took an irrational pleasure in our old truck, though. The pickup was part of the place for me, and the place reminded me subtly that I didn't have to live one particular way. In New York I worked at a magazine, endured blizzards, and deemed car ownership insane. But in Baja, the spot where my parents played out a new act, I felt like I still had choices about who I was going to be.

When, around 2012, my parents first said they were thinking about selling the house, I hoped they were just floating the idea, conducting a mental experiment. I felt a deep sense of possession, as though something that was rightfully mine was under threat. I argued with my dad. What he never said explicitly was that he had less energy these days. That caring for the house was draining him, physically and mentally. He had begun to feel the responsibility as a burden. I offered to take it over, to buy it. In fact, I didn't have the money to do this, but beyond my lack of funds, I sensed that he didn't want me to have it at any price. He preferred not to bequeath his children a remote, high-maintenance stucco house at risk of annual hurricane damage. The old, preretirement dad was back, the one who didn't dabble in luxuries, who preferred owning things that made sense on spreadsheets. I tried to reason him away from this point of view, with no luck.

They listed it, but it didn't sell. They stopped going to Baja, but I continued my annual pilgrimage.

When I first met Joe, another wandering writer, I told him during one of our earliest conversations that I would like to someday drive from Vancouver to Baja's southern cape. He said that sounded fun. Four years later, married and living on the West Coast again, we did. We covered the thousand-mile stretch south of Tijuana in three days, taking turns at the wheel of our nicked but sturdy Subaru, plunging through canyons of elephantine boulders, winding above the sea, pausing in missionary towns surrounded by lush oases.

On La Ventana bay, the pangas didn't buzz northward every morning anymore, due to a combination of overfishing and the lure of other trades. Fish were, paradoxically, easier to get, because instead of haggling with a lone fisherman, you could just go to the pescaderia in town. There was a proper tortilleria now, too, and well-marked trails all over the hills where you could run or ride a mountain bike. In winter, you could now take a yoga class any day of the week. Windsurfing had all but disappeared, but kiteboarding had boomed, and now we watched that sport's airborne sails move south along the bay every afternoon.

My polka-dotted boxfish, or its progeny, still lurked around the same rocky reef where I had always seen it. Manuel had passed away the previous fall at the age of seventy-nine, so I visited his widow at their compound to pay respects on behalf of myself and my parents.

The house entered into contract a month after we learned the cancer in my father's bowels was stage four. Joe and I were in Baja when he started chemotherapy. I felt glad I could be at the house one last time, but uneasy over the miles between my dad and me. I embraced the practical tasks that fell to me during that trip, like letting the realtor in to inventory the contents; they made me feel useful in the face of an otherwise helpless situation. For all my earlier railing against the idea of selling, I felt some relief when I looked at a crack in the wall and realized I didn't have to worry about whether it was caused by a shift in the foundation—it wasn't going to be my problem. This is what my father was unburdening me of, and now it was my job to help him.

The final time I left the Baja house, I took a last look at the sea from the roof, then descended the outdoor stairs and climbed into the car, which was fully packed for the 2,300-mile drive ahead. Joe had checked the oil, as he always does before a trip, and was seated at the wheel.

After I got in, he jumped out and ran to the courtyard gate, from where I heard a familiar, hollow tolling. A moment later he was back in the car, where he handed me the cow bell that had hung on our gate for so many years. We drove through El Sargento, now many times larger than it was during my first visit. We passed Manuel's home, the church, and the pescaderia, and drove from dirt onto paved road. Tawny hills met blue sky met dark blue sea, Baja's three-part color wheel. At a new building that housed the realtor's office, Joe pulled over, and I got out and dropped off the keys. My dad now had one less thing to worry about.

He passed away five months later. The cow bell now sits on my desk in our urban home. Occasionally, I ring it, and I'm back in Baja—my father fiddling with some repair, my mother puttering in the garden, and me at my desk, looking out at the pelicans and sails.

———

Elisabeth Eaves is the author of *Wanderlust: A Love Affair with Five Continents* and *Bare: The Naked Truth About Stripping*. Her writing has been anthologized in *The Best American Travel Writing* (2009), *The Best Women's Travel Writing* (2010), and Lonely Planet's *A Moveable Feast*, and she is the winner of three Lowell Thomas awards from the Society of American Travel Writers. An editor at the *Bulletin of the Atomic Scientists* and a former staff writer at *Forbes*, she has also written for *Afar*, *Marie Claire*, the *New York Times*, *Slate*, the *Wall Street Journal*, and many other publications. She is also the co-founder of Type Set, a co-working space for writers in Seattle. Elisabeth lives in Seattle with her husband, Joe.

We Carried Ourselves
Like Villagers

——

Catina Bacote

I go back and whole apartment buildings are gone. Brush completely covers the brook. There are no basketball courts, clotheslines, or cellar doors. The wooden logs that marked the bus stop have been taken up, too. Even the sign, green with white letters, EASTERN CIRCLE has been done away with. I watch a few kids run around in the cool evening air, under a darkening sky. My childhood here may not have been so different from theirs, but then again maybe it was, because even though the layout is the same—apartment buildings strung along a sloping hill, thin trees scattered here and there, and a handful of parking lots—the spirit of the place has changed.

The projects lie on the easternmost edge of the city and when I was growing up it seemed as far away from the mall, McDonald's, Burger King, and the Coliseum as any neighborhood could get while still being in New Haven. It felt like we were more in the country than in the city, and it wasn't just the shallow brook that we jumped across or the rust-colored cliffs that broke the skyline; it was the way we just about lived outside in the summer and how we could recognize someone from far away by the cut of his face or the curve of his back as an Allen or a Diamond or a Ricks. It seemed like only a dozen or so families lived in the neighborhood because so many of us had relatives there, whole clans with long-standing ties to the projects stretched from the top of the hill all the way to its bottom.

We carried ourselves like villagers—charming, quiet, territorial—and even though our well-being didn't hinge on the rotation of crops or a robust rainy season, our rhythms were still in tune with the seasons. Regardless of what the calendar announced, we marked summer from the first warm day of spring to the last balmy day of fall; winter was no more than a holding pattern, a time to cool down and rest, because as soon as the days got longer, Eastern Circle opened up.

Picture the first hint of clear skies and rising temperatures: shorts yanked from the bottom of drawers, feet slipped into dusty sandals, apartment doors thrown wide, and hundreds— and I mean hundreds—of kids waking up from a short slumber, a hypnotic haze, and fanning out across the projects. We didn't just settle for jump rope or Mother-May-I, we put our hands on everything Eastern Circle offered: stacking mud pies along the side of buildings, catching caterpillars in mason jars, and spreading eagle on the ground, one eye opened and the other closed, aiming our marble for the makeshift hole.

The ground below our feet and the sky hovering above our heads belonged to us and nothing in our line of sight was off limits, except the thicket of Slippery Elms and Red Pines that stirred behind the brick buildings. Once nighttime came slow and easy, and made its way over the day, snakes, dogs, skunks, raccoons, and possums scurried into the projects. Only the small striped skunks left something behind. And since I had lived in Eastern Circle all my life I recognized the stench of their spray—musk and rot—as easily as the mouthwatering smells of bacon and grits and sweet potato pie. But most of the time the shadowy world of knotted trees and thick branches served as only a backdrop to all our fun.

Except for the day my friend and I skidded back and forth in my grandparents' yard kicking up dirt. Around the time when I called *safe* and she whined *no fair*, the massive trunks and twisted branches unleashed a pack of dogs. They didn't seem to move toward us as much as drop down on us, a sudden hailstorm of muscled jaws, dark gums, and teeth. I ran one way and my friend ran another, and the dogs chased her. She stumbled up a rocky hill on the side of the yard before the dogs pinned her against a wall. Up on their hind legs, they growled in her face. She cried. They moved in closer. Her ponytails bobbed in and out of my sight. Hollering, I jumped up and down.

My grandfather rushed through his screen door with a huge wooden stick, charging right into the pack of dogs. His voice boomed. The span of his broad back widened. Dust rose as high as his cheekbones. And just as quickly as they had come, the dogs retreated.

Living in Eastern Circle and being under Dada's watchful eye were one and the same. Stories from my family and neighbors about his acts of rescue were varied: Dada found a finger that had been severed and flung into the grass. Dada caught the pregnant woman flying down a flight of stairs. Dada arrived a moment before the bully threw his first punch. And even if you hadn't heard any of the stories or spent time hanging out with him on his porch you knew his garden.

The twenty rows of fruits and vegetables stood out from everything around it. The projects' two-story brick apartment buildings looked identical. Each one had six apartments, all with the same white metal screen door. The garden broke up the monotony; its shades of emerald, ruby red, burnt orange, and gold deepened with the day's changing light; from week to week, buds spread and leaves unfurled. Even the dirt, raked and moist, yielded variation: smooth stones broken into bits, tiny sand crystals, dark clay.

People came by the house just to be near it.

I lived up the hill from my grandparents with my mother and brother. Whenever I walked to my grandparents' house Dada's garden slowly came into view: tomato plants wrapped around branches, yellow squash tucked between leaves, eggplant suspended from vines like dark half moons. The last time I visited him I was a teenager and his work from the morning had left its mark. The loosened soil and watered rose buds gave the yard a sweet, earthy smell.

We sat on the porch and dealt with matters big and small, like what kind of grades I had earned during my freshman year of high school and what he thought of my new boyfriend. He didn't go on and on about what needed to be done or spin corny homilies like *do your best* or *be careful*. It wasn't his style, plus he liked to hear me talk. He thought all my words lined up just right, even my beginner's Spanish. So with great exaggeration I shook my mouth loose and told him to repeat after me: *azul, marron, dorado, violeta*. Raising only one of his eyebrows and clearing his throat, he asked me if I was ready. I pretended to think about it before I nodded. He didn't speak Spanish, but he like to put on a show, so he gave a lot of weight to each word and rolled his r's way too long. I leaned into his shoulder and laughed.

I've come back to Eastern Circle because my memories of my grandfather rest here and even though it's been over twenty years since I lived in the projects I've never found a place that felt so much like home. My grandparents moved into the development the first year it opened, in 1960, and four generations of my family have settled on this land. Sometimes I conjure up the neighborhood as more mythical than real, and I let my memories have their way, because there is an understanding to be gained in the mythical too—a way to get at a truth that can't be reached any other way.

When my family lived in Eastern Circle it was one tight-knit neighborhood. Twenty-one apartment buildings and one hundred and twenty black families all held together by the circle: a ring-shaped street in the center of the projects. Now walkways and signs divide buildings into distinct sections. And the porches flanked by two white columns look separate from everything around them. The kids have fewer places to gather, too: most of the grass fields have been replaced by concrete. The neighborhood seems like a scattering of apartments with nothing at its center.

As I come closer to the building where my grandparents used to live, a strange sensation comes over me. It's not a feeling of dread or anxiety, but something else. I'm trying to understand exactly what's happening as the past comes into view: their front door, the porch, the two living room windows, the small dirt yard. I think I expected to feel only one thing when I got to their old apartment—comfort or distress, certainty or confusion—but I'm experiencing the pleasures of my childhood and the pain of my teenage years all at once. I abandoned this part of my life for so long that I have no idea how to walk back into it.

A couple of days after sitting with my grandfather on his porch and laughing at his showmanship I made a decision that I'm desperate to undo. I spotted my mother's journal on our stairway; it was brown with musical notes on the cover and for the first time ever I picked it up. I was searching for an answer, about how to deal with my feelings or at least understand them. Flipping through the pages I found the day, June 11, 1987.

My mother had only written: *My father died.*

I convinced myself that those words were enough. Dada had been shot and killed while breaking up a fight. I figured the only way to survive losing him was through restraint. I didn't talk about him to my friends, I wouldn't put up any photos that had him in them, and I've still never been to visit his grave—all a feeble attempt to move forward.

After Dada died and after I had left Eastern Circle for college, a mural went up in the projects. It was spray painted on the side of one of the apartment buildings, not far from where my grandparents used to live. The guys from the Circle chipped in to pay a graffiti artist from another neighborhood to paint it. The letters R.I.P. were huge and around it were the names of a handful of residents who had been killed. Like my best friend's brother who was nineteen years old and found shot to death in a nearby park. The mural was large enough to be seen from the circular street in the center of the projects, which was where I stood. I could make out Dada's name easily: *James Allen Jr.*

I thought it was *nice* of the guys to include Dada since his death wasn't a part of all that had happened. He had been killed right around the time that coke and heroin bowed down to crack, when users became addicts, and small guns were put aside for Glocks. The guys in Eastern Circle became the East View Posse to set themselves apart from the other gangs in the city. All these years later I've found out that the fight my grandfather was breaking up was between them and outsiders. At one time Eastern Circle, nestled away from the rest of New Haven, afforded us a safety we couldn't count on anywhere else. But it also meant that when drugs and guns flooded city streets we were on our own.

I look toward the brick wall that the mural had been painted on—the wall is still there, but of course, the mural isn't. I wander further up the hill taking in everything that's been revamped or done away with and wonder what it takes for an entire neighborhood to change course.

Twenty years after my grandfather's murder all the residents were made to leave Eastern Circle, and a demolition began. Nine apartment buildings came down and even part of the street that made up the circle was broken apart and carted off. What was left was built back up. Since my grandfather's death I've tried to start over, too, but have managed it in only fits and starts.

From my vantage point at the top of the hill I can see all the changes the housing authority has made to make the projects safer. Their office is very visible—as are the security cameras attached to the side of buildings—and the circular street was cut off because they figured it made it easy for people buying drugs to come in and out. At one time, the circle felt like a symbol for our lives in the projects. But maybe with its allusions to peace and harmony, it had promised too much.

The name of the street leading into the projects has been changed, too. Later I find out that it was named after Levi Jackson, who grew up in New Haven. In 1946 he enrolled at Yale University and joined its football team as its first black player.

Eastern Circle is now Jackson Lane. Renaming the street establishes a new beginning for New Haven and for the projects, and I understand the impulse to sever the past, to uproot it completely. But even so, some things remain: there's still so much sky and the smell, of bluegrass and dandelions, is even the same. And of course in the distance I can see East Rock, an ancient ridge of sandstone that shoots up three hundred feet in the air. Its brown ridges can be seen from anywhere in the projects. I've never been to the top, but I know that people go up there to take in a view of the city: the New Haven Harbor feeding into the Long Island Sound, the downtown office towers, the grand arches of Yale, the railroad tracks and lines of trains. From where I'm standing I can see the monument that rests on the highest summit of East Rock, a tribute to soldiers who gave their lives in war.

The city, like the nation, stamps the past with one battle or another. Statues are built to remember the fallen, to honor sacrifices, to recognize all the terrible losses, and I think there should be a marker for those who died in Eastern Circle, something more lasting than the mural that was painted on the brick wall.

I can't imagine a shrine or a heroic bust but I can envision a stone pillar etched with the story of what happened—an acknowledgment of the drug epidemic that swept the country and ravaged our community. It would make it harder for the violence to be forgotten, or denied, or justified, or diminished. I'd hold it in my mind as a stark contrast to all the monuments that put forward the idea that American splendor and victories serve everyone to the same degree. Throughout the country, in housing projects like Eastern Circle, the landscapes could be dotted with the pillars dedicated to those who died and those who survived. Each one, a record and a reminder.

———

Catina Bacote's nonfiction has appeared in the *Gettysburg Review,* the *Virginia Quarterly Review, TriQuarterly,* the *Common, The Sun,* the *Southern California Review,* and *Trace: Transcultural Styles + Ideas.* She wrote a companion guide to the documentary *Banished: American Ethnic Cleansings* and has received fellowships from the MacDowell Colony, the Millay Colony, the Headlands Center for the Arts, Hedgebrook, and Ragdale. Catina holds an MFA from the University of Iowa, where she was admitted as a Dean's Fellow and subsequently served as the Provost's Visiting Writer in Nonfiction. She is a professor of creative writing at Warren Wilson College.

Acknowledgments

To Cleveland, Lewiston, London, Morningside Heights, Brooklyn, Seattle, and Lopez.

To Stephanie Knapp, Sharon Kunz, Michael Clark, Jack Lenzo, Martha Whitt, and the whole team at Seal, thank you for helping us make the best possible book.

Thanks to Andrew Blauner, Columbia University's School of the Arts, and Seattle's excellent literary community—especially Seattle Arts & Lectures, Richard Hugo House, the Mayor's Office of Arts & Culture, King County 4Culture, Jack Straw, Humanities Washington, Seattle Public Library, and Type Set.

Thanks to the MLK studio crew and MW, for all the good reads.

To everyone who contributed an essay to this collection and to Kelly, I've loved every minute of this with you. Thank you.

To my parents, thanks for making home a place of creativity and inspiration.

To Scott, *thanks* is too small a word for all the things. I'm home with you anywhere, but I'm grateful we agree about the mountains and fruit trees.

And to Toby, my sweet boy, thank you for coming up with the title for this book. I love that you think home is the *best* place.

—Margot

With gratitude and thanks:

To Shirley, Vassar, Brooklyn, Great Jones, Honesdale, Lancaster, and now Port Washington.

To my friends, colleagues, and students at Columbia University, Franklin & Marshall College, and Hofstra University.

To the entire Seal team, especially Michael Clark for his enthusiastic calm, Sharon Kunz for her wisdom and cool, Stephanie Knapp for her patience and taking a chance.

To friends of the book from the start: Andrew Blauner, Lauren Cerand, Melissa Connolly, Michele Filgate, Sam Freeman, Pete Gudwin, Taylor Larson, M., Katie Machen, Laura McManus, Martha McPhee, Patty O'Toole, Keaton Ramjit, Noah Ross, Sammé, Jennifer Shapiro-Lee, and, as ever, Anna Stein.

To my tribe of women who have taught and continue to teach me how to mother and make home, including: Rachel Anderson, Dardana Henci, Megana Hosein, Brandy Keenan, Melissa Merendino, Marci Nelligan, Margaret Parker, Andrea Romano, Momoko Yagishita, and each and every one of your mothers.

To Valentina Venegas and Christina Paizis, without whom nothing would get done.

To my parents, who built every home they ever made with safety and love.

To my sons, my everything.

To Margot, and all our beautiful and fierce contributors: I am so honored to share these pages with you. Thank you.

—Kelly

About the Editors

Margot Kahn is the author of *Horses That Buck*, winner of the High Plains Book Award. Her essays and reviews have appeared in *Tablet, River Teeth: A Journal of Narrative Nonfiction*, the *Los Angeles Review, Publishers Weekly*, and elsewhere. A graduate of Columbia University's MFA program, she has received grants and residencies from the Seattle Mayor's Office of Arts & Culture, King County 4Culture, the Ohioana Library Association, the Bread Loaf Writers' Conference, and the Jack Straw Writers Program. She lives in Seattle. www.margotkahn.com.

Kelly McMasters is a former bookshop owner and the author of *Welcome to Shirley: A Memoir from an Atomic Town*, the basis for the documentary film *The Atomic States of America*. She is the recipient of a Pushcart Prize nomination and an Orion Book Award nomination. Her essays and reviews have appeared in the *New York Times*, the *Washington Post* Magazine, *Paris Review* Daily, *American Scholar, River Teeth: A Journal of Narrative Nonfiction*, and *Newsday*, among others. She holds a BA from Vassar College and an MFA in nonfiction writing from Columbia's School of the Arts and is an Assistant Professor of English and Director of Publishing Studies at Hofstra University in New York. www.kellymcmasters.com.